Herb & Spice Handbook

Special Thanks To:

Writer

Karen Miles

Editor

Chris D. Baker

Contributing Editors

Kathy Krezek-Larson
Timothy Moley
Steve Phillips

Cover Artist

Kermit Solheim

Artist

Judy Waterman

Published by
Frontier Cooperative Herbs, P.O. Box 299, Norway, Iowa 52318

ISBN Number: 0-9616218-1-8
Library of Congress Catalog Number: 87-82555
Printed in the United States of America
Third Edition, Copyright 1987
2nd Printing, March 1989

Preface

The purpose of this Herb & Spice Handbook is to provide you with valuable information about herbs, spices, and related products. Inside you will find descriptive, historical, interesting, and (above all) useful information about Frontier's herbs and spices, blends, sprouting seeds, dried broths and vegetables, cooking and baking products, sea vegetables, teas, oils, cosmetic and craft items. We have tried to answer the most common questions about non-medicinal uses for these items, and have provided abundant cooking, craft, and body care information - both in the product section, and in special sections devoted entirely to these topics. In addition, we have given you a glimpse of Frontier itself - our history, goals, and the herb and spice trade in which we work.

We hope you will find this a useful resource. Please write us with your comments and suggestions. We are always happy to hear from you.

Table of Contents

Herbs & Spices

Introduction

This section of our guide contains product information for the herbs and spices we sell. The entries are presented in alphabetical order, in the following format: **Common name and part of plant sold (Form of product) - Botanical name / Other common names / Geographical source / Text / FDA status.** Here is a brief explanation of the entry items:

Common name and part of plant sold - The common name we use here is the name generally accepted by the herb and spice trade. Also included is the part or parts of the plant we are selling. Below are the terms used for plant parts and a brief description of each.

-Root: A broad classification for the part of the plant that grows beneath the ground and in some cases includes roots, rootlets, rhizomes, and tubers. All are washed and freed of above-ground stem.

-Herb: When used to describe the part of the plant being sold, herb means the dried, above-ground portion of the plant. This includes the stems and flower tops.

-Bark: Taken mainly from young trees, the exterior bark is scraped off and freed of any adhering wood.

-Berries: Picked just before they are ripe, the fruit is dried to the correct moisture for storage.

-Seeds: Plant seeds are harvested ripe and carefully cleaned of chaff and freed of whiskers or adhering flower parts.

-Buds and flowers: The single flowers, or sometimes the flower clusters, arc harvested just before, or shortly after, the buds open.

-Petals: Each flower petal is freed of other flower parts.

-Gums: Cleaned and sorted, freed of bark, and graded according to size and purity, gums are the dried exudates (saps) from trees.

-Leaves: Collected just before the end of their growing season, leaves refer to the foliage or outgrowth of the stems. Leaves that are partially dried, discolored, or injured are excluded before drying.

Form of product sold - We sell herbs and spices in various forms. The most commonly available are:

-Whole: The plant part has not been purposely cut or changed in form. Whole herbs other than roots are fragile, however, and some breakage will occur in handling.

-Cut and sifted: The plant part has been chopped to a size ranging from 1/6 inch to 3/8 inch and then sifted to produce more uniform particles. The resulting size is easy to use and retains some of the valuable and sometimes volatile properties that may otherwise be lost in powdered products.

-Granulated: This type of cut produces a product particle that is somewhat square in shape. The size of the particle ranges from 1/8 inch to 1/32 inch. Granulated products have had more plant surface area exposed, thereby improving the release of flavor and aroma.

-Powdered: Smaller than 1/32 inch, powders are usually ground in a mill to obtain a fine grind, but may also be a result of the cutting and sifting process. Powders are convenient to use, mix well, and disperse flavor evenly in cooking.

-Kibbled: This is a large cut which, in the case of carob pods, results in the removal of most of the seeds.

-Roasted: Roasting converts some bitter flavors to mellow ones, often in order to improve the flavor of brewed beverages.

-Decorticated: Decorticating removes the shell or the pod, which allows for convenient use of a seed.

Botanical name - For identification purposes, we have included the genus and species name of each product. Occasionally, we have provided a variety (a subcategory of species) for further identification.

Other common names - Sometimes different names are used in different areas, or at different times. We have tried to provide you with the most commonly used names for each product.

Geographical source - This is the usual geographical origin of our product. Depending upon availability, the sources may vary from time to time.

Text - In this section of each entry we have provided you with factual and interesting product information: descriptions, uses, historical information, recipes, etc. You will find that many of the items we sell have culinary, craft, and cosmetic uses. We have purposely included no medicinal information in our entries. Because Frontier is neither a physician nor a drug company, FDA regulations prohibit us from suggesting or implying the herbs we package are "intended for use in the diagnosis, cure, mitigation, treatment, or prevention of disease" or "intended to affect the structure and function of the body."

Frontier is a reliable source for quality herbs and spices. Our primary intention here is to provide you with a description, as accurate and complete as possible, of the herbs and spices we sell. In addition, to help you use our products in a wise and informed manner, we have compiled a bibliography for sources of general information on herbs and spices.

FDA status - This section notes the FDA safety and use classification for each herb and spice. For more details see *Regulations/Quality Control*, page 183.

Herbs & Spices

AGRIMONY HERB (cut & sifted) - *Agrimonia eupatoria* / Germany / *Agrimonia eupatoria* is the European species of this plant and *Agrimonia gryposepalo* is native to America. The plants have similar properties and uses. Agrimony has been used to produce yellow dye. *No FDA designation for safe use in food.*

ALFALFA LEAF (cut & sifted, powdered) - *Medicago sativa* / lucerne, buffalo herb, purple medick / U.S. / Alfalfa is a perennial member of the legume order. It is valued for its nutritive properties, and is grown for livestock feed and as a soil conditioner. A popular tea herb, it is rich in vitamins A, D, and K, as well as calcium, magnesium, phosphorus, and potassium. *FDA approved as a spice and for flavoring foods.*

ALLSPICE (ground, whole) - *Pimenta dioica* / Jamaica / Allspice (known as "pimento" outside the U.S.) is so named because its flavor is similar to a combination of cinnamon, nutmeg, and cloves. It is indigenous to the Western hemisphere; attempts at transplanting it to similar climates in the East have failed. The Mayans used allspice in embalming. The Scandinavians use it today to preserve barrels of fish in transport. Ground allspice can be used in desserts, relishes, sausages and preserves. Try it with custard, pineapple, chutneys, and marmalades. It is also found as a flavoring agent in chartreuse and benedictine. Whole allspice is used as a flavoring in meats, broths, gravies, stews, and pickling liquids. The small, round, dark brown seeds are sometimes used for texture and aroma in herbal craft projects such as potpourri. *FDA approved as a spice and for flavoring foods.*

ALOES (CAPE) POWDER - *Aloe ferox* / aloe vera / East and South Africa / Although known botanically as *Aloe ferox*, cape aloes powder is actually prepared (in the Cape Colonies) from several species of succulents of the lily family: *Aloe ferox, Aloe spicata, Aloe africana, Aloe platylepia, Aloe arborescons*, and *Aloe purpascens.* It was used as early as the 4th century BC and is now cultivated commercially in Africa and the Caribbean. Also grown as a houseplant, the leaf blades are very fleshy and contain a gelatinous material used for a variety of purposes, including shampoos, creams, and rinses. Its bitter flavor is used in beverages and liqueurs. The powder hardens easily; often it has begun to harden when it arrives at Frontier. Cape aloes powder is best stored in an airtight container in a cool place. *FDA approved for flavoring foods.*

ANGELICA ROOT (cut & sifted) - *Angelica archangelica* / Syria / Used extensively in the Middle Ages, angelica was thought to fight pestilence and witchcraft. Known for its celery-like, herbal aroma, angelica is often used in herbal teas and bath sachets. Angelica is also used as a flavoring agent, most notably in chartreuse and French absinthe. The fresh root seeps a resinous gum which can be substituted for gum benzoin. *FDA approved as a spice and for flavoring foods.*

ANISE SEED (ground, whole) - *Pimpinella anisum* / Spain / Anise is a seed-like fruit grown in the world's temperate climates. The flavor of anise is delicious in cookies, cakes, fruit dishes, coleslaw, rye bread, apple pie, and meats. A fragrant tea, it is also used commercially as a flavoring in cough drops, French anisette, and aguardiente (a popular Latin American drink). Murtaceus, a spiced cake made by Romans, was flavored with anise and baked in bay leaves. Although anise is often used to give a licorice flavor and aroma to products, anise and licorice are unrelated. The small, oblong anise seed is sometimes used for aroma and texture in crafts projects such as potpourri. *FDA approved as a spice and for flavoring foods.*

Fancy Figs Recipe
It's the anise seeds that "fancify" these figs.
1 pound dried figs
1 1/2 cups water
2 tablespoons honey
3/4 teaspoon anise seeds, crushed
1 teaspoon vanilla extract
In a 2 quart saucepan combine the figs, water, honey, anise and vanilla; cover and simmer over low heat for 45 minutes. Serve warm or cold. Serves 4.
—from ***Cooking With the Healthful Herbs*** *by Jean Rogers*

ANISE STAR (ground, whole) - *Illicium verum* / China / This star-shaped spice is the dried seed cluster plus the pod of the anise shrub. One inch in diameter, with an orange-brown color and sweet spicy aroma, it is used for texture, aroma, and color in herbal crafts projects. In cooking it is used for simmering meats and poultry. Star anise will stay fresh indefinitely in an air-tight container. *FDA approved as a spice and for flavoring foods.*

ANNATTO SEED (whole) - *Bixa orellana* / Kenya / Known in Mexico as *achiote*, these small, reddish-brown seeds of the annatto tree are used to impart a rich yellow color and mild, distinctive flavor to foods such as rice and sauces. To use, cover seeds with water and simmer for five minutes. Turn off the heat and soak in water for an hour. Cool before grinding. In the Yucatan and southern Mexico, *recado rojo* ("red seasoning"), made from annatto seeds and oil, is used primarily in seasoning pastes for meats and fish. Some products on the market are naturally colored with Annato. Examples include butter, margarine, cheese, candies, and shampoos. Small and flat, the seeds are brick red and are sometimes used to add color and texture to potpourris. *FDA approved for flavoring foods and coloring when used as an extract.*

ARNICA FLOWERS (whole) - *Arnica montana* / Mexico / Arnica flowers are delicately scented and are commonly used to impart texture and color to potpourris. Their fuzzy appearance is reminiscent of dandelions gone to seed. Externally it is an irritant and may cause skin inflammation. *FDA approved for flavoring alcoholic beverages.*

ASAFOETIDA POWDER - *Ferula asafoetida* / hing / Pakistan / This resinous gum is extruded from the roots of several species of the *Ferula* genus, which is native to Southeast Asia. Used extensively in Indian and Middle Eastern cooking, it has a strong odor and taste, and is often used in place of onion or garlic. One clove of garlic or 1/4 cup chopped onion is the equivalent of about 1/8 teaspoon of asafoetida powder, so use sparingly! Its flavor enriches soups, stews, gravies, casseroles, meats, and vegetables. True asafoetida is a thick paste which turns hard very quickly; we carry a blend of rice flour, asafoetida, and gum arabic. Our asafoetida is available in two-ounce jars and in bulk. *FDA approved for flavoring foods when used as an extract or tea.*

BALM OF GILEAD BUDS (whole) - *Populus balsamifera* / tacamahac, tacomahaca / U.S., China / This plant has a bitter taste and a fragrant, balsamic odor. The one-inch cones are glossy orange-green-brown, and are used for texture, aroma, and color in herbal crafts projects. Balm of Gilead buds are imported into Europe under the name "tacomahaca." *Populus balsamifera* and *Populus candicans* can be used interchangeably. *FDA approved for flavoring alcoholic beverages.*

BARBERRY ROOT BARK (cut & sifted) - *Berberis vulgaris* / sowberry / U.S./ Barberry root is used as a yellow dye for wool, linen and leather. It was cultivated in medieval times near monasteries and churches. The small pieces of yellow and tan bark are used for their color and texture in crafts projects. *No FDA designation for safe use in food.*

BASIL LEAF (cut & sifted, ground) - *Ocimum basilicum* /sweet basil / domestic from California, and imported from Egypt / The taste of basil is strong and pungent. Hindus have been buried with basil on their breasts, as a passport to paradise. A member of the mint family, it was introduced to Europe from the East in the 16th century as a culinary herb and is still used as such today. Try it in Italian and other Mediterranean dishes, soups and sauces, egg dishes, and with spinach, tomatoes, zucchini, eggplant, broccoli, peas, and green beans. We sell domestic basil cut and sifted and imported basil both cut and sifted and ground. The domestic is a higher quality basil. *FDA approved as a spice for flavoring foods.*

Pesto Sauce Recipe
2 tablespoons pine nuts, minced
1/2 cup basil, cut and sifted, Californian
1/2 teaspoon garlic powder
1 1/2 cups grated Parmesan cheese
1 1/2 cups olive oil
1 stick butter
Soak basil in 1/2 cup water until all the water has been absorbed. Blend well with blender or mortar and pestle: nuts, basil, garlic powder, cheese. While still blending add oil, a little at a time. Add butter one piece at a time, still blending, until mixture becomes pasty. Press into a jar and refrigerate. (To seal well, coat top with melted butter.) Serve on piping hot pasta.

BAY LEAF (ground, whole) - *Laurus nobilis* / bay laurel, sweet bay / Turkey / The laurel leaf has been considered a symbol of victory and the Latin name reflects this. *Laurus* means "praise" and *nobilus* means "renowned." It has a spicy, aromatic scent. Bay is used to flavor soups and stocks. Craftspersons often use these two-inch oblong leaves, with their spicy, menthol scent, in potpourris. *FDA approved as a spice for flavoring foods.*

BAYBERRY BARK (cut & sifted, powdered) - *Myrica pensylvanica* / wax myrtle, candleberry, tallow shrub / U.S. / Bayberry bark has a bitter, woodsy aroma which is sometimes used in potpourri crafting, to scent various cosmetics, and in the making of candles and soaps. *No FDA designation for safe use in food.*

BIRCH BARK (cut & sifted) - *Betula alba* / white birch, canoe birch, paper birch / U.S. / The birch tree was sacred to northern Europeans, and dedicated to Thor, god of thunder, by Germanic peoples. American Indians used this water-resistant substance for canoes and wigwams. As a natural dye, a creamy yellow color results when alum is used as a mordant with birch bark. The bark is also used in lotions, rinses and creams for its fragrant scent. *No FDA designation for safe* *use in food.*

BLACK COHOSH ROOT (cut & sifted) - *Cimicifuga racemosa* / black snakeroot, bugbane, squawroot, cimicifuga, rattleroot, rattleweed / North America / Indigenous to the U.S., black cohosh is commonly found in the eastern half of North America. It was used extensively by Native Americans, who introduced it to settlers. Blue and black cohosh are dissimilar plants, blue being of the order *berberidaceae* and black of the order *ranunculaceae. No FDA designation for safe use in food.*

BLACK CURRANT LEAF (cut & sifted) - *Ribes nigrum* / Hungary / An infusion of black currant leaves is similar to that of green tea, and is used to change the flavor of black tea. Siberians use young black currant leaves to make a drink akin to brandy. *FDA approved for flavoring foods.*

BLACK WALNUT HULL (powdered) and **LEAF** (cut & sifted) - *Juglans nigra* / Eastern North America / Black walnut leaves have been a source of dye for many centuries. Gathered in late spring, they produce colors ranging from yellow-tan to gold-green, depending on the mordant being used. The powdered hulls, on the other hand, may be used to produce a black dye. We sell the hull powdered, and the leaf cut and sifted. *FDA approved for flavoring foods.*

BLACKBERRY LEAF (cut & sifted) - *Rubus* spp. / bramble, cloudberry / U.S., Poland / Blackberry grows wild throughout the U.S. and is used in facials, masks, and lotions. *No FDA designation for safe use in food.*

BLESSED THISTLE HERB (cut & sifted) - *Cnicus benedictus*, also known as *Centaurea benedicta, Carduus benedictus*, and *Carbenia benedicta* / St. Benedict thistle, cardin, holy thistle, spotted thistle / U.S. / *Cnicus* is the Latin name for safflower, which was once the name given to the thistle family. Blessed thistle is mixed with wine to make an aperitif. *FDA approved only for flavoring alcoholic beverages.*

BLOODROOT ROOT (cut & sifted) - *Sanguinaria canadensis* / Indian paint, red root, red pucoon / U.S. / American Indians used the orange-red juice of the bloodroot rootstock to produce a bright red dye with which they painted their bodies and dyed their baskets. Wooden implements were colored orange by rubbing them with the fresh root. Today, a natural orange dye is obtained by using alum and cream of tartar as a mordant with bloodroot root. *FDA prohibited for use in food due to naturally occurring toxins.*

BLUE COHOSH ROOT (cut & sifted, powdered) - *Caulophyllum thalictroides* / beechdrops, blueberry, blue ginseng, yellow ginseng, squaw root / U.S. and Canada / Blue cohosh contains the minerals potassium, magnesium, calcium, iron and phosphorus. It was used extensively by native Americans. *No FDA designation for safe use in food.*

BLUEBERRY LEAF (cut & sifted) - *Vaccinum ovatum* / bilberry, wineberry, whortleberry, huckleberry / Europe / The myrtle-shaped leaves of this plant have been used to flavor certain liqueurs. *No FDA designation for safe use in food.*

BONESET HERB (cut & sifted) - *Eupatorium perfoliatum* / thoroughwort, feverwort, Indian sage / U.S. / An herb used by numerous American Indian tribes, the Shakers, American settlers, and Civil War troops, boneset is now chiefly regarded as a weed throughout the eastern half of America where it grows. *No FDA designation for safe use in food.*

BORAGE LEAF (cut & sifted) - *Borago officinalis* / beebread, star flower, bugloss / Hungary / Borage has long been appreciated for its cooling quality and refreshing flavor. In ancient times, and during the Middle Ages, it was put into drinks and salads. Fresh borage leaves are still used in salads, and have a cucumber-like taste. The star-shaped, blue-purple flowers are used often in dried flower arrangements. *No FDA designation for safe use in food.*

BOUGANVILLIER FLOWERS (whole) - *Botanical name unavailable* / India / Bouganvillier is a very large, light petal that is similar in texture to tissue paper. Because these petals are so very light, .15 pounds equals about three gallons of petals by volume. Available in purple (a rose/purple color) and white (a cream color), bouganvillier petals hold their color well and are a lovely, economical addition to potpourris. *No FDA designation for safe use in food.*

BROOM FLOWERS (whole) - *Genista tinctoria* / dyer's weed / Albania / The yellow flowers of this plant bloom in late summer and fall, yielding a yellow dye which is especially good for coloring wool. These 1/2-inch petals, with their sweet, grain aroma and golden brown color are used in other crafts projects as well. This is not the same plant as broom tops. *No FDA designation for safe use in food.*

BROOM TOPS (cut & sifted) - *Cytisus scoparis* / butcher's broom tops, Jew's myrtle, box holly / Europe / A member of the Lily family, this plant grows wild as well as horticulturally. Its common name, butcher's broom tops, is derived from its long association with the meat trade. From the 16th through 19th centuries it was used as a broom to scrub chopping blocks, and as a decoration for holiday meats. *FDA prohibited for use in food due to naturally occurring toxins.*

BUCHU LEAF (whole) - *Barosma butulina* / South Africa / These attractive, 1/2-inch, lance-shaped leaves are green, with a pungent, earthy scent. They are used for aroma and texture in herbal crafts projects. *FDA approved for flavoring foods.*

BUCKTHORN BARK (cut & sifted) - *Rhamnus cathartica* / alder buckthorn, black dogwood, frangula bark / Yugoslavia / Buckthorn bark yields a yellow dye which is quite popular in Russia. The dye turns red when mixed with the salts of iron. Gunpowder manufacturers prefer the charcoal of this shrub over most other types and named it "black dogwood." *No FDA designation for safe use in food.*

BURDOCK ROOT (cut & sifted) - *Arctium lappa* / gypsy's rhubarb, gig's rhubarb, snake's rhubarb, beggar's buttons / West Germany, Yugoslavia, Belguim / Burdock, which resembles rhubarb, is cultivated commercially in Japan for use as a vegetable. Growing deeply into the soil, it is rich in iron, calcium, and vitamins A, B, and C. The botanical name is derived from the Greek *arktos*, "a bear." The roots, which contain starch, are mucilaginous, and are used for cosmetic purposes. *No FDA designation for safe use in food.*

CALAMUS ROOT (cut & sifted) - *Acorus calamus* / sweet flag / Germany / Calamus is an ancient herb of the East and was widely distributed at the end of the 16th century. Used as a fixative in potpourris, its warm, woody scent and 1/4-inch tan-brown chunks also impart aroma and texture. Commercially, calamus root is used in cosmetics. *FDA prohibited for use in food due to naturally occurring toxins.*

CALCATRIPPAE FLOWERS (whole) - *Calcatrippae* spp. / Hungary / This product consists of calcatrippae stem and petal strands. Purple and green with a light floral aroma, they are used for color, texture and scent in potpourris. *No FDA designation for safe use in food.*

CALENDULA FLOWERS (whole) - *Calendula officinalis* / Mary bud, garden marigold / Egypt, U.S. / Calendula petals are used for tea and as a substitute for saffron in coloring cheese and butter. The flowers are one inch in diameter and aster-like, with a light, corn scent and orange-yellow color. The texture and color is appreciated by potpourri crafters. A yellow dye is produced by boiling the petals. *FDA approved as a spice and for flavoring foods.*

CANADA SNAKE ROOT (cut & sifted) - *Asarum canadense* / wild ginger, false coltsfoot, Indian ginger, catsfoot / U.S. / Canada snakeroot smells like ginger. Its oil is used in perfumes, and as a flavoring agent. *FDA approved for flavoring foods.*

CARAWAY SEED (ground, whole) - *Carum carvi* / Holland / The name caraway is derived from "*karawya* ," the name given to the fruit by the ancient Arabs. Of all the condiments in Europe, caraway is believed to have been cultivated and consumed for the longest period of time. Caraway's warm, sweet, acrid flavor is used in sauerkraut, applesauce, soup, canned goods, cheese, sausage, potatoes, carrots, green beans, and rye breads, and is sometimes enjoyed as a fragrant tea. *FDA approved as a spice and for flavoring foods.*

Quick Slaw Recipe
1 small head cabbage
2 carrots
1/2 cup raisins
2 tablespoons caraway seeds
1 cup mayonnaise
1/2 cup vinegar
1/2 teaspoon sea salt

Coarsely grate cabbage into a bowl. Add grated carrots, raisins, caraway seed, and salt. In a separate bowl, combine mayonnaise with vinegar. Pour mayonnaise mixture over slaw. Mix well. Chill and serve.

CARDAMOM POD (whole) and **SEED** (ground, whole) - *Elettaria cardamomum* / Guatemala / Cardamom was one of the most popular spices in Roman cuisine. Today cardamom remains an indispensable seasoning of Indian, Scandinavian, and Arab countries. It is found in Egyptian cardamon coffee, Swedish meatballs, *garam masala* (a spice blend), and many cakes and cookies. Try it with custard, apples, melons, peaches, strawberries, and raspberries. Potpourri crafters use the oblong, 1/2 inch pods for their texture and menthol aroma. Frontier carries cardamom in several forms - whole green pods, decorticated ground seeds, decorticated whole seeds, and white cardamom pods. The whole green pods are kiln dried and unshelled, each capsule containing 15-20 hard brownish-black seeds. Decorticated seeds, which have the pods removed, are available either ground or whole. Ten pounds of pods equal six pounds of decorticated seeds. Fifty-thousand cardamom seeds equal one pound! White cardamom pods, the most expensive of the cardamoms, are chemically bleached by fuming with burning sulfur or by hydrogen peroxide. While white cardamoms are not used as often as the green pods or the seed, they are preferred by some gourmet cooks. *FDA approved as a spice and for flavoring foods.*

CARDAMOM POD, BLACK (whole) - *Elettaria cardamomum major* / ilchai, Ceylon cardamom / India / Although unrelated to true cardamom, this plant is known as black cardamom because of its dark color and mild flavor which is reminiscent of true cardamom. Grown in India, this item is used in Indian cooking. *FDA approved as a spice and for flavoring foods.*

CASCARA SAGRADA BARK (cut & sifted) - *Rhamnus purshiana* / California buckthorn, sacred bark / U.S. / The reddish-brown bark of this deciduous tree is often covered with grey lichen. Native to North American mountains, the tree grows from 15 to 25 feet high. Early Spanish settlers learned about this plant from the Indians and named it *cascara sagrada*, meaning "sacred bark." *FDA approved for flavoring foods.*

CASSIA BUDS (whole) - *Cinnamomum cassia* / Indonesia / Indonesian brides are traditionally given - for good luck - a beverage containing a pair of cassia buds that grew side by side. The dried, unripe fruits of the cassia (cinnamon) tree, these dark brown, 1/4-inch buds add texture and aroma to herbal crafts projects, and are especially good in simmering potpourris. Their hot, spicy flavor is used in pickles and confections, and they are good to snack on! *FDA approved as a spice and for flavoring foods.*

CATNIP HERB (cut & sifted) - *Nepeta cataria* / catmint, catnep, nep, catrup / U.S. / Catnip is a perennial herb of the mint family. Because of its scent, cats are strangely fascinated with catnip, and it has been commonly used to stuff toy mice. *No FDA designation for safe use in food.*

CAYENNE (ground) - *Capsicum frutescens* / red pepper / Cayenne is the ground product of pepper varieties grown in the U.S., Africa, China, Mexico, Japan, and India. Cayenne or red pepper is orange-red and varies in degree of hotness, measured in heat units (h.u.). Cayenne may range in hotness from 10,000 heat units to 120,000 heat units. We sell two cayennes. One, which measures 30,000 heat units, is a blend of domestic and foreign peppers. The second, with a heat unit of 90,000 or hotter, is made of ground peppers from China or Pakistan. Capsicum products are best stored in cool, dry, dark, conditions to insure color and flavor. (See *Capsicum*, page 13.) Cayenne frequents Mexican dishes and sauces, soups, stews, curries, potatoes, meats, and eggs. Add a pinch of cayenne to two cups stewed tomatoes for a special zing. Or add 1/16 teaspoon cayenne to eight ounces cream cheese, blending well. Cayenne is *very* hot - use with caution! *FDA approved as a spice and for flavoring foods.*

CEDAR RED (chips, shavings) - *Juniperous virginiana* / U.S. / These thin, 1/2-inch shavings have a woodsy aroma and are used for scent, color, and texture in herbal crafts projects. *No FDA designation for safe use in food.*

CEDAR TIPS GREEN (whole) - *Juniperous virginiana* / U.S. / Cedar tips are an attractive and very aromatic addition to potpourris, sachets, and other craft items. This product consists of the green and brown, one-inch branch tips and berries. *No FDA designation for safe use in food.*

CELERY SEED (ground, whole) - *Apium graveolens* / India / Although they are not identical in taste, celery seed is often substituted for the fresh vegetable to add celery flavor. The tiny, pleasantly-flavored seeds (75,000 of them per pound) can be added whole to almost any dish. Try them in coleslaw, tomato juice, soups, relishes, sauerkraut, curries, stuffings, dressings, breads, vegetable dishes, and eggs. *FDA approved as a spice and for flavoring foods.*

Herbed Green Beans Recipe
1 pound steamed green beans
3/4 cup chopped onion
2 tablespoons sesame seeds
1 teaspoon celery seed
1/4 teaspoon whole rosemary

1/4 teaspoon basil leaves

Saute' onion, sesame seeds, and celery seed for five minutes. Add rosemary and basil and simmer five minutes more. Add green beans and heat.

CELOSIA FLOWERS (whole) -*Celosia argentea* var. *cristata* / cockscomb / Orient / These attractive, purple flowers are velvety and fan-shaped. They have no scent, but are used for color and texture in herbal crafts projects such as potpourri. They are bulky and a little goes a long way! *No FDA designation for safe use in food.*

CENTAURY HERB (cut & sifted) - *Centaurea centaurium* / Europe / Considered a lucky plant by the Celtics of Europe, centaury was widely grown and used in the Middle Ages. An annual herb with smooth, shiny leaves, it is used today as an ingredient in vermouth and bitter herb liqueurs. *FDA approved only for flavoring alcoholic beverages.*

CHAMOMILE FLOWERS (whole) - *Matricaria chamomilla* / camomile, chamomilla, wild chamomile / Egypt / The ancient Germanic tribes considered chamomile sacred and dedicated it to Baldur, their sun god. The flower's yellow center and white surrounding petals seemed to represent the sun's forces. Today chamomile is used extensively by the cosmetic industry in bath, skin, and hair preparations as well as to make a delicious herbal tea. The color, texture, and softly fruity aroma is lovely in potpourri blends. Combined with alum and cream of tartar as a mordant, chamomile flowers produce a natural yellow dye. *FDA approved as a spice and for flavoring foods.*

CHAMOMILE FLOWERS, ROMAN (whole) - *Anthemis noblis* / Poland / These cream-colored flowers, 1/2-inch round, and many-rayed, are used to add color and texture to potpourris. Grown commercially in Europe, Roman chamomile flowers can be used in the same manner as regular chamomile when blending teas. They have also been used to lighten hair and in beer manufacturing. *FDA approved as a spice and for flavoring foods.*

CHAPARRAL LEAF (cut & sifted, powdered) - *Larrea tridentata* / greasewood, creosote bush / Mexico, U.S. / This erect, aromatic shrub has a white bark, yellow flowers, and disagreeable odor. It grows in alkaline soil (generally unfit for planting) and contains a resinous gum which has been used by the Papago Indians of the southwest U.S. for many purposes: to affix arrowheads to shafts, to patch cracked pottery, as a hair tonic, and to waterproof woven grass baskets. *No FDA designation for safe use in food.*

CHASTE TREE BERRIES (whole) - *Vitex agnus - castus* / monk's pepper / Europe / Native to southern Europe, these berries are irregular and angular, with oily kernels. The common name, monk's pepper, is derived from the fact that, historically, monks in Europe ground the seed to use as pepper. *No FDA designation for safe use in food.*

CHERVIL LEAF (cut & sifted) - *Anthriscus cerefolium* / Holland / Chervil was used extensively by the Romans. Today in France, it is used as fresh parsley is used elsewhere. Used with other herbs, it enhances the flavors with which it is combined. Its light, anise-licorice flavor is good in cream soups, egg salads, dressings, sauces, and as a garnish. Add chervil to your dish at the last minute, as its delicate flavor is destroyed by cooking. *FDA approved as a spice and for flavoring foods.*

CHESTNUT LEAF (cut & sifted) - *Castanea dentata* / Spanish chestnut / Europe / This tree is native to southern Europe, and is used primarily for lumber and nuts. Its leaves are odorless, with an astringent taste and are sometimes used as a flavoring. *FDA approved for flavoring in foods.*

CHIA SEED (whole) - *Salvia hispanica* / Central America / Several species of this sage plant are found in Central and South America, as well as the southern U.S. The seeds are somewhat mucilaginous, and were used as food by native Americans. *No FDA designation for safe use in food.*

CHICKWEED HERB (cut & sifted) - *Stellaria media* / stitchwort, starweed, adder's mouth / West Germany / This plant has light green leaves, tiny white flowers, and small hairs on the stems which switch sides at leaf joints. It grows in cool, moist, shady areas. *No FDA designation for safe use in food.*

CHICORY ROOT (cut & sifted, granulated) - *Cichorium intybus* / succory, blue diamond / France / Chicory is a perennial plant, commonly cultivated and found wild in the U.S. and Europe. It is often roasted and used with coffee, or as a coffee substitute. Brewed together with coffee, the resulting beverage has a richer flavor, deeper color, and less caffeine than coffee. For percolator or drip-method coffee makers, use chicory alone, or substitute one tablespoon chicory for two tablespoons ground coffee when brewing. For variation, serve with one cinnamon stick or one cardamom seed in each cup. We sell cut and sifted raw chicory root and granulated chicory root, which has been roasted. *FDA approved for flavoring foods when used as an extract or tea.*

CHILI PEPPERS (crushed, diced, ground, whole) - *Capsicum frutescens* / U.S., India / (See *Capsicum*, page 12.) Chili peppers are used around the world to add color and tang to many food staples which might otherwise be considered rather bland (rice, beans, corn, cassava). They are particularly enjoyed in hot, tropical climates because of their ability to increase body heat, thereby causing the surrounding hot air to seem cooler by comparison. Used extensively in Southwestern, Mexican, Oriental, and Caribbean cooking, more chili peppers are produced and consumed than any other spice in the world. They are grown throughout the U.S., but particularly in the valleys of California, Arizona, and New Mexico. Depending upon soil and climatic conditions, the hotness of these peppers varies. The volatile oils contained in chili peppers may burn the skin, so care should be taken in handling- rubber gloves are recommended.

A wide variety of chili peppers is available. We sell the following :

ANCHO - The Ancho, or "Mexican" pepper, is about four inches long, and heart-shaped, with a uniform dark red color and measures 2,000 heat units. It has a mild, sweet taste that is widely used in Mexican and Southwestern cooking.

CRUSHED - These crushed peppers are 1/8 inch pieces of *Capsicum frutescens* which have 10,000 heat units. They are very popular for sprinkling on pizza.

GREEN CHILI PEPPERS - Green chilies are very popular in Tex-Mex and Szechwanese cooking. They are mild and add a distinct chili flavor to sauces, beans, tacos, eggs, and cheese dishes. These 1/4-inch diced peppers have 500-1,000 heat units.

GROUND - The same peppers as are in the crushed product above (10,000 heat units) are ground to a fine powder.

WHOLE - These chilies measure 2,000 heat units. They are mild and large, measuring five to seven inches in length. In addition to their culinary use, they are also found in decorative crafts such as kitchen wreaths.

Whole Hot - These chilies measure 60,000 heat units. Small and very hot, they are used extensively in Chinese and Southeast Asian cooking. (Use chili peppers with the seeds for full hotness.)

Jalapeno - With a heat unit measurement of 70,000 - twice as hot as mild cayenne- these very hot chilies are used extensively in ethnic (especially Mexican) cooking. The red jalapenos are a bright to dark red color, the green an olive color. They are available crushed (red and green) and ground (red only).

All peppers are FDA approved as a spice and for flavoring foods.

CAPSICUM

The genus *Capsicum* is a member of the *Solanaceae* (nightshade) family and includes five species and over 300 varieties of plants. Two of the primary species are *Capsicum annuum* and *Capsicum frutescens. C. annuum* is an annual, herbaceous plant which grows three feet tall and yields yellow, brown, purple, or red fruits ranging in size from 1/2 inch to 11 inches. It includes some hot, and all sweet varieties of peppers grown in the U.S. *C. frutescens*, on the other hand, is a perennial which reaches six feet in height and produces small, thin-skinned peppers. Grown primarily in the tropics, this plant yields the hottest peppers commercially available.

Sweet and hot peppers differ in appearance - sweet usually have rounded, lobed, broad bottoms, while most hot chilies are tapered. All capsicum products, however (paprika, cayenne, sweet bell peppers, chili peppers), contain the crystalline, pungent substance capsaicin. The higher the capsaicin content, the hotter the pepper. In some varieties, such as the sweet bell pepper, the capsaicin content is very low, and the tang is minimal. Heat units (h.u.) are used to describe the range of hotness of capsicum peppers. The range for mild chili peppers is about 500-1,000, while some of the hottest measure over 100,000 HU.

To retain color and freshness, all capsicums are best stored in cool, dark, dry conditions (38° F with 50% humidity is ideal).

CHIVES (dehydrated cut & sifted, freeze-dried cut & sifted) - *Allium schoenoprasum* / garden chive, ciboulette, onion grass / Taiwan, U.S. / We carry two types of chives; freeze-dried, which are domestic, and dehydrated, which are from Taiwan. They grow from a bulbous root, similar to onions. The leaves are hollow and have a mild onion taste. Gypsies have used chives in fortune-telling rites and often hung clumps from ceilings and bedposts to drive away diseases and evil spirits. Chives are used in soups, salads and dips, in sour cream or cottage cheese, eggs, casseroles, sauces, fish dishes, and in dressings. They may be rehydrated by soaking in water for just one minute. One tablespoon of chives rehydrates to ten tablespoons. Dry chives may be used directly in wet dishes. Generally, freeze-dried chives retain their color and flavor better than dehydrated chives. *FDA approved as a spice and for flavoring foods.*

CHRYSANTHEMUM FLOWERS (whole) - *Chrysanthemum parthenium* / feverfew / Taiwan / These 3/4-inch round flowers have a faint scent and are used to add color and texture to herbal crafts projects. We sell chrysanthemum flowers in two colors - white and yellow. *No FDA designation for safe use in food.*

CILANTRO LEAF (cut & sifted) - *Coriandrum sativum* / Chinese parsley, Mexican parsley, fresh coriander / California / Cilantro is a culinary herb, popular in Mexican cooking,

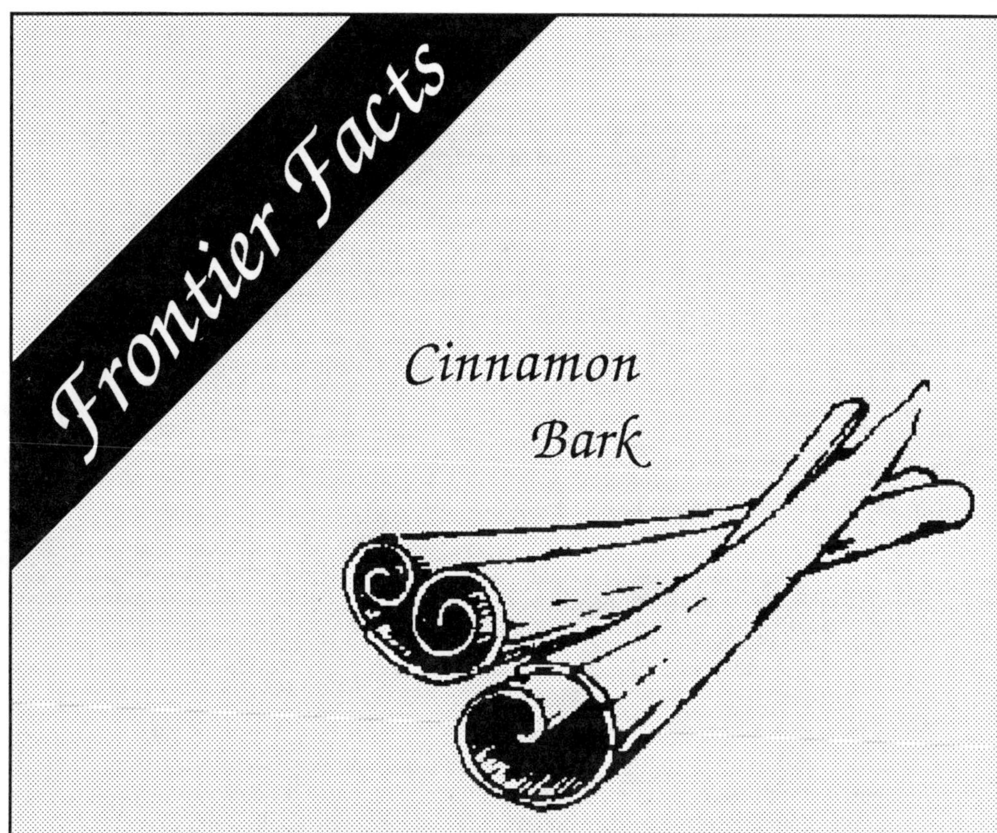

Cinnamon is ground from the sun-dried bark of evergreen trees belonging to the *Cinnamomum* family. The two trees most commonly used are *Cinnamomum zeylanicum*, native to Ceylon, and *Cinnamomum cassia*, from Indonesia, China, and Viet Nam. (See *Cinnamon (sticks) Ceylon*, page 15) Most of the cinnamon used in the U.S. today is cassia, a reddish-brown product with a distinctive aroma and taste. The cassia we sell is from Indonesia, which produces "Korintje" type (our ground cinnamon and cinnamon chips) and "Batavia" type (cinnamon sticks).

A component in numerous spice blends, cinnamon is used to flavor beverages, meats, pickles, fruits, and many baked goods and desserts. One teaspoon of cinnamon contains 28 grams calcium, 11 grams potassium, 6 I.U.'s vitamin A and 1 gram each of magnesium, phosphorus, and sodium. It lends its warm rich odor to potpourris, sachets, and perfumes, and the sticks are often used in teas and craft projects. Cinnamon granules are convenient for tea blending, sachets, and small-textured potpourris. Because they release their scent quickly, granules are also good for simmering potpourris.

We sell cinnamon in a variety of forms: chips (1/4 - 1/2 inch cut and 1/2 - one inch cut), granules, ground, and sticks (one , two and three-fourths, six, 10, and 16-inch lengths).

where it is used as both a garnish and seasoning. It is very aromatic, with a distinctive, strong flavor. Cilantro is the leaf of the same plant from which coriander seed is harvested. *FDA approved as a spice and for flavoring foods.*

CINNAMON (chips, granules, ground, sticks) - *Cinnamomum cassia* / cassia, Chinese cinnamon, bastard cinnamon, sweetwood / Indonesia / With a history of 5,000 years, cinnamon is one of today's most popular spices. A major goal of 15th and 16th century exploration, it played an important role in the development of imperialistic policies. (See *Cinnamon Bark*, page 14.) *FDA approved as a spice and for flavoring foods.*

CINNAMON (sticks) Ceylon - *Cinnamomum zeylanicum* / true cinnamon / Sri Lanka / This cinnamon is native to Ceylon and was known only to natives there until it was discovered by the Dutch. Its flavor is more delicate, sweet, and less pungent than that of *Cinnamomum cassia* (see above entry). In some countries, such as England, only Ceylon cinnamon may legally be sold as "cinnamon" while cassia is considered an impostor. Generally, however, both are sold as cinnamon, and consumers' preferences are guided by what they are accustomed to tasting. The Ceylon cinnamon sticks we sell are three inches long, and are also known as "soft cinnamon sticks." *FDA approved as a spice and for flavoring foods.*

CLARY SAGE TOPS - *Salvia sclarea* / muscatel sage, clear eye / Europe / Clary sage is grown as a source of muscatel oil which is used in flavoring and perfumery. In Germany it is used to give wines a musky bouquet. *FDA approved as a spice and for flavoring foods.*

CLEAVERS HERB (cut & sifted) - *Galium aparine* / bedstraw, goose grass, clivers, catchweed, scratweed / Hungary / Cleavers is a low perennial found in damp woods and swamplands. It is related to woodruff and the roots will produce a red dye. *No FDA designation for safe use in food.*

CLOVES (ground, whole) - *Syzygium aromaticum* / Zanzibar, Brazil / Clove varieties are known by the names of the localities in which they are grown. The word "clove" is derived from the French *clou*, meaning "nail." In the Moluccas (Spice Islands), parents planted a clove tree when a child was born in order to keep a rough record of the child's age. If the tree was destroyed, the parents believed the child was in danger. The Dutch, who governed the islands in the 17th century, decreed that clove trees were only to be grown on one island and destroyed all clove trees on other islands.

Cloves have a strong, pungent, sweet flavor. Ground cloves are popular in baked goods such as nut breads and gingerbread, and vegetables such as squash and beets, as well as curries and beverages. The French add cloves to soup stock. Americans stud ham and pork with whole cloves, and add them to pickled fruits, spicy sweet syrups, meat gravies, and cranberry punch. Stud an onion with whole cloves and add to stews or lentil soup for a subtle taste difference. Or add cloves to fruit as it cooks. In crafts projects, these dark brown, torch-shaped whole beads are used for texture and a spicy scent. *FDA approved as a spice and for flavoring foods.*

COLTSFOOT LEAF (cut & sifted) - *Tussilago farfara* / British tobacco, bullsfoot, butterbur, coughwort, flower valure, foal's foot, horse-foot, horsehoof / Yugoslavia / The coltsfoot leaf, which is shaped like a hoof, was painted on doorways in France as a logo for druggists. *No FDA designation for safe use in food.*

COMFREY LEAF (cut & sifted) and **ROOT** (cut & sifted, powdered) - *Symphytum officinale* / blackwort, bruisewort, knitbone, healing herb, knitback, salsify, slippery root, wallwort / U.S., West Germany / Comfrey is rich in vitamin B12 and protein. Research has sought to develop this hardy perennial as a food source because of its prolific growth under a wide variety of growing conditions. It has also been used as cattle food, and its active ingredient, allantoin, makes it a useful emollient for lotions, creams, salves, ointments, hair rinses, and body oils. *No FDA designation for safe use in food.*

CORIANDER SEED (ground, whole) - *Coriandrum sativum* / Morocco / The people of Latin America, especially Peru, regard coriander as a delicious flavoring. It has a warm, distinctive, fragrant odor and pleasant taste - mild and sweet, yet slightly pungent. In the East it is used as a condiment. Ground, it is used in curry powder, other spice mixtures, sausages, and in baked goods. Certain types of alcohol, especially gin, are flavored with it. The whole seed, which is small, rigid, and light brown, is used for texture and color in potpourri crafting. In cooking, it is used in pickling spice, and by confectioners. *FDA approved as a spice and for food flavoring.*

CORNFLOWERS (whole) - *Centaurea cyanus* / Yugoslavia / Cornflowers are used for color and texture in herbal crafts projects. We sell them both with and without calyx. The green-brown calyx is topped by a swirl of blue-purple petals. Removal of the calyx results in a delicate mass of blue-purple petals. *No FDA designation for safe use in food.*

CORNSILK (cut & sifted) - *Zea mays* / maize, Indian corn / Europe / A native to South America, this plant is now widely cultivated as a nutritious food plant. Cornsilk is the stigmas from the female flowers. It can be used fresh, or dried, to make a tea sweetened with molasses. *FDA approved for flavoring foods when used as an extract or tea.*

CRAMP BARK (cut & sifted) - *Vibrunum opulus* / guelder rose, cranberry tree / U.S. / Cramp bark was popular in early 19th century America. The bark, collected in thin strips, is greyish-brown with a strong odor and bitter taste. In Norway, a liquor has been distilled from the fruit. *No FDA designation for safe use in food.*

CRANESBILL ROOT (cut & sifted) - *Geranium maculatum* / alum root, crowfoot, geranium, storksbill / U.S. / Cranesbill is a native American plant which is found in rich woods, meadows, and fence rows. The leaves and roots contain tannin. *No FDA designation for safe use in food.*

CUBEB BERRY (whole) - *Piper cubeba* / tailed pepper, Java pepper / Malaya and Indonesia / The cubeb berry is closely related to black pepper, but has a "tail" leading to the stem. The taste, though bitter, is reminiscent of allspice and is good in fruit dishes. Black and grey with a sharp spicy scent, cubeb berries are sometimes used in potpourri crafting. *FDA approved for flavoring foods.*

CUMIN SEED (ground, whole) - *Cuminum cyminum* / India / The seed of the cumin plant, an annual member of the parsley family, is very popular for use in cooking. An essential ingredient in most chili powder blends, it is a wonderful seasoning for beans, avocadoes, beets, cabbage, dairy foods, eggs, pickles, potatoes, curries, chili, breads, rice, and soup. Kümmel is a liqueur flavored with cumin. Although the cumin seed has been disregarded by European cooks for the last 300 years (after extensive use in the Middle Ages), it enjoys a wide popularity in Oriental, Indian, Mexican, and American cooking today. The whole seeds may be roasted to release their full flavor. *FDA approved as a spice and for flavoring food.*

DAMIANA LEAF (cut & sifted) - *Turnera diffusa* / Mexico / Damiana is a small shrub, the leaves of which have been used in tea by South Americans for a number of years. Mexicans refer to damiana as *hierba de la pastora.* It has also been used to flavor liqueurs. *FDA approved for flavoring foods.*

DANDELION LEAF (cut & sifted) and **ROOT** (cut & sifted, granulated) - *Taraxacum officinale* / Germany, Yugoslavia / The French term for lion's tooth, *dent-de-lion*, was given to this plant because of its jagged, irregularly-toothed leaves. A European native, dandelion now grows wild all over North America. The leaves are often used as a spring tonic, as they are high in iron and vitamins A, B, and C. Dandelion beer was a popular European beverage, and the blossoms of dandelion are gathered today to make a lovely pale yellow wine. Dandelion leaves are used to make a mild, slightly bitter tea that blends well with other herbs, especially mints. Dried and roasted dandelion roots are a nutritious substitute for coffee. We sell dandelion root raw (cut & sifted) and roasted (cut & sifted, granulated). *FDA approved for flavoring foods when used as an extract or tea.*

Dandelion Coffee Recipe

Perk or drip method: Use one teaspoon roasted dandelion root per cup of water, or pour boiling water over dandelion root, steep for five minutes, and strain before serving.

DEER'S TONGUE LEAF (whole) - *Trilisa oderatissima* / dog's tongue, vanilla leaf, vanilla plant / U.S. / This aromatic herb has a vanilla-like fragrance and is used for scent and as a fixative in potpourris and other herbal crafts. *FDA prohibited for use in food due to naturally occurring toxins.*

DEVIL'S CLAW TUBER (powdered) - *Harpagophyton procumbens* / unicorn plant, grapple / South Africa / The devil's claw plant has branching woody fruit equipped with barbs reminiscent of claws or grapples. This plant has one or two sets of tubers where water is stored to carry the plant through droughts. The black fiber of the devil's claw plant was used by the Indians of the southwest U.S. to form patterns in coiled basketry. The tubers are the part of the plant we sell, in powdered form. *No FDA designation for safe use in food.*

DILL SEED (ground, whole) - *Anethum graveolens* / India / The dill fruit or seed is famous for the flavor it imparts to dill pickles. The whole or ground seed is also used in potato and carrot salads, as well as in breads, sauerkraut, soups, dressings, egg and potato dishes, cabbage and meat dishes. The name is derived from old Norse *dilla*, which means "to lull." *FDA approved as a spice and for flavoring foods.*

DILL WEED (cut & sifted) - *Anethum graveolens* / U.S. / The weed, or dried leaf, can be used in salads, soups, fish dishes, sauces, dressings, or on vegetables. It is sometimes enjoyed as a fragrant tea as well. The name is derived from old Norse *dilla*, which means "to lull." The dill weed we carry is domestic. *FDA approved as a spice and for flavoring foods.*

DOG GRASS HERB (cut & sifted) - *Agropyrum repens* / couchgrass, witchgrass, quackgrass / Europe / A European native, this plant is now naturalized all over the U.S., its spreading rhizomes causing it to be declared a primary noxious weed in some places. Dog grass derives its common name from the fact that animals can be seen eating its leaves as a tonic in the spring. *FDA approved for flavoring foods when used as an extract or tea.*

DON QUAI ROOT (powdered) - *Angelica polymorpha* / Tang kuei / China / Dong Quai root has been used by the Chinese for years. Some of its characteristics are similar to the western herb angelica. Its bitter, though pleasant flavor is used as a tea, and in flavoring. *FDA approved as a spice and for flavoring foods.*

ECHINACEA ANGUSTIFOLIA ROOT (cut & sifted, powdered, whole) - *Echinacea angustifolia* / hedgehog coneflower, purple coneflower, sampson root / U.S. / This plant's common name, hedgehog coneflower, is derived from the bristly texture of its seedhead. It is a native perennial found in the midwest prairie states. Angustifolia is the best known of the echinacea's nine species. True angustifolia has declined in availability due to intense harvesting in the wild. This has led to high prices and the substitution of other echinaceas or other plants. However, continued market demand is popularizing the cultivation of this wilfdlower as a commercial crop. *No FDA designation for safe use in food.*

ECHINACEA PURPUREA ROOT (cut & sifted, powdered) - *Echinacea purpurea* / U.S. / Of the nine species of echinacea, purpurea is the most commonly cultivated. In its natural habitat Echinacia purpurea may be found growing in moderately rich soil along creek beds or seepage, often under dappled shade. It flowers from June through October from Louisiana and eastern Oklahoma, north through Ohio and Michigan. Some believe echinacea angustifolia to be the true, preferred species of this plant (see above entry); others suggest angustifolia and purpurea are comparable. *No FDA designation for safe use in food.*

ELDER BERRIES (whole) and **FLOWERS** (whole) - *Sambucus nigra* / Yugoslavia, Hungary / Elder has been found in Stone and Bronze Age excavations. The elder has craft, culinary, and cosmetic uses. The berries are dark purple, with a sweet, fruity aroma. They are used for texture, scent, and color in herbal crafts. *No FDA designation for safe use in food.*

The tiny flowers are yellow-tan and are used for texture and color in herbal crafts. *FDA approved as a spice and for flavoring foods.*

> ***Elder Flower Milk Recipe***
> *Pour 4 cups boiling water over:*
> *4 teaspoons elder flowers*
> *1 teaspoon lemon balm*
> *Steep 7 minutes. Strain. Add milk and honey and drink warm.*

ELECAMPANE ROOT (cut & sifted) - *Inula helenium* / elfdock, elfwort, horse-elder, horse-heal, scabwort / China / The Latin *helenium* is a reference to Helen of Troy, who is believed to have been carrying the plant when she was abducted. This plant has huge leaves offset by orange, daisy-like flowers with fringe borders. It grows from four to ten feet in height. A wine was once made by an infusion of elecampane roots, sugar, and currants in white port. The roots are still used to flavor wines and liqueurs in Europe. A natural black dye can be made by combining the bruised root with ashes and whortleberries. *FDA approved only for flavoring alcoholic beverages.*

EPHEDRA (cut & sifted) - *Ephedra viridis* / Morman tea / Russia / A plant from the dry regions of the southwest. *No FDA designation for safe use in food.*

EUCALYPTUS LEAF (cut & sifted, whole) - *Eucalyptus globulus* / blue gum / Spain / The

Greek *eucalyptos* means "a well and a lid" and refers to the sepals and petals of the plant, while *globulus* signifies the shape of the fruit. The tree is native to Australia and Tasmania, and its leaves are studded with glands containing a fragrant volatile oil. We sell eucalyptus leaves whole (1/2 inch wide and four to six inches long) and cut and sifted (1/4 inch pieces). They have a menthol aroma, and are sometimes used in potpourri and other crafts for texture and scent. *FDA approved for flavoring foods.*

EYEBRIGHT HERB (cut & sifted) - *Euphrasia officinalis* / euphrasy, red eyebright / Bulgaria / Commonly found in the meadows of Europe and western Asia, eyebright has also naturalized in parts of the U.S. It is a small annual herb with red or purple and white flowers, said to give the appearance of a bloodshot eye. The name is derived from the Greek meaning "gladness." *No FDA designation for safe use in food.*

FENNEL SEED (ground, whole) - *Foeniculum vulgare* / large fennel, sweet fennel, wild fennel / India / Fennel is a relative of dill, one of the earliest known herbs. During the Middle Ages, fennel was used to stave off hunger during church fasts, and in 16th century Europe "to give fennel" meant to flatter or give false compliments. For cooking it has long been used in conjunction with fish, and is enjoyed as a fragrant tea. *FDA approved as a spice and for flavoring foods.*

FENUGREEK SEED (ground, whole) - *Trigonella foenum-graecum* / India / The Egyptians used fenugreek as a food and in incense. It is one of the oldest cultivated crops. The Latin *trigonella* means "little triangle," which is a reference to the shape of the seed. It is currently used in perfumery, for maple flavoring in confectionery, as an addition to curry and spice mixtures, as an ingredient in chutney, puddings, candy, and baked goods, as a yellow dye, and for sprouting. *FDA approved as a spice and for flavoring foods.*

FEVERFEW HERB (cut and sifted) - *Tanacetum parthenium* / U.S. / This attractive, robust perennial is many-branched with yellow-green, strongly-scented pinnate leaves. The abundant flowers are yellow discs with white rays. Feverfew grows wild on dry sites in any well-drained soil. *No FDA designation for safe use in food.*

FLAX SEED (whole) - *Linum usitatissimum* / linseed / U.S. / This seed is commonly pressed for its oil, which is edible, or used to produce a wood-finishing preparation (boiled linseed oil, which is not edible). Used as a food in ancient times, protein-rich flax is currently gaining popularity as an addition to such foods as cereal. The shiny, oval-shaped, golden-brown seeds are used in bird seed and livestock feed. A hair setting lotion may also be made using the mucilaginous properties of flax. *No FDA designation for safe use in food.*

FO-TI ROOT (powdered, sliced) - *Polygonum multiflorum* / minister Ho, outside scarlet vine, chicken-droppings vine, iron scale weight / China / Fo-ti is a perennial vine with fibrous roots and large flat tubers. It is used extensively by the Chinese, and has a pleasantly bitter, acrid taste. *No FDA designation for safe use in food.*

FRANKINCENSE POWDER AND TEARS - *Boswellia carteri* / oblibanum / Arabia / In ancient times frankincense was used by upper class Egyptians to ward off foul odors, which were associated with evil. Its primary use today is still in the manufacture of incense. Frankincense is a resin and needs an outside heat source to burn. It is easily burned with the use of incense charcoal. (See *Frankincense Incense,* page 170.) If you place it on a heated surface, such as a cookstove, protect the surface with foil. Frankincense tears are translucent yellow, with a sharp, balsamic scent. We offer frankincense tears, which are resinous drops from the tree, and frankincense powder, which is the ground tears. The frankincense powder contains silicon dioxide, a natural anti-caking agent. *FDA approved for flavoring foods.*

GALANGAL ROOT (cut & sifted) - *Alpinia galanga* / catarrh root, galanga, large galangal / Asia / Related to ginger, this plant is cultivated in China, southeast Asia, Indonesia, and Iran. It has a creeping rootstock, and, during flowering, reaches a height of three to five feet. An important flavoring in Southeast Asian cooking, this herb is used in stews, soups, and curries. *FDA approved only for flavoring alcoholic beverages.*

GARLIC (flaked, granulated, powdered, bulbs) - *Allium sativum* / U.S. / One of the earliest cultivated plants, garlic is thought to be native to central Asia. A small, pungent member of the onion family, as a seasoning it may be used for anything except sweets. It is especially flavorful with soups, salads, fish, poultry, meat, eggs, sauces, dressings, breads, grains, and vegetables. Use long, slow heat to soften the flavor of garlic, as high heat will produce a bitter flavor. (See *Garlic*, page 21.) *FDA approved as a spice and for flavoring foods.*

GENTIAN ROOT (cut & sifted) - *Gentiana lutea* / bitter root, bitterwort, pale gentian / Spain / A perennial found in mountain meadows and pastures, this plant is thought to be named after Gentius, King of Allyria. Fermented gentian root is used as a bitter preparation in alcoholic drinks, and is the principle flavoring agent in angostura bitters. *FDA approved for flavoring foods.*

GERMANDER HERB (cut & sifted) - *Teucrium canadense* / U.S. / Germander seed pods are fluted, with toothed ends. Germander is often sold (incorrectly) as scullcap; though germander and scullcap are from the same family (*labiatae*), they are different genera. *No FDA designation for safe use in food.*

GINGER ROOT (crystallized, cut & sifted, ground, whole) - *Zingiber officinale* / black ginger, race ginger, African ginger / China, India / Ginger is used in pickling, and as an ingredient in syrups, soups, meats, vegetables, sweets, squash, sweet potatoes, roasts, poultry, carrots, fruit mixtures, seafood, beverages, preserves, and sauces. It is an essential ingredient in Oriental cooking, as well as in such traditional western favorites as gingerbread and ginger snaps. Also used to diminish undesirable tastes such as fishiness, it is spicy, hot, and pungent. Pickled ginger is a popular Chinese and Japanese condiment. For a good dipping sauce, mix minced ginger with soy sauce and scallions or crushed garlic. To preserve ginger's aroma and taste, store in an airtight container, in a dry place, away from light. To use fresh ginger, lightly scrape the skin and slice. Then mince or prepare according to the recipe directions. Dried ginger root may be substituted for fresh in recipes, and when neither is available, ginger powder may be used at the rate of 1/8 teaspoon powder per tablespoon of fresh ginger. The spicy, sharp aroma is sometimes used to scent potpourris. Crystallized ginger is a sweetened ginger which can be used in cooking and eaten as a candy. To make crystallized ginger, fresh ginger is peeled, boiled, and preserved in a sugar solution. It contains ginger and sugar and the preservative sulfur dioxide. *FDA approved as a spice and for flavoring foods.*

GINSENG

A perennial plant known as the "root of life," ginseng has been used for centuries in the Orient. *Panax quinquefolius* is the species of ginseng found in the U.S. and Canada, while *Panax Ginseng*, the Oriental variety, is found primarily in Korea, China, and Siberia. (Siberian ginseng is known as *Eleutherococcus senticosus* and is closely related to *Panax ginseng.*)

Frontier sells dried garlic, from California, in three forms. It has not been organically grown, but has been tested to insure that there is no detectible chemical residue. Store garlic in a tightly-closed container in a cool, dry place.

Garlic flakes may be used whenever a garlic flavor and uniform garlic texture is desired. They are successfully used in casseroles, sauces and gravies, marinades, pickles, and dressings. These flakes may be added directly to most foods or rehydrated by soaking in cool water for 30 minutes. Substitute 3/4 teaspoon of garlic flakes for each fresh garlic clove required by your recipe.

Granulated garlic is more readily dispersible than garlic flakes, and provides more bulk and thickening properties than powdered garlic. Use it when a garlic flavor, but not texture, is important. It works well in blends, and with canned, frozen, and dry packaged foods, as well as with meat products. Try this form if you have trouble with powdered garlic caking (due to excess moisture). Granulated garlic may be added directly to most foods, or blended with other dry seasonings. To add to hot foods, or foods lacking enough water for rehydration, first mix with enough cool water to make a smooth paste. To obtain maximum fresh garlic flavor, the paste should be added toward the end of the cooking time. One teaspoon of garlic granules is equivalent to one clove of fresh garlic.

Powdered garlic, a potent and convenient form, may be used whenever a garlic flavor and aroma, but no garlic texture or additional bulk, is required. Its uniform appearance makes it desirable for salt blends or white sauces. It disperses easily into liquids, and retains its flavor even in hot or acid foods. Try it in tomato base products, salad dressings, sausage, snacks, and seasoning blends. You may add powdered garlic directly to hot and cold foods, and other dry seasonings. A paste may be made, to approximate the appearance of crushed fresh garlic, by mixing one part garlic to two parts water. When substituting for fresh garlic in recipes, use 1/2 teaspoon powder per garlic clove.

While dried garlic is very convenient, some cooks depend heavily on a supply of fresh garlic. While our supply lasts, we also sell fresh garlic bulbs in the fall. Certified organic, these are from New York State, and are available in five pound and forty pound quantities. We also sell elephant garlic, a large, mild bulb appreciated by many cooks. You can easily store garlic bulbs through the winter in a cool, dark, dry place. Cloves may be planted in the garden in either spring or late summer. To plant, place two inches deep, about six inches apart in sandy-loam soil in a sunny spot. Pull and dry in the fall for winter storage, or when planting in late summer, harvest the following fall. (Mulch with dry leaves or straw over winter.)

ginseng is known as *Eleutherococcus senticosus* and is closely related to *Panax ginseng*.)

Containing vitamins, minerals, amino acids, enzymes and saponins, ginseng is cultivated in Korea, Russia, and the U.S., and is found growing wild in sheltered North American forests. To insure potency, roots are traditionally harvested at about six years of age. Yellowish-white when pulled from the ground, they taste like raw turnips and will later vary in color depending upon the method of curing. Steam curing produces brownish-red roots, for example, and roots dried in the sun are white.

Ginseng root, American wild (whole) - *Panax quinquefolius* / Iowa / This fine-quality ginseng is hand dug by local gatherers in Iowa woods. Harvested in late summer, the roots are air-dried and purchased by Frontier in the fall. Many people prefer wild ginseng to cultivated, believing it to be more potent. We sell American wild ginseng root whole in one-ounce packages. *No FDA designation for safe use in food.*

Ginseng root, Korean white (powdered) - *Panax ginseng* / Korea / Cultivation of Korean ginseng is thought to have begun more than 1,000 years ago. It has been used for centuries for culinary purposes, especially in soups, and as a tonic. *No FDA designation for safe use in food.*

GLOBE AMARANTH FLOWERS - *Gomphrena globosa* / India / These pink-white or red-purple one inch spheres are similar in shape to a clover blossom and are used for color and texture in potpourris. As these flowers are very light, a little goes a long way. We estimate 650-700 flowers to a half pound. *No FDA designation for safe use in food.*

GOLDENROD HERB (cut & sifted) - *Solidago virgaurea* / European goldenrod / Poland / Americans have used goldenrod with alum and cream of tartar or chrome (as mordants) when making yellow dye. There are more than 80 species of goldenrod, of which all but one grow in the U.S. *No FDA designation for safe use in food.*

GOLDENSEAL LEAF (cut & sifted) and **ROOT** (powdered, whole) - *Hydrastis canadensis* / eyebalm, yellowroot / U.S. / Goldenseal was used by the American Indians as a yellow dye for clothing and weapons. Once plentiful in American forests, it was harvested almost to extinction by collectors in the 1930's. *No FDA designation for safe use in food.*

GOTU KOLA HERB (cut & sifted, powdered) - *Hydrocotyle asiatica* / Indian pennywort, hydrocotyle / India / An exotic cousin of the common pennywort, gotu kola is indigenous to the swampy tropical areas of Africa, India and South America. In the Philippines only, it is used as a cover crop on tea and rubber plantations and is eaten raw or cooked in salads and curries. The "kola" portion of this herb's name should not be confused with "kolanuts" (*Cola nitida*), which contain caffeine. Gotu kola contains neither kolanuts nor caffeine. Gota kola is occasionally used in herbal bath mixtures. *No FDA designation for safe use in food.*

GRAINS OF PARADISE SEED (whole) - *Aframomum melegueta* / Melegueta pepper / West Africa / Served as a spice in medieval European cuisine, this item was known as *grana paradisi* because it was imported from distant lands. Because of its hot and peppery taste, it has long been used as a pepper substitute when real pepper was not available. *FDA approved as a spice and for flavoring foods.*

GUARANA SEED (ground, whole) - *Paullinia cupana* / Brazilian cocoa, uabano / Brazil /

Guarana, often drunk as a tea, contains three times as much caffeine as coffee. Used for thousands of years by the Indians of the Amazon, and as currency in the Bolivian area, it is often referred to as the "soft drink of Brazil." *FDA approved for flavoring foods.*

HAWTHORN BERRIES (whole), **LEAVES** and **FLOWERS** - *Crataegus oxycanthus* / maythorn, whitethorn, May blossom / Europe, U.S. / The ship Mayflower was named for this very showy bush, which blooms in May. Hawthorn refers to the sharp thorns all along the twiggy branches of the plant. The deep red berries are 1/2 inch, deep red ovals, and are found adding texture and color to potpourris. Historically, the leaves and flowers have been used in European teas. *No FDA designation for safe use in food.*

HEAL ALL HERB (cut & sifted) - *Scrophularia marilandica* / figwort, knotted figwort, carpenter's square, kennelwort / U.S. / Known for its detergent properties, heal all is a perennial with tuberous roots and dark purple flowers. *No FDA designation for safe use in food.*

HEATHER FLOWERS (whole) - *Calluna vulgaris* / France / These tiny flowers are lavender and green, and add lovely color and texture to herbal craft projects. *No FDA designation for safe use in food.*

HELONIAS ROOT (cut & sifted) - *Chamaelirium luteum*, also known as *Helonias dioica* / false unicorn root, devil's bit, fairy want / U.S. / Easily cultivated, this plant is indigenous to North America, and likes wet meadows, rich woods and thickets. It has densely-packed clusters of tiny white flowers and a wand-like stem, often drooping at the tip. *No FDA designation for safe use in food.*

HENNA LEAF, RED (powdered) - *Lawsonia alba* / Iran / Henna has been used since ancient times to color nails and hair (It is thought to have been used by Cleopatra!). This true henna is a natural red dye and is used as a conditioning and natural coloring agent for hair. (See *Henna Treatment*, page 179.) *FDA approved as a hair dye.*

HIBISCUS FLOWERS (cut & sifted, whole) - *Hibiscus sabdariffa* / China, Sudan / Hibiscus grows wild in temperate and tropical areas of the world. Often used in potpourris, hibiscus flowers have no scent, but are a lovely pink-red to deep red color. They lend this color as well as delicious tart, tangy flavor to teas, fruit juices, and punches. We sell hibiscus flowers whole and hibiscus flowers cut and sifted, which are more convenient for tea making. *FDA approved only for flavoring alcoholic beverages.*

Hibiscus Blend Tea Recipe
Bring 4 cups of water to a boil and pour over:
4 teaspoons hibiscus flowers
1 teaspoon spearmint leaves
1 vanilla bean
3 cloves
1 stick cinnamon
Steep 10 minutes. Sweeten with honey and serve hot or iced.

HOPS FLOWERS SWEET (whole) - *Humulus lupulus* / U.S. / Hop is a vine which is used to provide a bitter flavor to beer and ale. Sweet hops are from the unfertilized female flower clusters, while acid hops are from the fertilized female. Fertilization increases yield, but produces a poor quality flavor which is disfavored in the brewing industry. These papery, pale green sweet hops flowers have a light, grassy scent, and add texture and color to potpourris. *FDA approved for flavoring foods when used as an extract or tea.*

HOREHOUND HERB (cut & sifted) - *Marrubium vulgare* / hoarhound, marrubium, white horehound / Bulgaria, Germany / This plant was dedicated by the ancient Egyptians to Horus, god of sky and light. At Passover, it was one of the bitter herbs taken by the Jews. It is now used as a flavoring for candy, and makes an appealing tea when blended with honey, peppermint, and hyssop. *FDA approved as a spice and for flavoring foods.*

HORSERADISH ROOT (granulated, powdered) - *Armoracia lapathifolia* / red cole / U.S. / "Horseradish" suggests a coarse, strong, pungent, radish, as opposed to the edible radish. Rehydrate the granules by soaking in water for 30 minutes. The granules may also be reconstituted and preserved in white wine vinegar. One pound rehydrates to five pounds. They are most often used in cocktail sauces and fish entrees, with meat, and in pickles, horseradish vinegar, and breads. The powdered form is best used to add heat and pungency to spicy sauces, mustards, deviled eggs, sour cream, and German sausage. The root is high in vitamin C. The root we sell contains sodium bisulfite as a preservative. *FDA approved as a spice and for flavoring foods.*

Herb Cheese Recipe
1 clove garlic
1 tablespoon parsley flakes
1 - 8 oz. pkg. cream cheese
1/4 cup butter
dash fresh ground pepper
1-1/2 teaspoon horseradish root powder

Mince garlic clove in food processor. Add other ingredients and blend until smooth. Refrigerate. Serve on cucumber slices or crackers.

—Recipe by Ruth E. Ohlsen, ***The Flavor Connection****, Inc., Glenwood, IL*

HYDRANGEA ROOT (cut & sifted) - *Hydrangea arborescens* / seven barks / U.S. / This native North American shrub is found on dry slopes, in shady woods, and on streambanks. The stems grow from three to ten feet high and are covered with thin layers of different colored bark. *No FDA designation for safe use in food.*

HYSSOP HERB (cut & sifted) - *Hyssopus officinalis* / Yugoslavia, Germany / Of Greek origin, hyssop was used to purify sacred places, and is alluded to in the scriptures: "Purge me with hyssop, and I shall be clean." It is a traditional staple of Middle Eastern cuisine, where it is used in pita bread, and a spicy blend known as *zatyr*. (*Zatyr* consists of hyssop, sesame seed, wheat, parsley, chickpeas, salt, elm-leaved sumac, soya oil, and lemon.) It is also used in salads, fried eggs, fish, cheese, and meats. *FDA approved as a spice and for flavoring foods.*

JASMINE FLOWERS (whole) - *Jasminum officinale* / Taiwan / Jasmine flowers are famous for the perfumes made from their oil. This product consists of 1/2 inch, yellow-tan flowers and petals. Jasmine flowers have a light, sweet, aroma and are used for their texture and scent in craft projects such as potpourri. They are also used to blend fragrant herbal teas. Jasmine black tea, one of the best-known scented teas, is made by blending black tea with jasmine flowers until the tea has absorbed the flavor and aroma of the flowers. The flowers are then removed, or left in for visual appeal. *FDA approved for flavoring foods when used an extract as long as daily intake does not exceed 300 mg.*

JUNIPER BERRIES (whole) - *Juniperus communis* / Yugoslavia / Juniper berries are connected both with legends of evil spirits and with holy legends from the Bible. In the 19th century, the air in schoolrooms was sweetened by putting juniper berries on red-hot burning coals. Its distinctive, evergreen-like flavor is also used to season foods; as a fragrant component in soaps, detergents, creams, lotions, and perfumes; and as a main flavoring ingredient in gin. *FDA approved for flavoring foods when used as an extract or tea.*

KAVA KAVA ROOT (cut & sifted, powdered) - *Piper methysticum* / ava, ava pepper / Polynesia / Popular beverage in Fiji and other Pacific countries. *FDA approved for flavoring foods when used as an extract as long as daily intake does not exceed 300 mg.*

KESU FLOWERS (whole) - *Kesu* spp. / India / These one-inch swirls of brown, yellow, and orange flowers have a faint aroma and are used for color and texure in herbal crafts such as potpourri. *No FDA designation for safe use in food.*

KOLA NUTS (cut & sifted, powdered) - *Cola nitida* / guru nut, caffeine nut, cola seed, bissy nut / Sudan / An important part of inland commerce in tropical Africa, kola nuts are used to improve the flavor of whatever is eaten after them, and to make water more palatable. As a flavoring, they are used in bitters, carbonated beverages, and desserts. Caffeine is found only in fresh kola nuts. *FDA approved only for flavoring food when used as an extract or a tea.*

LADY'S MANTLE HERB (cut & sifted) - *Alchemilla vulgaris* / lion's foot, bear's foot, nine hooks / U.S. / This plant was named lady's mantle in the Middle Ages when it was associated with the Virgin Mary, and the lobes of its leaves were thought to resemble the scalloped edges of her mantle. The Latin name *alchemilla* is derived from *alkemelych*, which is Arabic for "alchemy." It is sometimes used for cosmetic purposes such as herbal baths. *No FDA designation for safe use in food.*

LADY'S SLIPPER ROOT (cut & sifted) - *Cypripedium pubescens* / nerve root, American valerian, Noah's ark / U.S. / American Indians climbed high into the Rocky Mountains to collect lady's slipper . The golden-yellow flowers, lined with purple, have a lower lip that forms an inflated sac, suggesting the shape of a moccasin. Hunted to near extinction, this plant is an endangered species in some states. *No FDA designation for safe use in food.*

LAVENDER FLOWERS (whole) - *Lavandula officinalis* / English lavender / France / Lavender was used in ancient times to scent bath water; the Latin *lavandus* means "to be washed." The small, lance-like flowers are blue-purple in color and have a sweet, perfume scent. Lavender is used for aroma and texture in herbal crafts such as potpourri. Its aroma is also enjoyed in perfumes, and its flavor in teas such as jasmine. We sell two grades of lavender flowers - regular and select. Select lavender flowers are similar in aroma and shape to our regular flowers, but are of exceptional color. *FDA approved as a spice and for flavoring foods.*

Lavender Water Mix (Toilet Water)
1 oz. lavender oil
30 oz. isopropyl alcohol
Shake ingredients together and let set for 48 hours. Shake again and let set for another 48 hours, then bottle tightly.

LEMON BALM LEAF (cut & sifted) - *Melissa officinalis* / balm mint, garden balm, bee balm, melissa, cure-all / Albania / Lemon balm, which grows profusely, is considered a weed by many. Its uses are both cosmetic and culinary. Its fragrant aroma makes it a popular potpourri ingredient and the soft lemony flavor is delightful in hot or cold tea. *FDA approved as a spice and for flavoring foods.*

LEMON GRASS (cut & sifted) - *Cymbopogon citratum* / sweet rush / U.S., Central America / A tropical grass grown in the western U.S., lemon grass has a fresh lemon scent and mild, cool, lemon flavor. It is delicious in herbal tea blends and broths, and is especially compatible with mints, hibiscus, black tea, and alfalfa. This citrus-scented herb is found in Indonesian, Malaysian, Indochinese, and Thai cooking. Lemon grass contains citral (citronella), an essential oil used in perfumes. It is used in shampoos and skin tonics, and is sometimes found in potpourris. *FDA approved for flavoring foods when used as an extract or tea.*

Lemon Herb Tea Recipe
Steep 5 minutes in 3 cups of boiling water:
4 tablespoons mint
4 tablespoons lemongrass
Add honey and ice.

LEMON PEEL (cut & sifted, granulated, powdered) - *Citrus limon* / Spain / Dried lemon peel is versatile and comes in many forms. Store it in an airtight container in a cool, dry place.

Cut and sifted lemon peel is used in cooking when chunks of peel, as well as the flavor and aroma of lemon, are desired. To rehydrate, soak one part peel in three parts cool water for about 30 minutes. One-half teaspoon of cut and sifted lemon peel equals one teaspoon of freshly grated peel, or 1/2 teaspoon of extract. Try this form in marmalades, tea blends, jellies, and cookie fillings. These 1/4-inch, brown-yellow chunks are also used in potpourri crafting for their texture and citrus aroma.

Granulated lemon peel is easily measured and dispersed. Use this form whenever a lemon taste and aroma, but not texture, is required. Each granule is approximately 1/8 inch square. To rehydrate, soak one volume of granules in three and one half volumes of water for about 30 minutes. Drain if necessary and use promptly. Or use directly in wet recipes by adding an additional one and one-half parts of water for each part granules. One-half teaspoon lemon granules equals one teaspoon freshly grated lemon, or 1/2 teaspoon lemon extract. Try this form in meringue pies, puddings, cheesecakes, doughnut icings, jellies, with baked fish and clams, and seasoning mixes.

Powdered lemon peel is a convenient form which is used to add lemon color, aroma, and flavor to recipes. Use the powdered form when no lemon peel texture is required. Add the powder directly to dry ingredients, or to baking batter. Try this form in cakes and frostings, cookie fillings, pie fillings, jellies, marmalades, and seasoning mixes. To substitute for one teaspoon of freshly grated lemon peel, or 1/2 teaspoon of extract, use 1/4 teaspoon of powder. *FDA approved for flavoring foods.*

LEMON THYME (cut and sifted) - *Thymus citriodorus* / U.S. / This culinary herb is especially good in Mexican foods, meat, poultry, and fish dishes. It combines well with mints, especially spearmint, for a refreshing tea. Try adding some spiced apple cider to your next cup, hot or cold. The tiny, bright green leaves have a soft lemon-herbal scent and are used to add aroma, color, and texture to potpourris. *No FDA designation for safe use in food.*

LEMON VERBENA LEAF (cut & sifted, whole) - *Aloysia triphylla* / lemon-scented verbena / France / Lemon verbena is commonly used in potpourris, sachets, and perfumes. Its three-inch, lance-like leaves are medium green in color and lemony in aroma. Its mild lemon taste and aroma is perfect in tea blends. *FDA approved only for flavoring alcoholic beverages.*

LICORICE ROOT (cut & sifted, powdered) and **STICK** (whole) - *Glycyrrhiza glabra* / sweetwood / Turkey and southern Europe / Licorice root is four times sweeter than cane sugar. The roots are dug in the autumn of their fourth year, preferably from plants that have not borne fruit as these are the sweetest. Licorice is used as a food flavoring and sweetener in soft drinks, teas, syrups, candies, liqueurs, ice cream, puddings, bakery products, soy sauce, soybean meat substitutes, beers, mouthwashes, and toothpastes. Licorice sticks are often chewed or sucked on for their sweet, licorice flavor. The whole licorice sticks we sell are eight inches long. *FDA approved as a spice and for flavoring foods.*

LICORICE STICK, CHINESE (whole) - *Glycyrrhiza uralensis* / China / These licorice sticks, which are about six inches long, are thinner, softer, and more fibrous than Italian or Turkish licorice sticks (above). They were popular in China as toothbrushes because the stiff fibers cleaned the teeth while the flavor sweetened the breath. *FDA approved as a spice and for flavoring foods.*

LIFE EVERLASTING FLOWERS (whole) - *Helichrysum stoechas* / cat's ear, cudweed, catsfoot, American everlasting / Russia, Hungary / These bright yellow, 1/2-inch flower clumps are used in dried flower arrangements and potpourris. *No FDA designation for safe use in food.*

LIME PEEL (cut & sifted) - *Citrus aurantifolia* / Europe / This lime has excellent flavor and can be used in cooking or in simmering potpourris. For use in cooking, rehydrate by soaking in cool water for one hour. Lime turns very dark when dried naturally and is not appropriate when a green color is needed. *FDA approved for flavoring foods when used as an extract or tea.*

LINDEN FLOWER (whole) - *Tilia europaea* / European linden, basswood, European lime tree / Yugoslavia, Romania / The name linden is derived from the Latin *lentus*, meaning "flexible." This is a reference to the plant's pliable, fibrous inner bark, which was used in ancient times for binding vines. Linden foliage has been dried like hay for winter animal feed and linden flowers made into wine. *FDA approved as a spice and for flavoring foods.*

LOBELIA HERB (cut & sifted) - *Lobelia inflata* / bladderpod, Indian tobacco, gag-root, vomit root / U.S. / Used extensively by Native Americans, lobelia was discovered by early colonists and named by the botanist Matthias de Lobel. It was exported to England by the Shakers. Its common name, Indian tobacco, is derived from the fact that it was formerly smoked by North American Indians. The FDA does not permit the sale of this product for human consumption. *FDA prohibited for use in food due to naturally occurring toxins.*

LOVAGE ROOT (cut & sifted) - *Levisticum officinale* / European lovage, love parsley, sea parsley / Europe / This plant was used as a love charm in Europe, and thus became known as love parsley. Its celery-like flavor has been used to flavor teas, vinegars, poultry, meat, fish, egg dishes, chowders, sauces, and vegetables. *FDA approved for flavoring foods.*

LUNGWORT LEAF (cut & sifted) - *Pulmonaria officinalis* / cowslip, Jerusalem sage, spotted comfrey / Europe / The name lungwort is derived from the fact that this plant's oval, hairy leaves with whitish spots resemble diseased lungs. *FDA approved for flavoring foods.*

MACE (cut & sifted, ground, whole) - *Myristica fragrans* / Indonesia, Sri Lanka / Mace is the net-like membrane (arvil) surrounding the shell of the nutmeg. It is used in pickling, stews, and baked goods. East Indian mace, the variety we carry, is a brighter orange, has a higher essential oil content, and a richer flavor than West Indian mace. With a spicy nutmeg aroma, and attractive reddish-orange color, mace (especially the whole form which comes from Sri Lanka) is sometimes used in herbal crafts such as potpourri. *FDA approved as a spice and for flavoring foods.*

MAIDENHAIR FERN (whole) - *Adiantum pedatum* / rock fern, maiden fern, hair fern / U.S. / The Latin name Adiantum comes from the Greek *Adian-tum*, or "unwetted." This is a reference to the fact that the maidenhair fern glistens when immersed in water, and remains dry when removed. The taste of this delicate fern is terribly bitter. It grows throughout the eastern U.S. in moist, shady woods, particularly heavily-limed areas. *FDA approved only for flavoring in alcoholic beverages.*

MALVA FLOWERS, BLACK (whole) - *Althea rosea* / Yugoslavia, Romania / These one-inch flowers are composed of black petals in a pale green base. They have a sweet raspberry scent and are used to add color and texture to potpourri and other herbal crafts such as floral necklaces. *No FDA designation for safe use in food.*

MALVA FLOWERS, BLUE (whole) - *Lavatera thuringiaca* / common mallow, high mallow, cheese flower, country mallow / Yugoslavia, Hungary / These malva flowers are a mauve-purple, with one-inch papery flowers. They have long been used for garlands on May day, and are beautiful in herbal craft projects. *No FDA designation for safe use in food.*

MALVA LEAF (whole) - *Malva rotundifolia* / U.S. / The Latin name malva refers to the soft, emollient leaves of this plant. It has long been cultivated as a garden herb, and was once highly respected as a foodstuff. *No FDA designation for safe use in food.*

MANDRAKE ROOT (cut & sifted) - *Podophyllum peltatum* / May apple, raccoonberry, wild lemon / North America / Mandrake has been considered a mystical plant since ancient times and was thought to be the medieval witch's most utilized plant. *FDA prohibited for use in food due to naturally occurring toxins.*

MARJORAM LEAF (cut & sifted, ground) - *Marjorana hortensis* / knotted marjoram, sweet marjoram / Egypt / Marjoram was believed to have been cultivated by Aphrodite, and was a favorite herb of the Greeks. A member of the mint family, marjoram is mild, sweet, and aromatic, and is often used as a flavoring for vegetables, meats, soups, sauces, and some cheeses. One of the most important of all western culinary herbs, it is also delicious as an herb butter. *FDA approved as a spice and for flavoring foods.*

MARSHMALLOW ROOT (cut & sifted) - *Althaea officinalis* / althea, mallards, mallows / Hungary / Marshmallows were originally made of the mucilaginous extract of marshmallow root and were considered a medicine rather than a food. Romans enjoyed boiled marshmallow roots, which are said to be delicious fried with onions and butter. English bakers today prepare a confectionary paste from these roots, and the Chinese still eat mallows in some of their dishes. As an emollient, marshmallow root is sometimes used in the preparation of creams and lotions. *FDA approved for flavoring foods.*

MISTLETOE LEAF (cut & sifted) - *Viscum album* / all-heat, birdlime, devil's fuge, European mistletoe / Hungary / Because it has no roots in the ground, ancients believed mistletoe came from heaven, in a flash of lightning. According to Scandinavian legend, Balder (god of peace) was slain with an arrow made of mistletoe. He was restored to life and mistletoe was given to the goddess of love for safekeeping. It was then ordained that everyone who passed under it should receive a kiss, to show that the branch had become an emblem of love and not of hate. Mistletoe is commonly used in craft projects, especially winter decorations. *FDA prohibited for use in food due to naturally occurring toxins.*

MOSS, DARK GREEN, DYED - / U.S. / For use in potpourri and other herbal crafts, this is a moss that has been dyed a very dark bright green. *No FDA designation for safe use in food.*

MOTHERWORT HERB (cut & sifted) - *Leonurus cardiaca* / lion's ear, lion's tail, throwwort / Europe / The leaves of this member of the mint family have a pungent, but aromatic odor and bitter taste. The latin name *leonurus* means "lion's tail," and is thought to refer to a resemblance in the plant. Motherwort has been used as a source for dark green dye. *No FDA designation for safe use in food.*

MUGWORT HERB (cut & sifted) - *Artemisia vulgaris* / common mugwort, felon herb, sailor's tobacco / Yugoslavia / Once known as "the mother of herbs," mugwort was one of the nine herbs used in pre-Christian times to repel demons. It has long been used as an ingredient in dream pillows and in herbal bath mixtures, especially in combination with chamomile and agrimony. *FDA prohibited for use in food due to naturally occurring toxins.*

MUIRA PUAMA ROOT (cut & sifted) - *Ptychopetalum olacoides* / marapuama / Brazil / Found in the Amazon, muira puama is a shrub whose young stems and roots are used by natives. *Ptycho* refers to the folds or deep grooves in the leaves, *petalum* refers to the single petals, and *olacoides* means "resembling olive." *No FDA designation for safe use in food.*

MULLEIN LEAF (cut & sifted) and **FLOWERS** (whole) - *Verbascum thapsus* / black mullein / Bulgaria, Egypt / Because it was reportedly used by witches in the Middle Ages, mullein was known as "hag taper." The leaves are used to add bulk and interesting shape to winter bouquets and potpourris. *No FDA designation for safe use in food.*

The flowers are 1/2 inch and bright yellow, with a downy underside. Romans mixed the flowers with lye to dye their hair blond, and they are still used cosmetically today. Use the flowers carefully in crafts however, as they turn brown when oil is added to them. *FDA approved only for flavoring alcoholic beverages.*

MUSTARD SEED, BROWN (whole) - *Brassica juncea* / Canada / In cooking, black mustard seed is used interchangeably with brown mustard seed, both of which act as a preservative for mayonnaise, curries and salad dressings. Prepared mustard is a mixture of ground mustard seed, salt, vinegar, turmeric and other spices. French mustard paste is made from brown or black seeds ground in vinegar; Italians mix orange and lemon peel with the seed. Mustard seed is also a popular pickling spice. *FDA approved as a spice and for flavoring foods.*

MUSTARD, HOT ORIENTAL (ground) - *Brassica hirta* / Western Canada / This Chinese mustard is much hotter than our yellow mustard and is served as a condiment with Oriental meals. To make, moisten mustard powder with warm water to form a thin paste. Allow to stand for 10 minutes to develop hotness and pungency. Because the pungency dissipates within a few hours unless vinegar or other acidic liquid is added, plan to use within an hour. For variety, soy sauce may be used as the liquid instead of water. Use within an hour. A blend of Oriental and Canadian mustard seeds, this is a hot and spicy blend. *FDA approved as a spice and for flavoring foods.*

MUSTARD SEED, YELLOW (ground, whole) - *Brassica hirta* / Canada / Yellow (or white) mustard is milder than brown mustard, with a tangy flavor that develops after the seed has been moistened. Whole seeds are used in pickling, and boiled with vegetables, especially cabbage and beets. Ground yellow mustard is used in sauces, dressings, prepared mustard, and mayonnaise. Ground mustard must be moistened with water or another low-acid liquid for ten minutes in order to develop its flavor. If it is to be stored, the mustard preparation should be acidified with vinegar or lemon. Add prepared mustard to sauces, dips, eggs, cheese dishes, tofu, grain dishes, and salad dressings. *FDA approved as a spice and for flavoring foods.*

MYRRH GUM (cut & sifted, powdered) - *Commiphora molmol* / northern Africa / Myrrh has been used since ancient times in incense, perfumes, and fumigants. The name myrrh comes form the Arabic *mur*, or "bitter," referring to the spice's bitter taste. Today it is found in incense and mouthwashes, as well as some herbal crafts. The 1/2-inch rough chunks are brown-red, with a sweet aroma when heated (on a charcoal disk or other outside heat source, for example). The powdered form contains silicon dioxide, an anti-caking agent. *FDA approved for flavoring foods.*

NETTLES LEAF (cut & sifted) - *Urtica dioica* / common nettle, common stinging nettle, great stinging nettle / West Germany / Before the introduction of flax, nettle was used for thread, and the Anglo-Saxon name netel is derived from noedl (a needle). *Urtica urens* is a small, dwarf nettle, while *Urtica dioica* is a greater nettle. Nettles contain vitamins A and C, as well as calcium, iron, and potassium. Nettle is commonly found in herbal shampoos and rinses. The leaves are also used in facial steams. *No FDA designation for safe use in food.*

NUTMEG (ground, pieces, whole) - *Myristica fragrans* / Indonesia, (East Indies), Grenada (West Indies) / Nutmeg is the seed of an evergreen tree indigenous to the islands of the East Indian Archipelago. East Indian nutmeg yields a higher essential oil content and is more piquant in flavor than milder West Indian nutmeg. West Indian nutmegs are "unassorted," or mixed sizes. These are the nutmegs we sell whole. East Indian nutmeg (our ground variety), is softer and therefore usually used for grinding. This spice is used to flavor baked goods, sauces, fruit pies, confectionery, liqueurs and dairy products such as eggnog and pudding. Whole nutmeg and nutmeg pieces (which are about 1/2 inch) add aroma and texture to potpourris, and the oil is used in the production of soap and perfumes. The pieces are also used in some blends such as mulling spices. To use whole nutmeg in cooking, simply grate as needed. Caution: Large, concentrated quantities of pure nutmeg can be toxic. *FDA approved as a spice and for flavoring foods.*

OAK MOSS - *Evernia prunastri* / Europe / Oak moss serves many functions in potpourri crafting; it is used for color, texture, aroma, and as a fixative. The 1/2-inch feathery strips are silver to dark-grey and have a soft, sweet moss scent; they are especially nice in floral potpourris. Powdered oak moss is used as the basis for body powder, while the resin is used in perfumery and soapmaking. *No FDA designation for safe use in food.*

OAT STRAW (cut & sifted) - *Avena sativa* / U.S. / Avena is the old Latin name for oats and is often added to bathwater by Europeans. *No FDA designation for safe use in food.*

ONION (flaked, granulated, powdered, sliced) - *Allium cepa* / U.S. / Like garlic, onions are one of the earliest cultivated plants. A member of the lily family, onions were probably cultivated in Egypt, China, and India before the beginning of recorded history. Today they may be used to season all dishes except sweets. They are especially good in soups, stews, salads, with eggs, fish, poultry, grains, and vegetables. We sell dried onion in many forms. Store them in an airtight container in a cool, dry place. (See *Onions*, page 33.) *FDA approved as a spice and for flavoring foods.*

ONION GREEN (minced) - *Allium fistulosum* / U. S. / These dried green onions add lovely color and mild onion flavor to a wide variety of dishes. Try them on salads, in soups, cheese or cream sauces, casseroles, or on baked potatoes. They may be added directly to foods containing liquids, or reconstituted (for use on salads, for example) by soaking in cool water for just a few minutes. *FDA approved as a spice and for flavoring foods.*

ORANGE PEEL (cut & sifted, granulated, potpourri cut, powdered) - *Citrus sinensis* / Spain / We sell orange peel in a variety of dried forms. Store it in an airtight container in a cool, dry place. Granulated orange peel is easily measured and dispersed. It is suitable for use when an orange flavor and aroma, but not texture, is required. Each granule is approximately 1/8 inch square. Use directly in baking by adding one part of peel in batter or filling, with about equal parts water. To rehydrate (for addition to dishes without enough liquid for rehydration), soak one volume of granules in about three volumes of water for 30 minutes. Drain, if necessary, and use as soon as possible. One-half teaspoon orange peel granulated equals one teaspoon fresh orange peel, which equals 1/2 teaspoon of extract. Try granules in orange marinades (as for poultry, meat, or fish) and marmalades, glazes, sauces, tea blends, cakes, frostings, custards, hot pastries, cookies, and pies. Sprinkle granules directly on top of fruit pies to enhance their overall flavor.

Orange peel cut and sifted is suitable for use when larger chunks of peel are desired. It imparts an orange flavor and aroma as well as texture to recipes. Rehydrate by soaking peels in three times their volume of cool water for 30 minutes. One-half teaspoon orange peel cut and sifted equals one teaspoon fresh orange peel, or 1/2 teaspoon of extract. These 1/4-inch orange pieces are also used in herb or black teas and to add aroma, texture, and color to herbal crafts projects such as potpourri.

Our potpourri cut of orange peel consists of 1/2 to 3/4 inch chunks, and is especially well-suited to potpourri when larger chunks are needed.

Powdered orange peel is a convenient form which is used to add orange color, aroma, and flavor to recipes. Use the powdered form when no orange peel texture is required. Add the powder directly to dry ingredients, or to baking batter with an equal volume of additional liquid. It is primarily used in cakes and frostings. For each teaspoon of fresh orange peel or 1/2 teaspoon of extract required, substitute 1/4 teaspoon powder. *FDA approved for flavoring foods when used as an extract or a tea.*

ORANGE PETALS SWEET (whole) - *Citrus aurantium* / Spain, Mexico / The first mention of the orange tree is found in writings of the Arabs. It is a small tree, with fruit a little darker and rougher than the common orange, and more strongly scented flowers. The yellow-tan petals have a very sweet, orange scent, and are used for their aroma and color in potpourris, and as a flavoring in teas. *FDA approved for flavoring foods when used as an extract or a tea.*

OREGANO LEAF MEDITERRANEAN (ground) and **GREEK** (cut & sifted) - *Origanum vulgare* / wild marjoram, Greek oregano, organy / Greece, Turkey / Since the end of WW II, when the G.I.'s returning from Italy started the demand for "pizza spice," the sale of oregano has increased 6,000%. Before 1940 it was referred to as "wild marjoram." *Origanum vulgare* has been more popular than *Lippia graveolens* (Mexican oregano) for use in Italian dishes; it has a more subtle flavor. It is used in pizza and other tomato dishes, omelettes, gravies, beef stew, and lamb dishes. *FDA approved for flavoring foods when used as an extract or tea.*

OREGANO LEAF MEXICAN (cut & sifted) - *Lippia graveolens* / Mexican marjoram, Mexican wild sage / Mexico / This oregano, more aromatic and pungent than Greek oregano, is used in chili powder, chili con carne, and other Mexican dishes. *FDA approved as a spice and for flavoring foods.*

OREGON GRAPE ROOT (cut & sifted) - *Mahonia nervosa* / Rocky Mt. grape, trailing mahonia, holly mahonia, California barberry / U.S. / Oregon's state flower, this plant was used to produce a yellow dye and as a tea by the Indians of the northern Pacific Coast. Around larger towns and cities, this plant was almost exterminated when the roots were used for domestic purposes by settlers. *No FDA designation for safe use in food.*

ORRIS ROOT NATURAL (cut & sifted, granulated, powdered) and **PEELED** (cut & sifted, powdered) - *Iris germanica* var. *florentina* / yellow flag, iris / Italy / Orris has a very astringent taste, and is found in dentrifices, cosmetics, and herbal crafts. We sell natural orris root and peeled orris root. Both forms are available powdered, and cut and sifted, and the natural root is also available in granulated form. *FDA approved for flavoring foods.*

Powdered orris is used as a fixative in sachets, while the cut and sifted is used in potpourris. (It is an especially nice fixative for floral potpourris.)

Granulated orris root is a convenient form for small-particle potpourris or sachets.

The natural orris root is generally darker than the peeled, as it still contains some of the root skin. It is also less aromatic, because the root skin itself has no aroma.

(Caution: Many people are allergic to orris. Do a skin test on a small patch of skin before using this product for cosmetic purposes.)

OSHA ROOT (whole) - *Ligisticum porteri* / Colorado cough root, porter's lovage / U.S. / Related to the European lovage plant, osha is harvested in the mountains of New Mexico, Montana, Wyoming, Colorado, and Arizona. The root is dark brown, with a camphor and celery aroma and a thick, hairy appearance. It is sometimes confused with poison hemlock, which has a hairless root and purplish splotches on the stem just above ground level. *No FDA designation for safe use in food.*

PAPAYA LEAF (cut & sifted) - *Carica papaya* / paw, paw, melon tree / India / Papaya leaves have been used as a soap substitute and as an ingredient in herbal facials. *No FDA designation for safe use in food.*

PAPRIKA HUNGARIAN, SPANISH, DOMESTIC - *Capsicum annuum* / pimiento, sweet pepper / Hungary, Spain, U.S. / (See *Capsicum*, page 13.) The fruit of several varieties of *Capsicum annuum* are ground to make paprika, a spice used for its coloring properties and delicate flavor. Soon after the discovery of the Americas, Europe was introduced to capsicum seeds from the fiery hot peppers found among the natives by Columbus. Because of different soils, climates, and cross breedings, the resulting European capsicums were very different from their American relatives. In Hungary, for example, the capsicums, while still pungent, were much milder, and Spain produced from their seeds a sweet product with no heat at all.

Today, the paprika produced by Hungary and Spain are more similar, as Hungarian cultiva-

Onion flakes are successfully used when an onion flavor, aroma, and texture is desired. To reconstitute, soak in cold water (three times their volume) for at least 30 minutes. When sufficient liquid is present, flakes may be added dry toward the end of the cooking process. Try onion flakes in casseroles, soups, sauces, canned foods, meat and bean loaves, frozen vegetables, relishes, onion rolls, and stuffings. For each onion required by your recipe, substitute 1/4 cup onion flakes.

Granulated onion provides an easily dispersible onion flavor for blends, meat products, canned, frozen, and dry packaged goods. This form also provides more bulk and thickening properties than powdered garlic and is more easily measured than flakes. Try this form if you have trouble with your powdered onion caking (due to excess moisture). Use it when an onion flavor, but not appearance, is important. Granulated onion may be added directly to most foods, or rehydrated before being added to foods that are hot or lacking enough water for rehydration. To rehydrate, mix with enough cool water to make a smooth paste. Add the paste toward the end of cooking time. To substitute for one onion in a recipe, use 1 and 1/2 tablespoons onion granules.

Onion powder is a convenient form that may be used when an onion flavor and aroma, but not texture, is desired. Use it with canned foods, meat products, gravies, sauces, spice blends, soups, and spreads. Add powdered onion directly to most foods, or rehydrate before adding to hot foods, or foods lacking enough water for rehydration. Rehydrate by mixing with enough cool water to make a smooth paste. To obtain maximum onion flavor, add the paste toward the end of cooking time. Use in place of fresh onion by substituting 1 and1/3 tablespoons onion powder for each onion required.

Onion slices are great in soups, sauces, casseroles, and on pizzas - anywhere full onion slices are desired for taste and prominent onion appearance. Add these slices directly to most dishes, or rehydrate first by soaking in cool water for 30 minutes. Rehydration is necessary when adding to foods that do not contain sufficient liquid for rehydration. Substitute 1/4 cup sliced onion for each fresh onion required.

tors strive to reproduce the characteristic sweetness of Spanish paprika. In Europe, Hungarian paprika is used almost exclusively as a spice rather than a coloring agent, while Spanish paprika is cultivated with color range and sweetness in mind. Domestic paprika, grown in southern California, is standardized to insure uniform color and taste.

Paprika is used to add color and mild flavor to cheese, eggs, potatoes, pasta, and sauces. Commercially it is a vital ingredient in salad dressings, soups, and sausage. Famous European dishes made with paprika include Hungarian goulash and rosenpaprika. Higher in vitamin C than citrus fruits, it should be stored carefully to prevent deterioration in flavor, color, and vitamin content. Ideal storage conditions are 38° F in a dark, dry (50% humidity) area. *FDA approved as a spice and for flavoring foods.*

PARSLEY LEAF (flakes, powdered) and **ROOT** (cut & sifted) - *Petroselinum crispum* / California / Parsley leaf flakes are made from freshly harvested parsley which has been washed, trimmed, diced and dried. The flake size is 1/4 to 3/8 inches square. One teaspoon of parsley leaf flakes equals one tablespoon of fresh parsley. Reconstitute dehydrated parsley by soaking one part parsley in two parts ice water for five to ten minutes. Drain and use as you would fresh parsley to enhance the color and flavor of foods. It is delicious in dips, salad dressings, stuffings, sauces, gravies, butters, and fine herb mixtures. Our parsley flakes are bright green, with a fresh, mild, clean flavor. They serve well as a garnish.

Powdered parsley leaf may be used when a parsley aroma and taste are desired, without added texture. Try it with canned foods, meat products, sauces, spice blends, and spreads. Add powdered parsley directly to most foods, or rehydrate by mixing with enough cool water to make a smooth paste. One-half teaspoon powdered parsley leaf may be substituted for each 1/4 cup fresh parsley required. *FDA approved as a spice and for flavoring foods.*

Parsley root is a white taproot, long and thick, and best harvested its second year. *No FDA designation for safe use in food.*

PASSION FLOWER HERB (cut & sifted) - *Passiflora incarnata* / America / This genus has about 400 species, the majority of which are native to the Americas. Its climbing vine has tendrils and large white or yellow flowers with purple centers. Early settlers thought the corona in the center of this plant's flower resembled Christ's crown of thorns and named it passion flower. This flower is used in massage oils, herbal bath mixtures, and teas. *FDA approved for flavoring foods.*

PATCHOULI HERB (cut & sifted) - *Pogostemon cablin* / pucha-pat / Germany / Patchouli is highly aromatic and its principal use is as a perfume. It has an earthy, pungent aroma and is used to scent soaps, cosmetics, sachets, and potpourris. *FDA approved for flavoring foods.*

PAU D' ARCO BARK (cut & sifted) - *Tabebuia impetiginosa* / bowstick, taheebo, ipe, lapacho morado / Brazil / Pau d' arco is the shredded bark from a tall tree whose hard wood is used to make archery bows. Used by Native South Americans for years, it has recently been "rediscovered" and is being popularized in the U.S. The Pau d' arco we sell is obtained from the inner bark. *No FDA designation for safe use in food.*

PEACH LEAF (cut & sifted) - *Prunus persica* / U.S. / In Italy it was once believed that if fresh peach leaves were applied to warts and then buried, the warts would fall off by the time the buried leaves decayed. In the Taoist religion, it is the most important sacred plant, symbolizing immortality. Peach leaves are used for cosmetic purposes, and to produce a yellow dye. *FDA prohibited for use in food due to naturally occurring toxins.*

PENNYROYAL HERB (cut & sifted) - *Mentha pulegium* / squaw balm, tickweed, fleabane /

Europe / European pennyroyal is not the same plant as American pennyroyal (*Hedeoma pulegioides*), although they have many of the same uses and properties. Its menthol, minty aroma is sometimes used in potpourris. Pennyroyal has, in small quantities, been used as a flavoring agent in puddings, and as a weak tea. It is also used in scented products such as sachets. In the eastern Mediterranean area, pennyroyal has been used to produced a natural dye. *FDA approved for flavoring foods.*

PEONY FLOWERS (whole) and **ROOT** (cut & sifted) - *Paeonia officinalis* / Korea / The peony plant is named after Paeon, the physician of the Greek gods. The large flowers are pink-purple with yellow centers and are used for color and texture in potpourris. *No FDA designation for safe use in food.*

PEPPER - *Piper nigrum* / India, Indonesia / *Piper nigrum* is a woody, climbing vine native to Indonesia and cultivated in the tropics as well. No relation to pod peppers (capsicums), pepper berries (peppercorns) grow in spike-like clusters of four to six inches in length and turn from green to yellow to red as they ripen. The U.S. consumes more peppers than any other nation on earth. This popular spice was a medium of exchange in medieval times. *FDA approved as a spice and for flavoring foods.*

We sell a variety of peppers:

Black pepper (ground, whole) - To produce black pepper, the immature berries are picked, fermented, and dried, and the entire peppercorn - after wrinkling and turning brown/ black - is ground. The result is a combination of a dark skin and light-colored core (a "salt & pepper effect"). Black pepper, generally preferred over white in the U.S., can be used in all foods except sweets. Our ground black pepper is available in regular (pepper-shaker) grind, and a flavorful coarse grind. Whole black peppercorns are used in meats, sausages, gravies, salad dressings soups, salads, and vegetables. They may be ground in a peppermill for seasoning almost any food.

Tellicherry peppers, from the tellicherry coast of India, are considered the highest quality gourmet black pepper. Prized for their large, very regular and flavorful berries, they have long been used by Italian sausage makers. We sell whole Tellichery peppercorns.

White pepper (ground, whole) - White pepper is produced by allowing the berries to ripen longer on the vine, harvesting and soaking them, removing the red outer skin, and sun drying the white core. Containing more starch and less ash than black pepper, white pepper has a milder, finer flavor. It has been used extensively in Europe, and some in the U.S. to season light-colored foods such as white sauces.

Green peppercorns (whole) - These peppercorns, picked while still green, are dehydrated. They are used for their color and special taste in gourmet cooking. To preserve them, they contain sodium sulfite and/or sodium bisulfite.

PEPPERCORNS PINK - *Schinus terebinthifolius* / Brazilian pepper tree / Reunion Islands / These whole pink berries are a gourmet item in French cooking, where they are used for their sweet peppery flavor and lovely color. Pink peppercorns are not related in any way to true peppercorns. *(Banned from use in the U.S. by the FDA until recently. Some controversy still exists about their safety because of a close relationship to the poison ivy family. There is some research which indicates that some people are sensitive to this item, especially if they are sensitive to poison ivy.)*

PEPPERCORNS SZECHAUN - *Xanthophyllum piperitum* / Anise pepper / China / This Chinese spice has a sweet, balsam-like taste which leaves a tingling sensation. Reddish, with a slightly different shape than that of black and white peppercorns, it is often used in marinades and sauces. Our Szechuan peppercorns are available in 1/4 pound bags. *No FDA designation for safe use in food.*

PEPPERMINT LEAF (cut & sifted) - *Mentha piperita* / lamb mint, brandy mint / U.S. / The familiar taste of peppermint is used to flavor a wide variety of products, from desserts, liqueurs, chewing gum, sauces, and fruits, to medicines, toothpastes, and mouthwash. Peppermint is among the most popular tea herbs and complements most other herbs. Its clean, refreshing flavor is equally good iced in the summer and hot in the winter. *FDA approved as a spice and for flavoring foods.*

PERIWINKLE HERB (cut & sifted) - *Vinca minor* / great periwinkle, early-flowering periwinkle, lesser periwinkle / Yugoslavia / Historically, periwinkle has served varied purposes. It has been used in making chains and love philters, and in the exorcism of evil spirits. Known as the "flower of death," it was made into garlands for the caskets of children. It was known as the "flower of immortality" to the Germans, and to the French it represented friendship. Often planted as an ornamental ground cover, it is still used in garlands and wreaths. *FDA prohibited for use in foods due to naturally occurring toxins.*

PIPSISSEWA (cut and sifted) - *Chimpaphila umbellata* / Prince's Pine, love in winter, winter green / U.S. / The name *chimaphila* is derived from the Greek words for "winter" and "to love." The dry leaves have only a slight odor, but the freshly rubbed leaves are sweet smelling. This herb has been made, along with powdered ginger, into a beer. *FDA approved for flavoring foods when used as an extract or tea.*

PLAINTAIN LEAF (Cut & sifted)- *Plantago major*/ way bread, white man's foot, round-leaved plaintain / West Germany/ American Indians found plaintain spreading wherever Europeans went, and named it "white man's foot." Now considered a weed by gardeners, it has a great reputation in herbal folklore and is mentioned in the writings of Chaucer and Shakespeare. *No FDA designation for safe use in food.*

PLEURISY ROOT (cut & sifted) - *Asclepias tuberosa* / butterfly weed, flux root, tuber root / U.S. / There are about eighty species of this plant, most of which are native to North America. It grows in dry, sandy soils, and is of the same genus as common milkweed. *No FDA designation for safe use in food.*

POPPY FLOWERS (whole) - *Papaver rhoeas* / Romania / Large papery flowers with a deep red and burgundy color, poppy flowers are used for color and texture in potpourris. *No FDA designation for safe use in food.*

POPPY SEED (whole) - *Papaver somniferum* / Holland / The species name of this plant is derived from the "sleep-bearing" properties of its flowers, although the seeds do not share this quality. Poppy is grown in most temperate regions of the world, but Dutch blue poppy, which we stock, is said to produce the best seeds. These tiny, slate-blue seeds are used as a condiment on breads, pastries and rolls, crushed in fillings, or added to salad dressings and stuffings. The nutty, sweet flavor of poppy seeds is fully released when the seeds are warmed. They yield a fine salad oil when pressed. To glaze any baked goods with poppy seeds, simply beat one egg and spread on rolls, breads, etc., with a pastry brush. Sprinkle on the poppy seeds and bake as usual. How many poppy seeds are there in a one pound sack? Roughly 900,000! *FDA approved as a spice and for flavoring foods.*

Poppy Seed Waffles Recipe
1 cup poppy seeds
3 cups milk
2 tablespoons oil
1 tablespoon honey
2 eggs
1/2 cup wheat germ
2 cups flour
2 teaspoon baking powder
1 teaspoon sea salt

Heat poppy seeds in milk. Simmer for five minutes. Cool. Combine milk and poppy seeds with oil, honey, and eggs. In a separate bowl, combine: wheat germ, flour, baking powder, and salt. Add liquid ingredients to dry ingredients and mix.

Cook according to directions for your waffle iron. Makes 8 waffles.

PRICKLY ASH BARK (cut & sifted) - *Zanthoxylum clavus herculis* (southern) and *Zanthoxylum americanum* (northern) / northern prickly ash, toothache tree / U.S. / There are two principal varieties of prickly ash - northern and southern - which have been used for similar purposes by Native and early Americans. They are small, aromatic trees with spines on their stems and petioles. The bark has been used to make alcoholic beverages. Another tree, *Aralia spinosa*, is sometimes substituted for prickly ash. Although the two small trees are similar in appearance, the difference between the two is obvious under microscopic examination. True prickly ash may also be detected by the numbing of the mucous tissue after several minutes of chewing. We sell only true prickly ash. *FDA approved for flavoring foods when used as an extract or tea.*

PSYLLIUM SEED HUSK (powdered, whole) **SEED** (whole) - *Plantago ovata* / India / Psyllium husk is a thin, membrane-like layer coating each psyllium seed. When water is added, the husk swells to form a gelatinous mass. We sell blond psyllium, which is used as a thickener in foods. *FDA approved as a spice and for flavoring foods.*

Fruit Gel Recipe
1 cup fresh or frozen fruit (cherries or blueberries work well)
1 tablespoon psyllium seed husk powder
1/3 cup honey
1 teaspoon vanilla extract
1 teaspoon lemon juice
Mix all ingredients well in a blender. Refrigerate at least half an hour to gel.

QUEEN OF THE MEADOW HERB (cut & sifted) - *Eupatorium purpureum* / Joe Pye, gravel root, meadowsweet / U.S. / This herb became well known in the eastern U.S. as "Joe Pye weed" because of its extensive use by an Indian named Joe Pye. When the plant is well established, it predominates an area, and thus earned the name queen of the meadow. Used to flavor mead in the Middle Ages, it also came to be known as meadowsweet. The flowers have a faint almond aroma, and may be used in scented articles. A black dye is made using queen of the meadow and a copper mordant. *No FDA designation for safe use in food.*

RASPBERRY LEAF (cut & sifted) - *Rubus idaeus* / European red raspberry, garden raspberry, hindberry, bramble of Mt. Ida / Yugoslavia, U.S. / A member of the rose family, raspberry is a shrub which has been believed to belong to Venus. The leaves are used in herbal

Popular Herbs/Spices

Anise

Allspice

Alfalfa

Bay

Basil

Caraway

Burdock

Cardamom

Cayenne

Black Pepper

Celery

Catnip

Chamomile

Chives

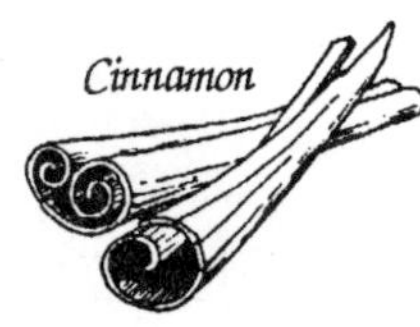
Cinnamon

Clove

Chicory Root

Dandelion Root

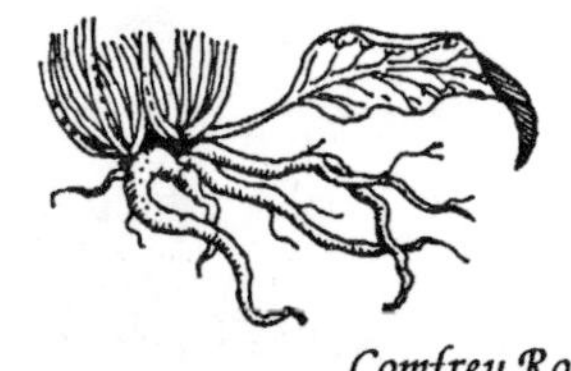
Comfrey Root

Dandelion Leaf

Coriander

Fennel

Comfrey

Cumin

Dill Weed

Echinacea Herb

Echinancea Root

Whole Dill

Fenugreek

Flax

Garlic

Eucalyptus

Hibiscus

Nutmeg

Gotu Kola

Kelp

Goldenseal

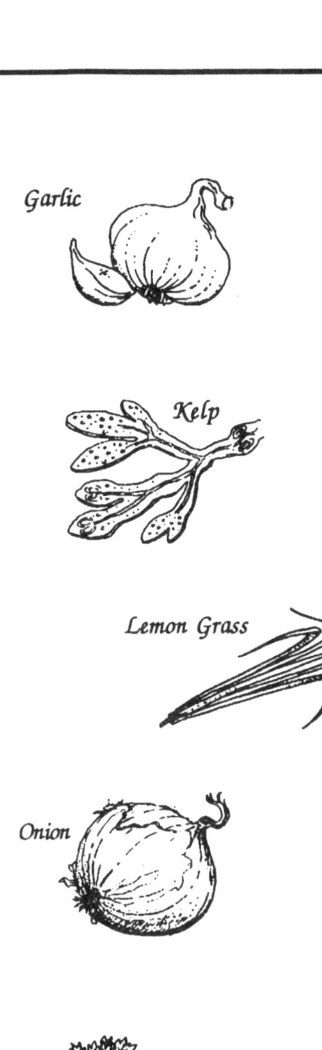

Licorice Root

Lemon Grass

Nettle

Marjoram

(Yellow) Mustard Seed

Oregano

Onion

Paprika

Peppermint

Poppy

Pau D'Arco

Parsley

Red Clover

Psyllium

Rosehip

Raspberry

Rosemary

Senna

Slippery Elm Bark

Sage

Thyme

Spearmint

Turragon

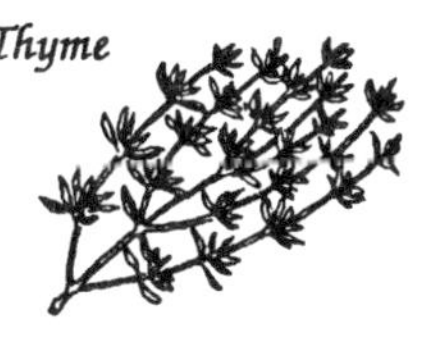

Valerian Root

hair, facial, and bath mixtures. *No FDA designation for safe use in food.*

RED CLOVER HERB (cut and sifted) and **TOPS** (whole) - *Trifolium pratense* / U.S., Bulgaria / Because of its three leaves, red clover was known to the ancients as *trifolium*. It is a short-lived perennial native to Europe. After its introduction to America, it became naturalized and was used by American Indians. Today red clover is important agriculturally, as a forest and cover crop. The herb is valued for the delicate, sweet flavor it imparts to herbal teas. This flavor combines especially well with dried rosehips, lemon, and wild mint. Red clover tops are used for texture and color in potpourri and other herbal craft projects. *FDA approved as a spice and for flavoring foods.*

RED ROOT (cut & sifted) - *Ceanothus americana* / Jersey root, Jersey tea, wild snowball / U.S. / Used as a tea during the Revolutionary War, red root has also been used to dye wool a cinnamon color. *No FDA designation for safe use in food.*

RHUBARB ROOT (cut & sifted) - *Rheum officinale* / Chinese rhubarb, turkey rhubarb, Russian rhubarb, East Indian rhubarb / Bulgaria / The commercial names of rhubarb indicate the routes by which it formerly reached the European market; the geographical sources are the same. Rhubarb is a perennial herb which resembles the common garden rhubarb and is cultivated outside its native Tibet and China. Rha is the ancient name of the Volga, on whose banks the plant grows. It has been added as a bitter to tonic wines, and used as a dye by Canadian wool dyers. *FDA approved for flavoring foods.*

ROSEBUDS AND PETALS (whole) and **ROSEBUDS** (powdered) - *Rosa centifolia* (pink), *Rosa gallica* (red) / Morocco, Pakistan / This large, sweet-scented rose is available in red or pink, and becomes white towards the base. When dried, a soft floral aroma remains, which is lovely in potpourris. Rosebuds are also used in commercial rosewater and perfumery, and French liqueurs. The Romans cultivated *Rosa gallica*, and fable suggests that it was derived from the blood of Adonis. *FDA approved for flavoring foods when used as an extract or tea.*

ROSEHIPS (cut & sifted, powdered, whole) - *Rosa canina* / Chile, Bulgaria / Rosehips, or "hips of the dog rose," impart a red color and tart flavor to teas. The hip is an achene, or small, dry fruit which bears the seed of the rose and is high in Vitamin C before drying. Chilean rosehips are a bright red color with a faint, fruity aroma. Bulgarian rosehips are darker but have a sweeter flavor. They are also used for color and texture in potpourri crafting. The cut & sifted rosehips we sell have most of the seeds removed. *FDA approved for flavoring foods when used as an extract or tea.*

ROSEMARY LEAF (ground, whole) - *Rosmarinum officinalis* / Spain, Yugoslavia / This plant has been named *Rosmarinum* (dew of the sea) because of its blue flowers, and its affinity for the seashore. Associated since ancient times with remembrance, fidelity, and love, rosemary is still worn by some brides in Europe today. In 17th and 18th century Europe it was a funeral flower, symbolizing the memories of loved ones. As a culinary herb, its clean, fresh, bittersweet flavor is commonly used to flavor vegetables, meats, breads, soups, stews, and fish dishes. The 3/4-inch needles have an herbal, menthol scent and are used for texture and aroma in potpourris. Rosemary is also found in many herbal shampoos and hair rinses. *FDA approved as a spice and for flavoring foods.*

RUE HERB (cut & sifted) - *Ruta graveolens* / Herb of Grace / Germany / This bitter herb has long been a symbol of sorrow and repentance. Thought to be a protector against witchcraft and magic, rue was an ingredient in the poison antidotes of Mithridates. The gray leaves of this plant served as the model for the suit of clubs in playing cards. Formerly used in a mead called sack, rue is employed today in the production of an Italian grape wine known as *Grappa con ruta*. The oil of rue is used in perfumery, and fresh leaves are used sparingly in salads. *FDA approved as a spice and for flavoring foods.*

SAFFLOWER PETALS (whole) - *Carthamus tinctorius* / American saffron, false saffron, bastard saffron, carhami, dyer's saffron / Europe, China / As one can easily see by the various common names for safflower, it is used as a substitute for saffron. It was introduced by the Mormons to the Southwest around 1870, and used by the Hopi Indians to color their wafer bread yellow. Although the color is similar, it is not an acceptable culinary substitute for saffron. The red-orange, thread-like petals are successfully used for color and texture in potpourris. *No FDA designation for safe use in food.*

SAFFRON, SPANISH (whole) - *Crocus sativa* / crocus, karcom, drokos, zaffer, hay saffron, valencia saffron, gatinais saffron / Spain / Saffron was used by the Greeks to produce a royal dye color and to perfume streets, buildings, baths, and homes. From the 14th to 18th centuries, spice dealers were known as "saffron grocers." Saffron is the world's most expensive spice. These red and gold threads are the hand-picked stigmas from flowers, and it takes over 200,000 dried stigmas from more than 70,000 flowers to make one pound. From one acre of plants, only eight to twelve pounds are yielded. Its color, aroma, and taste are distinctive. It is used today in rice, chicken, and bread, producing a bright yellow color and a delightful pungent flavor. Our saffron is available in 1/2 ounce packages, 1/2 gram bottles, and one gram bottles. *FDA approved as a spice and for flavoring foods.*

SAGE LEAF (ground, rubbed, whole) - *Salvia officinalis* / Yugoslavia, Albania / There are over 500 species of sage. *Salvia officinalis* is the most popular for culinary use. Sage is a perennial mint and is native to the northern shore of the Mediterranean. Dalmatian sage, reputed to have the finest flavor, comes from Dalmatia (Yugoslavia). Sage from Albania is grown in the same region and is also of excellent quality. We carry either one, depending on availability. Until World War II, sage was the most popular culinary herb in America. (Oregano displaced it at that time.) Sage is highly aromatic and fragrant, and the taste is pungent and slightly bitter. It is often used with fats, such as sausage, pork dishes, and processed meats. It is also good in salad dressings, chowder, stuffings, fish dishes, cheeses, and many seasoning blends. In medieval Europe, sage was the favorite hot beverage, and it was added to ale. A delicious herb tea can be made from sage leaves alone or in combination with other herbs. The grey-green 1/2-inch leaves have a woodsy, sharp scent and are used for aroma, color and texture in herbal crafts. We carry sage in three forms: whole (whole leaves), rubbed (leaves are crushed, yielding a fluffy consistency), and ground (a fine powder). *FDA approved as a spice and for flavoring foods.*

ST. JOHN'S WORT HERB (cut & sifted) - *Hypericum perforatum* / Europe / The species name, *perforatum* , refers to the small, hole-like dots on the leaves of this plant. St. John's wort is native to Europe and is not naturalized in the U.S. It is one of the best known of a group of herbs which were smoked in fires on St. John's Eve in medieval times. The purpose was to purify the air of evil spirits. The flowers of this plant have been used to produce both yellow and pink dyes. *FDA prohibited for use in food due to naturally occurring toxins.*

SALT FROM THE SEA - Sodium chloride (NaCL) / U.S. / Salt is not a spice, but a mineral. Our sea salt currently comes from the West Coast and is 99% salt (NaCL), with no additives or iodine. (The salt commonly purchased in grocery stores contains sodium silico aluminate, dextrose, and potassium iodide.) It can be used for brining and pickling solutions, as well as seasoning. Salt has traditionally been used to preserve foods such as pickled vegetables, brined meats, and dried cheeses. It has also been used in common household cleaners. A paste of vinegar and salt makes a good brass and copper cleaner, and salt sprinkled over hot oven spills helps clean up after the oven cools. *FDA approved as a spice and for flavoring foods.*

SANDALWOOD YELLOW (chips, powdered) - *Santalum album* / India / Sandalwood is valued for its fragrance, and is used to make perfumes and incense. Only the trunk of this small tree is valued; trimmed of branches, it is left on the ground for several months during which time white ants eat away the otherwise worthless sapwood. White sandalwood comes from young trees, yellow from mature trees. The 1/4-inch chips have a woodsy scent and are often used for aroma in herbal bath mixtures and aroma and texture in potpourris. *FDA approved for flavoring foods.*

SANDALWOOD RED (cut & sifted) - *Pterocarpus santalinus* / sanders, red sanders, santal / West Germany / These bright red 1/4-inch shreds are used for color and texture in herbal crafts. Because of their size, they are nicely suited to small textured potpourris. Unlike yellow sandalwood, red sandalwood is not especially aromatic, but can be used as a natural dye. On cottons and woolens, sandalwood can produce a red color, and it may be used as an under-hue for indigo as well. *FDA approved only for flavoring alcoholic beverages.*

SANICLE HERB (cut & sifted) - *Sanicula* spp. / wood sanicle, European sanicle / Yugoslavia / Sanicle derives its name from *sanus*, meaning "to heal." It is a perennial plant, found in shady, moist, European forests. *No FDA designation for safe use in food.*

SARSAPARILLA ROOT (cut & sifted, powdered) - *Smilax regelii* / Jamaica / American, or false sarsaparilla, is what was used to make the elixirs sold in the U.S. during the 1800's. The variety of sarsaparilla we carry is in the lily family and is used to flavor the soft drink sarsaparilla. It is also used in herbal bath mixtures. *FDA approved for flavoring foods.*

SASSAFRAS ROOT BARK (cut & sifted) - *Sassafras albidium* / ague tree, tea tree, mitten tree, cinnamonwood, fennel wood / U.S. / Sassafras has been one of the most important export items in U.S. history. The tree is an aromatic member of the laurel, or bay family. According to the book, *Trees and Shrubs of Massachusetts 1894*, the aroma of sassafras trees reached Columbus on the sea before land was actually in sight. The red-brown chunks have a root-beer scent and are used for aroma in potpourris. Although commonly used as an herb tea by colonists and later in the south, sassafras contains safrole, which is cited as a cancer-causing substance by the FDA. *FDA prohibited for use in food due to naturally occurring toxins.*

SAVORY LEAF WINTER (ground, whole) - *Satureja montana* / France / Savory is one of the plants that was brought to America by English colonists to remind them of the gardens they left behind. It is aromatic and warming, used both for soap and culinary purposes. In the kitchen, savory is a common ingredient in bread stuffings and dressings, and is often boiled with beans and peas. The leaf is an important ingredient in salami, and the oil is used commercially as a flavoring. *FDA approved as a spice and for flavoring foods.*

SAW PALMETTO BERRIES (whole) - *Serenoa repens* / sabal / U.S. / This low-growing fan palm is found in swampy lowlands along the Atlantic coast and southern California. Its name is derived from the saw-toothed look of its leaves. The 1/2-inch black ovals have a sharp, cheesy scent and are used for texture and aroma in herbal crafts projects. *No FDA designation for safe use in food.*

SCULLCAP HERB (cut & sifted) - *Scutellaria laterflora* / Virginian scullcap, true blue, mad-dog scullcap, madweed, blue scullcap, helmet flower, toque / U.S. / The Latin name for this plant is derived from the word *scutella*, which means "a little dish." This is because of the peculiar bowl-shape of the seed pods. Scullcap is very similar in structure to germander and germander is sometimes sold as scullcap by misinformed or unscrupulous dealers. It is very hard to tell the difference once the herb has been cut. *No FDA designation for safe use in food.*

SENNA LEAF (cut & sifted, powdered, whole) and **PODS** (whole) - *Cassia angustifolia* / Tinnevilly senna / Egypt, India / First used by 9th century Arabians, the best senna was thought to come from Mecca. Senna is enjoyed as a tea, and is especially good with slices of ginger. The small, rather flat pods and whole leaves are sometimes used in potpourri crafting. *FDA approved for flavoring foods.*

SESAME SEEDS (whole) - *Sesamum indicum* / benne / Guatemala, Honduras, Central America / Sesame seeds were brought to America by slaves in the 17th and 18th centuries. In the tale of Ali Baba in *The Thousand and One Nights,* the magical command "Open Sesame" opens the door to the robber's den. China is the largest producer of the seeds, and most of the four million pounds produced annually is converted to oil. (See *Sesame*, page 44.) *FDA approved as a spice and for flavoring foods.*

SHAVEGRASS HERB (cut & sifted) - *Equisetum hyemale* / horsetail, bottle-brush, paddock-pipes, Dutch rushes, pewterwort, horsetails / West Germany / The *Equisetum* family is considered to be composed of primitive plants. They have jointed, hollow stems with no leaves and jointed branches. Because of the large quantitity of silica in the epidermis of the stem of this plant, it has been used for polishing metal. *No FDA designation for safe use in food.*

SHEPHERD'S PURSE HERB (cut & sifted) - *Capsella bursa pastoris* / pickpocket, mother's heart, pepper and salt, lady's purse / Hungary / Although native to Europe, it now grows as a weed over much of the U.S. *No FDA designation for safe use in food.*

SLIPPERY ELM BARK (cut & sifted, powdered) - *Ulmus fulva* / sweet elm, Indian elm, moose elm, rock elm, winged elm / U.S., West Germany / The slippery elm is a small tree native to North America. The bark we sell is the inner bark, obtained by stripping the bark from the tree in the spring and scraping off the outer layer. When this inner bark is soaked, it yields a mucilage which has been used (particularly in Appalacia) to soften and protect skin. *No FDA designation for safe use in food.*

SOAP TREE BARK (powdered) - *Quillaja saponaria* / soap bark, panama bark, cullay / Peru / In Peru, Chile, and Northern Hindustan, soap tree bark powder is used as a soap substitute in washing clothes. It is used elsewhere to clean delicate materials, and as a shampoo. Saponins, compounds in the plant, produce lather when the mashed plant parts are beaten in water. *No FDA designation for safe use in food.*

SOLOMON'S SEAL ROOT (cut & sifted) - *Polygonatum multiflorum* / drop berry, sealwort, seal root, Lady's seals, St. Mary's seal / U.S. / This plant is a close relative of Lily-of-the-Valley. The rootstock is knotty, with circular scars, or seals, left by the leaf stems of previous years. *Multiflorum* distinguishes this species, which has many flowers, from another

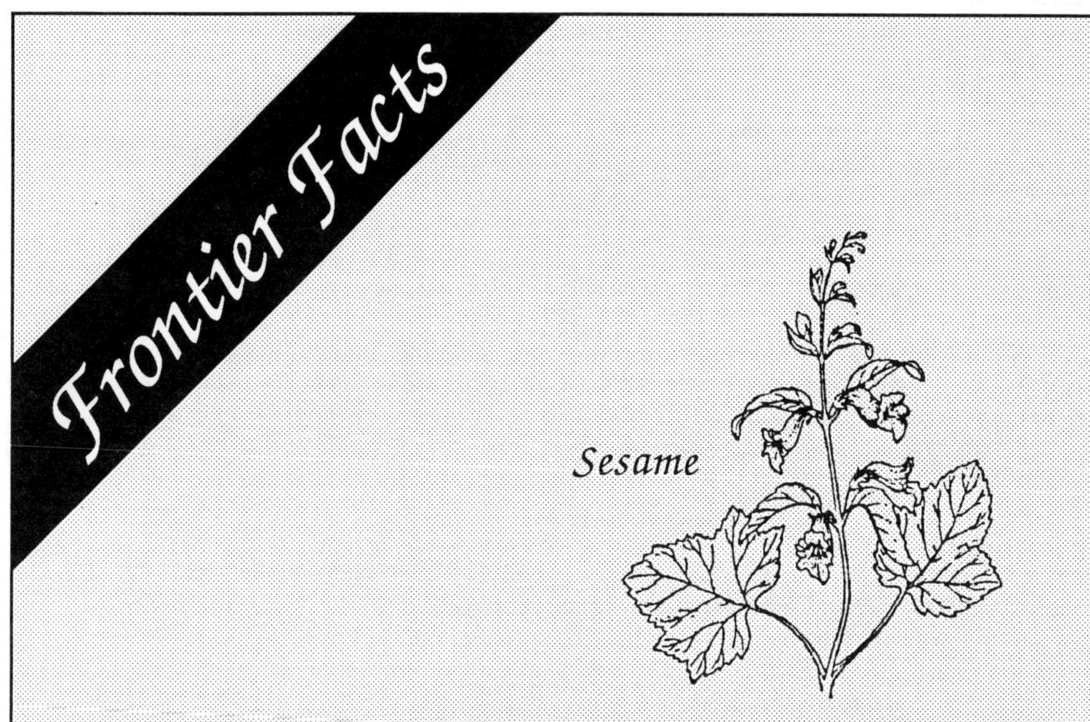

Many wonderful ethnic dishes are made with the seeds of the sesame. In the Near East, halva or sweetmeat is made with the ground seed. In the Middle East, sesame paste, or tahini, is used in cooking and on bread, in much the same way peanut butter is consumed. Tahini is also used in preparing hummus, a seasoned puree of chickpeas, and in blending *Baba gannouj*, an eggplant dip. In North American, sesame seed is commonly used by bakers much the way poppy seeds are used - sprinkled on rolls and breads, folded into biscuits and cakes. Pita bread is often topped with these seeds, as are hamburger buns, for which a high percentage of the seeds are used in the U.S.

In your own kitchen, sesame seeds can be added to a variety of dishes. Best when roasted lightly, try them sprinkled on rice, fish, chicken, or leafy vegetables. They may be added to stir-fried vegetables, or used to top casseroles. Added to salad dressings, cereals, yogurt, or sauces, sesame adds its special taste and aroma.

Sesame seeds are a good source of calcium, protein, and vitamins C and E. We sell whole, unhulled sesame seeds and hulled sesame seeds. The two forms are very similar in appearance, and may be used interchangeably. Unhulled sesame seeds are light brown, and preferred by some who believe the whole form of a product is more desirable. Hulled sesame seeds are white, and preferred by those who believe this form to be more digestible.

Gomasio Recipe

Mix 3/4 cups toasted sesame seeds and 1/4 cup sea salt. Grind. Store in refrigerator. Use as a table condiment. (Great on rice dishes.)

species, in which the blossoms are solitary. The mucilaginous root has been used by Italian women for cosmetic purposes, particularly in facial lotions and perfumes. *No FDA designation for safe use in food.*

SOUTHERNWOOD HERB (cut & sifted) - *Artemisia abrotanum* / Europe / A native of southern Europe, this is a leafy, lemon-smelling plant. Early American colonists carried sprigs of southernwood to church to help prevent drowsiness. Its pleasant smell is used in moth mixtures, and it is sometimes used in herbal crafts such as wreaths as well as herbal shampoos and hair rinses. *FDA prohibited for use in food due to naturally occurring toxins.*

SPEARMINT LEAF (cut & sifted) - *Mentha spicata* / garden mint, lamb mint, pea mint / U.S. / Menthe was a nymph, who because of Pluto's love for her was metamorphosed by Persephone into the plant we now call mint. Milder than peppermint, spearmint is a popular tea herb, and is used to flavor chewing gums, soaps, confections, and in making mint juleps and jelly. Its cool, aromatic fragrance is a favorite bath scent. *FDA approved as a spice and for flavoring foods.*

SPIKENARD ROOT (cut & sifted) - *Aralia racemosa* / petty morrel, Indian root, life-of-man / U.S. / The root of this plant is aromatic, with a spicy, balsamic taste. It is native to North America and was used extensively by American Indians. *No FDA designation for safe use in food.*

SPINA CRISTI (whole) - *Paulitus spina christi* / Yugoslavia / These one-inch conical hats are light green and tan and are found adding texture and color to potpourris. *No FDA designation for safe use in food.*

SQUAWVINE HERB (cut & sifted) - *Mitchella repens* / partridgeberry, squawberry, twinberry, checkerberry, winter clover / U.S. / A member of the Madder family, squawvine is a near relative of teasel, elderberry, and honeysuckle. It is the only species of its genus, and is fond of hemlock timbers. *No FDA designation for safe use in food.*

STATICE FLOWERS (whole) - *Limonium sinuatum* / U.S. / These 1/2-inch, fan-like flowers add color and texture to herbal crafts. We sell a variety of colors, depending on what is available each year. *No FDA designation for safe use in food.*

STEVIA HERB (cut & sifted) - *Stevia rebaudiana* / South America / A small, herbaceous shrub, stevia is a native of Paraguay, Brazil, and Argentina. In Japan, where it is approved for use as a sweetener, the sweetening substance stevioside is extracted and used to sweeten diet soft drinks. *No FDA designation for safe use in food although petitions have been filed with the FDA to allow its use as a food additive.*

STONE ROOT (cut & sifted) - *Collinsonia canadensis* / hardhack, horse weed, heal-all, knob grass, knob root, richweed / U.S. / The hard, knobby rootstock of this North American perennial sends up a quadrangular stem from one to four feet tall. The opposite, serrate leaves are heart shaped at the base. It is found in damp woods. *No FDA designation for safe use in food.*

STRAWBERRY LEAF (cut & sifted) - *Fragaria vesca* / wild strawberry, mountain strawberry, wood strawberry / Hungary / It is a common fallacy that the name strawberry is derived from the placing of straw under plants as the berries are ripening. Actually "straw" is derived from "to strew," referring to the tangle of vines with which the strawberry covers the ground. It is sometimes used as a herbal bath and in facial preparations. *No FDA designation for safe use in food.*

STRAWFLOWER (whole) - *Helichrysum bracteatum* / U.S. / These one-inch by one-inch flowers come in assorted colors, primarily fall shades of red and gold. Papery and large, they hold their shape well and are good for herbal crafts projects such as wreath making. *No FDA designation for safe use in food.*

SUMAC BERRIES (whole) - *Rhus glabra* / smooth sumac, dwarf sumac, mountain sumac, scarlet sumac / U.S. / Small and flattened, these rosy red berries have a fruity scent and are used for color and texture in potpourris. An infusion of sumac berries is an excellent dye for wool. *No FDA designation for safe use in food.*

SUNFLOWER PETALS (whole) - *Helianthus annus* / Yugoslavia, Pakistan / These one-inch narrow petals are golden brown and are sometimes used for texture and color in potpourris, as well as an ingredient in herbal hair rinses. They have no aroma. *No FDA designation for safe use in food.*

TANSY HERB (cut & sifted) - *Tanacetum vulgare* / bitter buttons, hindheal, parsley fern, yellow cedar / Germany / Tansy was a strewing herb used on the floors in the Middle Ages. Until the mid 19th century, this herb was used in pancakes known as "tansies." These were once served at Lent, and their bitterness served to remind one of Jesus' sufferings. *FDA prohibited for use in food due to naturally occurring toxins.*

TARRAGON LEAF (cut & sifted) - *Artemisia dracunculus* / U.S. / Tarragon is a shrub-like perennial with narrow, dark-green leaves. Native to Russia, true culinary tarragon must be propagated by cuttings. Its delicate, strong, sweet taste complements fowl, fish, dairy, and egg dishes. Tarragon vinegar is used for a true tartare sauce, and is also excellent for herb sauce. *FDA approved as a spice and for flavoring food.*

Tarragon Salad Dressing Recipe
1 cup apple cider vinegar
3 cups olive oil
4 teaspoons sea salt
1 tablespoon honey
1 teaspoon dry mustard
1 teaspoon black pepper
1 teaspoon paprika
1 tablespoon tarragon
1/4 cup parsley
1/4 teaspoon garlic powder

Combine all ingredients and blend well. Chill. Remove to room temperature 1/2 hour before serving, to liquify oil. Shake well.

THYME LEAF (cut & sifted, ground) - *Thymus vulgaris* / garden thyme / Spain / Thyme was thought in ancient and medievel times to inspire courage. According to legend, at midnight one midsummer night, the king of the fairies and his followers danced in beds of wild thyme. The strong, pleasant scent of thyme makes it appropriate for use in deodorants, perfumes, soaps, and herb cushions. It is also used as a moth preventative in closets and cupboards. As a culinary herb it is found in bouquet garni, soups, chowders, stuffings, fish dishes, tomato juice, in cheeses, and with carrots, celery, mushrooms, tomatoes, zucchini, potatoes and beets. Add a small amount of thyme to your favorite bread and biscuit doughs. *FDA approved as a spice and for flavoring foods.*

TILIA STAR FLOWERS (whole) - *Ternstroemia* spp. / Mexico / This genus contains a number of species known as lime trees in Europe and linden trees or basswoods in the U.S. The star-shaped, red-brown flowers add interesting shape and color to potpourris. *No FDA designation for safe use in food.*

TONKA BEANS (whole) - *Dipteryx odorata* / Venezuela / Tonka was once used in a concoction of imitation vanilla extract, and to adulterate real vanilla extract. It is now used in perfumes, and has the scent of newly-mown hay. The one-inch beans are also used as a fixative, and for aroma and texture in potpourris. *FDA prohibited for use in food due to naturally occurring toxins.*

TREE CONES

We sell a variety of evergreen cones. The available choices in sizes and shapes will provide you with diverse supplies for your crafts projects.

Black spruce cones (whole) - *Picea mariana* / U.S. / Black spruce cones, similar to hemlock cones, are used in herbal crafts such as potpourri and wreath making. They measure 1/2 inch by 1/2 inch. *No FDA designation for safe use in food.*

Hemlock Pine (whole) - *Tsuga canadensis* / U.S. / These 3/4-inch by 5/8-inch brown cones are used for texture and color. They are lovely in potpourris and add an especially nice touch to holiday crafts projects. *No FDA designation for safe use in food.*

Jeffrey Pine (whole) - *Pinus jeffries* / U.S. / Sold six to a package, these reddish brown cones measure eight inches by four inches by four inches, and are suitable for use in centerpieces, wreaths, and other crafts projects. *No FDA designation for safe use in food.*

TURMERIC ROOT (ground, whole) - *Curcurma longa* / India, China / Turmeric is quite versatile. It has a peculiar fragrant, bitter, acrid odor and rich color. Related to ginger, it flavors artichokes, potatoes, tea, eggs, fish, and pickled vegetables. It is a constituent in curry powder, and an essential ingredient in piccalilli. It is sometimes used as an adulterant of mustard as well as a pharmaceutical coloring agent. We sell Alleppey type turmeric root, which has excellent flavor and color properties. *FDA approved as a spice and for flavoring foods.*

UVA URSI LEAF (whole) - *Arctostaphylos uva-ursi* / bearberry, kinnickinnik / Spain / This plant has small, attractive, green-white leaves which are sometimes used to add color and texture to potpourris. *No FDA designation for safe use in food.*

VALERIAN ROOT (cut & sifted, powdered) - *Valeriana officinalis* / cat's valerian, set well, St. George's herb, all heal, capon's tail, garden heliotrophe, vandal root / Europe / Native to Europe and western Asia, valerian root has a musty odor and taste. It has been used as a seasoning (in small quantities), and to scent linen. In gardens it is employed in composts. *FDA approved for flavoring foods.*

The vanilla bean, harvested while ripe and golden-green, is about eight inches long and has no aroma. It is sun dried for ten days, yielding a brown/black color. The chemical vanillin is produced in the bean during a curing of four to five months; it is during this time the beans develop their characteristic aroma and flavor. Five pounds of beans are harvested to produce one pound of marketable beans.

You may detect small raised bumps on some vanilla beans. These are pinpricks made in the skin by growers (a process similar to branding livestock) in order to deter theft. You may also detect white crystals forming, especially on the ends, of vanilla beans. Resembling white fur, this crystalline substance is actually vanillin being exuded by the beans. It is completely harmless. In fact, it is a sign of a quality vanilla bean. The crystals will often dissolve when the beans become warm (when they are placed in the sun, for example).

One way to use whole vanilla beans, which are richer and more fragrant than extracts, is to infuse the bean in a liqiud, such as a syrup or beverage. Another is to make vanilla sugar by placing a bean in a closed canister of sugar. This vanilla sugar may be spinkled over berries or other fruits, or used in cakes or ice creams. A piece of vanilla bean may be placed with coffee grinds in a coffee filter for a special brew. Or use a vanilla bean to scent a linen drawer!

Vanilla beans are available individually, in tubes of three, and in bulk. Store beans in a plastic bag, in a cool place.

Vanilla powder, sold in bulk, is available in both starch and dextrose bases (no alcohol). The starch base contains cornstarch and vanilla bean extracts (no sugar). The dextrose base, derived from corn sugar, contains dextrose and vanilla bean extracts. Use these powders in baking and cooking, in place of extracts. One teaspoon powder equals one teaspoon extract.

FDA approved for flavoring foods.

VANILLA (beans, powdered, whole) - *Vanilla planifolia* / Madagascar / A member of the orchid family, this plant is pruned to a height of eight feet. Pollinated naturally only by a particular Mexican bee, most vanilla grown today is pollinated by hand, part of a labor-intensive routine in the production of vanilla. (See *Vanilla Beans*, page 48.) *FDA approved as a spice and for flavoring foods.*

VANILLA TAHITIAN (beans) - *Vanilla tahitensis* / Tahiti / Although also a member of the orchid family, this South Pacific plant is genetically different from vanilla grown elsewhere. Tahitian vanilla beans have been used for years by European gourmet cooks, and are gaining popularity with American cooks today. Very juicy and aromatic, these beans measure roughly six inches in length and 1/2 inch in diameter. Use as you would regular vanilla beans, but compare the difference! We sell these beans singly, and in bulk. *FDA approved as a spice and for flavoring foods.*

Vanilla Extract Recipe

There are two methods for making your own vanilla extract. One involves alcohol, the other water.

Method 1

2/3 cup warm water
4-8 vanilla beans
2 teaspoons lecithin (as an emulsifier)

Soak beans for several hours. Blend water and beans in a blender. Bring to a boil in a covered pan and immediately remove from the heat. Place in a tightly covered jar; let stand overnight or longer. Strain into blender and blend in lecithin at low speed. Pour into bottles and cap tightly. (This may produce extract which is slightly less potent than alcohol-base extract.)

Method 2

1 vanilla bean
8 ounces bourbon or rum

Slice the vanilla bean lengthwise, and soak in the bourbon or rum for one month. Remove bean. Pour into a bottle and cap tightly.

VERVAIN BLUE (cut & sifted) - *Verbena officinalis* / wild hyssop, Indian hyssop / U.S. / Ancient Egyptians believed that vervain originated from the tears of Isis. Roman heralds wore wreaths of vervain, and the Druids used it as a holy food in their rituals. This variety of vervain was used in Eurasia, and is mentioned in European herbals. Blue vervain is indigenous to the U.S. and was used extensively by native Americans. Today it is used in liqueurs and the oil is sometimes used in perfumery. *FDA approved only for flavoring alcoholic beverages.*

VETIVER ROOT (cut & sifted, powdered) -*Vetiveria zizanoides* / cuscus, kuskus, betivert / Dominican Republic / Vetiver has a woodsy scent. It is used as a fixative in potpourris, and in perfumes and incense. The cut and sifted form is preferred for potpourris, and the powdered form for sachets and incense cones. *FDA approved only for flavoring alcoholic beverages.*

VIOLET LEAF (cut & sifted) - *Viola odorata* / garden violet, sweet violet, sweet-scented violet / Yugoslavia / The essence of violet leaf is used mainly in perfumery, but also as a flavoring in desserts and some beverages. *FDA approved only for flavoring alcoholic beverages.*

VIRGINIA SNAKEROOT ROOT (cut & sifted) - *Aristolochia serpentaria* / pelican flower, red river snake root, sangree root, snakeweed, thick birthwort / U.S. / This plant is a twining, low-growing flowering shrub. It belongs to the same family as birthwort, and is found in acid soils, and peaty or rocky woods. *FDA approved only for flavoring alcoholic beverages.*

WHITE OAK BARK (cut & sifted) - *Quercus alba* / West Germany / The genus name *Quercus* is derived from the Celtic *quer* (fire) and *cuez* (tree). This tree produces a bark which is strongly astringent and bitter. It has been used to tan leather, and to produce a variety of natural dyes. *FDA approved for flavoring foods.*

WHITE PINE BARK (cut & sifted) - *Pinus strobus* / deal pine, soft pine, weymouth pine, pin du lord / America / This tree's European name of "weymouth pine" descends from lord Weymouth who planted many white pine trees shortly after their introduction to the U.S. in 1705. *FDA approved only for flavoring alcoholic beverages.*

WHITE WILLOW BARK (cut and sifted, powdered) - *Salix alba* / willow salacin, withe, withy, willow / U.S. / The branches and runners of this plant are used in basket weaving. It has also been used as an herbal deodorant, and in lotions, creams, facial washes, and herbal bath mixtures. *No FDA designation for safe use in food.*

WILD CHERRY BARK (cut & sifted) - *Prunus serotina* / choke berry / U.S. / This species is very similar to *Prunus virginana* in appearance and habitat; both are sold as wild cherry. The bark contains hydrocyanic acid which in large quantities may be poisonous. To remove this acid, Native Americans soaked the bark before drying. It has a tart, cherry-like flavor and the extract is used in the formulation of aromas for flavoring desserts and beverages. Wild cherry loses its flavor quickly and should be replaced after a year. *FDA approved for flavoring foods when used as an extract or tea.*

WILD LETTUCE LEAF (cut & sifted) - *Lactuca virosa* / prickly lettuce, acrid lettuce, poison lettuce / This prickly lettuce is a biennial plant with leafy, round stems. In its second year, it grows two to seven feet high. The whole plant is filled with a milky juice which is used for making soaps and lotions. *No FDA designation for safe use in food.*

WILD YAM ROOT (cut & sifted) - *Dioscorea villosa* / colic root, devil's bones, rheumatism root / U.S. / There are over one hundred and fifty species of *Dioscorea.* This herbaceous vine, found wild in damp woodlands and thickets, was used by Native Americans, southern slaves, and the Shakers. *No FDA designation for safe use in food.*

WINTERGREEN LEAF (cut & sifted) - *Gaultheria procumbens* / Canada tea, checkberry, ground berry, deerberry / India / This small plant is found growing under trees and shrubs, particularly evergreens. The oil has been used as a flavoring in pastry, candy, chewing gum and toothpaste, but has largely been replaced by methyl salicylate. It is also used in perfumery and potpourri crafting. *No FDA designation for safe use in food.*

WITCHHAZEL BARK (cut & sifted) and **LEAF** (cut & sifted) - *Hamamelis virginiana* / spotted Alder, winter bloom, snapping hazelnut / U.S. / Similar in appearance to another plant known as hazel, this plant, because it bloomed in November, earned the preface "witch." *No FDA designation for safe use in food.*

WOOD BETONY HERB (cut & sifted) - *Stachys officinalis* / bishopswort, betony, purple betony, lousewort / Yugoslavia / The surface of the leaves of this plant is dotted with glands containing bitter, aromatic oils. *No FDA designation for safe use in food.*

WOODRUFF HERB (cut & sifted, whole) - *Asperula odorata* / woodrove, waldmeister tea, star grass, hay plant, sweet grass, haw-hoof / Yugoslavia / Woodruff is used for aroma, texture, and as a fixative in potpourris. Its odor, which is not apparent until the plant is dried, is similar to new-mown hay, and the one inch, lance-like leaves are dark green. It is also used to flavor wine, to preserve linens from insects, as an ingredient in herbal bath and facial mixtures, and in the preparation of an aftershave rinse. *FDA prohibited for use in food due to naturally occurring toxins.*

WORMWOOD HERB (cut & sifted) - *Artemisia absinthium* / Poland / The goddess Diana (Artemis) supposedly discovered the virtues of wormwood and gave them to the world. One of the most bitter herbs known, in concentrated form it is a volatile poison. Today it is used as an ingredient in insect sprays to repel cabbage moths. *FDA prohibited for use in food due to naturally occurring toxins.*

YARROW FLOWERS (whole) - *Achillea millefolium* / milfoil / Hungary / The botanical name for yarrow is derived from the fact that Achilles supposedly healed his warriors with the leaves of this plant. Yarrow has been used for "I Ching" sticks. The yellow-tan flowers have a faint scent and come in one-inch clumps. They are often used to add texture to potpourris and as an ingredient in shampoos and hair rinses. *FDA prohibited for use in food due to naturally occurring toxins.*

YELLOWDOCK ROOT (cut & sifted) - *Rumex crispus* / curled dock, garden patience, narrow dock/ Europe / This perennial weed is found in fields and wastelands in the U.S., Europe, and southern Canada. The taproot, which is yellow and spindle-shaped, was used extensively by American Indians. *No FDA designation for safe use in food.*

YERBA MATE LEAF (cut & sifted) - *Ilex paraguariensis* / Brazil / The leaves and twigs of this evergreen shrub are used to brew a drink which contains less caffeine than coffee or black tea. Traditionally it was flavored with burnt sugar and lemon and sucked through a silver tube from a hollow gourd. We sell yerba mate both roasted and green (unroasted). *FDA approved for flavoring foods when used as an extract or tea.*

YERBA SANTA LEAF (cut & sifted) - *Eriodictyon californium* / holy weed / U.S. / This aromatic evergreen shrub was used as a mouthwash by Native Americans. The leaves were rolled into balls, dried in the sun and then chewed. A drink of water sweetened and cooled the taste of the leaves. *FDA approved for flavoring foods.*

Organic Herbs & Spices

In keeping with our quality standards at Frontier, one of our goals is to provide you with a choice of as many organic herbs and spices as possible. Our organic products must meet strict requirements to obtain certification.

What do we mean by organic, and how are products certified? There has been much confusion, controversy, and deception regarding organic products since they became a popular part of the health foods movement.

Because no uniform standards existed to define "organic," an individual producer, distributor, or retailer could legally label anything as organic. Consumers often paid a substantially higher price for a product that they believed to be organic. In reality, they may have been grown under the same conditions as the non-organic product next to it on the shelf.

On the other hand, these products may have been grown under the strictest organic conditions possible. Much to the dismay of legitimate producers of organic products, "organic" began to get a bad name. The result was the birth of the term "certified organic." Certified organic simply means that the product has been "certified" by some party other than the producer according to a set of pre-existing standards.

In our opinion the best way to obtain organic certification is through an independent third party. We use third party certification whenever possible; unfortunately, it is not always available in all areas of the country. When third-party certification is not available, Frontier will certify the crop through a grower's affidavit, questionnaire, lab tests, and inspections when necessary. Over the last several years a number of organizations and dedicated individuals have worked hard to bring certifying organizations together. Their purpose was to develop a common set of standards and make organic certification available across the country. We expect third-party certification to soon be available throughout the United States. This will enable us to offer you more certified organically-grown herbs.

The next challenge will be organic certification for overseas products. Several groups are already working on this. Frontier is working through various farmers' cooperatives researching the organic farming of spices in several parts of the world.

These are the standards we use when certifying products as organic:

Frontier's Standards for Organic Certification

1. Land upon which the crop is grown shall have been farmed in accordance with these standards continuously for at least 36 months from date of production harvest.

2. No synthetically compounded materials or chemically fortified materials may be applied to the soil or to the crop during planting, growing, harvesting, distribution, storage, processing or packaging. This includes fertilizers, pesticides, herbicides, growth regulators, fumigants, rodenticides, colorings, and preservatives.

3. Production records shall be kept by the farmer for a minimum of 36 months from the date of production harvest and be made available upon request.
4. Frontier reserves the right to conduct periodic inspection tours of farm and production facilities.
5. Frontier will do random testing for residues. Acceptable pesticide residue levels are a maximum of 10% of the level regarded as safe by the USFDA.
6. All production must meet the standards set by the USFDA.

This page contains a list of the organic herbs and spices available at the time of printing this Product Guide. This list is variable, however. Because of the possibility of crop failures, and a lack of backup organic suppliers, we cannot always insure adequate supplies. We are working to increase our list of organic sources, but this is not an easy task. (If you are interested in growing organic products for us, we'd be happy to hear from you!) At this time all our organic sources are domestic, though we are also investigating the possibility of importing organic products.

All of these items are available in bulk. In addition, those noted below with an * are available in smaller, "consumer packs" (See *Consumer Packs*, page 54). For more descriptive information, read the entries for these products in the prior chapter.

Common Name

Alfalfa leaf (cut and sifted) *
Alfalfa leaf (powdered)
Black mustard seed (whole)
Blessed thistle herb (cut and sifted)
Calendula flowers (whole)
Catnip herb (cut and sifted) *
Comfrey leaf (cut and sifted) *
Comfrey root (cut and sifted) *
Comfrey root (powdered)
Coriander seed (whole)
Dill seed (whole)
Echinacea herb purpurea (cut and sifted)
Flax seed (whole) *
Lemon grass (cut and sifted) *
Lemon thyme (cut and sifted)
Oregon grape root (cut and sifted)
Peppermint leaf (cut and sifted) *
Raspberry leaf (cut and sifted) *
Red clover herb (cut and sifted) *

Consumer Packs

Some Frontier products are now available in consumer-sized foil pouches, six pouches per case. Most pouches will fill a four-ounce spice jar. Items available in "consumer packs" include the following quality herbs, spices and seasonings, and Frontier blends. For more product information, see the *Herbs and Spices* and *Herb & Spice Blends* sections of this handbook.

Quality Herbs	Wt. Oz.
Alfalfa leaf (cut and sifted)	.6
Burdock root (cut and sifted)	1.3
Catnip leaf (cut and sifted)	.5
Chamomile flowers (whole)	.5
Chicory root roasted (granulated)	2.6
Comfrey leaf (cut and sifted)	.6
Comfrey root (cut and sifted)	2.7
Dandelion leaf (cut and sifted)	.6
Dandelion root roasted (cut and sifted)	1.25
Echinacea angustifolia root (cut and sifted)	1.10
Echinacea purpurea herb (cut and sifted)	1.0
Eucalyptus leaf (cut and sifted)	1.4
Flax seed (whole)	3.4
Goldenseal root (ground)	1.2
Gotu kola (cut and sifted)	.8
Hibiscus flowers (cut and sifted)	1.6
Lemon grass (cut and sifted)	.8
Licorice root (cut and sifted)	1.8
Nettle leaf (cut and sifted)	.5
Pau d'arco (cut and sifted)	1.0
Peppermint leaf (cut and sifted)	.6
Psyllium husk (ground)	2.6
Raspberry leaf (cut and sifted)	.6
Red clover herb	.6
Rosehips seedless (cut and sifted)	1.0
Sage leaf (cut and sifted)	.5
Senna leaf (cut and sifted)	.8
Slippery elm (ground)	1.4
Spearmint leaf (cut and sifted)	.6
Valerian root (cut and sifted)	3.0

Spices and Seasonings

Spices and Seasonings	Wt. Oz.
Allspice (ground)	1.8
Allspice (whole)	1.8
Anise seed (whole)	1.9
Basil California (cut and sifted)	.6
Caraway seed (whole)	2.4
Cardamom (ground)	1.25
Cayenne (red pepper)	1.9
Celery seed (whole)	2.4
Chives (dehydrated)	.3
Cinnamon (ground)	2.2
Cinnamon (sticks 3")	1.9
Cloves (ground)	2.1
Cloves (whole)	1.6
Coriander seed (ground)	1.8
Cumin (ground)	2.1
Cumin seed (whole)	2.1
Dill seed (whole)	1.9
Dill weed (cut and sifted)	.8
Fennel seed (whole)	2.1
Fenugreek seed (whole)	3.8
Garlic (granulated)	3.2
Ginger (ground)	1.8
Kelp (flakes)	3.2
Marjoram leaf (cut and sifted)	.75
Mustard seed yellow (ground)	1.9
Mustard seed yellow (whole)	3.7
Nutmeg (ground)	1.75
Onion (flakes)	1.8
Onion (granulated)	3.0
Oregano leaf Greek (cut and sifted)	.8
Paprika Hungarian	2.7
Parsley (flakes)	.3
Pepper black (coarse grind)	2.4
Pepper black (fine grind)	2.4
Peppercorns black	2.9
Poppy seed (whole)	3.0
Rosemary leaf (whole)	.8
Sage leaf (rubbed)	.6
Tarragon leaf (cut and sifted)	.6
Thyme leaf (cut and sifted)	.8
Turmeric (ground)	1.9

Frontier Blends

Frontier Blends	Wt. Oz.
Apple pie spice	2.2
Barbeque seasoning	2.4
Chili powder deluxe	2.4
Cider Mate	1.8
Curry powder	1.9

Spices and Seasonings	*Wt. Oz.*
Herbal seasoning	1.9
Italian seasoning	1.0
Lemon pepper	1.9
Mexican seasoning	2.4
Pickling spice	1.8
Pizza seasoning	1.1
Pumpkin pie spice	2.1

Salsas

Fiesta Oriente	
Hot	3.2
Medium	3.2
Mild	3.2
Picante Mexicana	
Hot	2.8
Medium	2.8
Mild	2.8
Tex-Mex	
Hot	2.8
Medium	2.8
Mild	2.8

Herb & Spice Blends

We are proud of the wide variety of fine products we blend at Frontier. Most are blended without salt, and all will add a special touch to your dishes. Here are the blends available, the ingredients contained in each, and recipes to inspire you!

ALL-SEASONS SALT - This very tasty blend of salt and spices can be used to season most any non-dessert dish, and makes an excellent table condiment in place of table salt. Ingredients: sea salt, Hungarian paprika, yellow mustard ground, Mediterranean oregano ground, garlic powder, onion powder, celery seed ground, hickory smoke.

Tofu Croutons Recipe
2 tablespoons oil
1 pound tofu, drained
Frontier All-Seasons Salt

Chop tofu into 1/4 inch pieces. Place in preheated oil, sprinkle with Frontier All-Seasons Salt. Cook until tofu is browned on all sides and firm. Use to top salads, potatoes, and casseroles.

APPLE PIE SPICE - This delectable seasoning can grace any dish containing apples or other fruit. Add it to puddings, fruit crisps and cobblers, cakes, cookies, and desserts.

Ingredients: cinnamon, fenugreek, lemon peel, ginger, cloves, and nutmeg.

Apple Whip Recipe
4 apples
2 pints of cream
1/4 cup honey
1 heaping tablespoon Frontier Apple Pie Spice

Core, skin, and bake apples until soft. Combine cooked apples with one pint of cream, honey, and Frontier Apple Pie Spice. Whip. In a separate bowl, whip another pint of cream. Fold together. Place in dessert dishes, and sprinkle with coconut flakes. Makes eight servings.

BARBECUE SEASONING (Bar-b-quick) - A spicy blend to provide the zing for your favorite barbecue sauce recipe! Frontier Barbecue Seasoning can also be added to a variety of other dishes for a robust hickory flavor. Try it with baked beans, grain dishes, cheesey casseroles, potatoes, tofu, eggs, dips, and appetizers.

Ingredients: chili peppers, garlic, nutritional yeast, onion, paprika, black pepper, cumin, nutmeg, cayenne, and hickory smoke (liquid smoke, modified food starch, and silica gel).

Barbecue Beans Recipe
2 cups cooked beans (pinto, kidney, or navy)
1 sliced and sautéed onion
1 grated carrot
1 cup of tomato sauce
2 tablespoons Frontier Barbecue Seasoning
1 tablespoon molasses
Combine beans, onion, and carrot. In a separate bowl, combine tomato sauce with Frontier Barbecue Seasoning and molasses. Combine sauce with beans and bake in 350° oven for one hour. Makes four servings.

CELERY SALT - This blend of ground, aromatic celery seeds and sea salt is perfect for seasoning soups, stews, salads, curry dishes, stuffing, fish, and meat dishes, vegetables, eggs, and breads.
Ingredients: sea salt, ground celery seed.

Fancy Tomato Sauce Recipe
2 tablespoons olive oil
1/2 cup chopped onion
1 clove garlic, finely chopped
1/2 green bell pepper, diced
1 bay leaf
1/4 cup tomato juice
1/8 teaspoon Frontier Celery Salt
1/8 teaspoon rosemary, ground
1/8 teaspoon thyme, ground
1/4 teaspoon oregano, ground
1/4 teaspoon basil, ground
1/4 cup tomato paste
Heat oil and sauté onion and garlic until tender. Add pepper, bay leaf, and tomato juice. Simmer 15 minutes. Mix together celery salt, rosemary, thyme, oregano, and basil. Add to sauce along with tomato paste. Simmer 20 minutes. Makes about 1 1/2 cups. This sauce is good on spaghetti or in casseroles.

CHILI POWDER - So that you may choose the chili powder most suited to your taste, we offer three varieties - a standard blend both with and without salt, and a "deluxe" blend which is salt-free. Each is a delicious combination of fresh and flavorful spices.
Ingredients:
Standard blend: chili peppers, salt, cumin, oregano, garlic, less than 2% silicon dioxide (a naturally-occurring compound which prevents caking).
Standard blend, no salt: chili peppers, cumin, oregano, garlic, less than 2% silicon dioxide (a naturally-occurring compound which prevents caking).
Deluxe blend: chili peppers, cumin, garlic powder, oregano, coriander, allspice, cloves.

Egg Tacos Recipe
12 eggs
1 cup milk
3 tablespoons soy grits (optional)
2 tablespoons Frontier Chili Powder

4 large taco shells
1 cup grated cheese
2 chopped tomatoes
1 small onion, chopped
1/2 cup plain yogurt
Frontier Salsa Grande

Blend well: eggs, milk, soy grits, Frontier Chili Powder. Scramble mixture in oiled fry pan and serve in taco shells. Top with cheese, tomato, onions, yogurt, and Frontier Salsa Grande. Makes four large servings.

CIDER MATE - A blend of sweet spices, Cider Mate perks up a variety of hot or cold fruit drinks, teas, and wines. Add to your favorite juice and let stand overnight; strain before serving. To speed up the process and release the full spice flavor, heat the juice and Cider Mate together, simmering 10-20 minutes. Strain and serve hot or chilled.

Ingredients: cinnamon, allspice, orange and lemon peel, star anise, nutmeg, cloves, fenugreek, and ginger.

Spiced Apple Tea Recipe
1 quart apple juice
1 quart peppermint tea
1 cup Frontier Cider Mate
honey to taste

Combine: juice, tea, and Frontier Cider Mate in a pot. Bring to a boil, reduce heat, and simmer for 20 minutes. Strain and sweeten as desired.

CURRY POWDER - Originally a specific blend of spices intended to flavor or "curry" a particular Indian dish, curry powder today signifies a fairly uniform spice blend used to flavor a host of dishes, including rice, eggs, vegetables, meat, dips, sauces, salad dressings, and soups. Our curry is available in both a hot and standard blend.

Ingredients: turmeric, coriander, paprika, fenugreek, black pepper, cumin, ginger, cloves, celery seed, caraway, and cayenne.

Crustless Curried Quiche Recipe
2 cups grated cheese (Swiss, Mozzarella, or Jack)
1 green pepper, sliced
1/2 cup mushrooms, sliced
8 eggs
1 cup milk
1 tablespoon Frontier Curry Powder

Fill a ten-inch quiche pan 2/3 full with grated cheese. Top with green pepper and mushroom slices. In a bowl, combine eggs, milk, and Frontier Curry Powder. Blend well and pour over cheese. Top with sliced tomatoes and bake at 350° until set (about 40 minutes). Makes eight servings.

FIVE SPICE POWDER - This fragrant, aromatic, sweet and spicy blend is used extensively in Chinese cooking, particularly with meats, poultry, and sauces. It can also be used in fruit desserts.

Ingredients: cinnamon ground, fennel seed ground, cloves ground, star anise ground, white pepper ground.

Stir Fried Vegetables Recipe
1 medium onion, sliced
6 stalks celery, cut in 1-inch diagonal slices
6 green onions, cut in half lengthwise
2 large bell peppers, sliced
1/2 cup water
1/3 cup soy sauce
2 tablespoons honey
1 teaspoon Frontier Five-Spice Powder
2 cups fresh mung bean sprouts
1/2 pound fresh mushrooms, sliced
In a wok or skillet, heat oil. Add onion, celery, green onion, and peppers. Cover and simmer for five minutes, stirring frequently. Mix together: water, soy sauce, honey, Frontier Five-Spice Powder. Pour this sauce over vegetables. Cover and cook for five minutes. Stir in mung bean sprouts and mushrooms, and cook another five minutes. Serve over hot rice. Makes four servings.

GARLIC SALT - Garlic may be used to flavor everything but sweets. This tasty garlic salt blend is excellent for soups, salads, stews, fish, poultry, meat, eggs, mayonnaise, salad dressings, breads, and vegetables. It is also good to have on hand for making your own spice blends. Taste before adding additional salt to your recipe when using this blend.
Ingredients: sea salt, garlic powder.

Italian Dressing Recipe
4 tablespoons olive or safflower oil
3 tablespoons mayonnaise or yogurt
2 tablespoons vinegar
1 tablespoon Frontier Italian Seasoning
1/2 teaspoon Frontier Garlic Salt
Mix well in a bowl. Refrigerate at least two hours before serving. Makes about 3/4 cup.

GUMBO FILÉ - This delicious powder is a necessary ingredient in creole gumbos. Since it contains sassafras, it should be added to hot dishes off the heat, and not boiled.
Ingredients: sassafras leaf powder, thyme leaf ground.

Gumbo Rice Recipe
1 onion, minced
1 tablespoon butter
3 cups chicken broth (Mix 3 cups water with 3 teaspoons Frontier Chicken-Flavored Broth Powder)
1 cup uncooked rice
1/2 teaspoon Frontier Gumbo Filé
In a skillet, saute' onion in butter. Add broth, rice, and Frontier Gumbo Filé. Bring to simmer. Remove and place in a large, covered casserole. Bake at 350° for one hour or until all of the liquid has been absorbed.

HERBAL SEASONING - Frontier's Herbal Seasoning contains no added salt. It is a tasty salt substitute in soups, stews, and salad dressings, and on salads, fish, vegetables, tofu, and

eggs. Blended with the finest, freshest herbs and spices, it may be served at your table with pride.
Ingredients: dill weed, kelp powder, nutritional yeast, oregano, spirulina, marjoram, garlic, and cayenne.

Fried Cheese Recipe
1/2 pound of your favorite cheese
1 egg
1/3 cup whole wheat flour
1 tablespoon Frontier Herbal Seasoning
Slice cheese into 1/2 inch slabs. In one small bowl, beat egg. In another, combine flour and Frontier Herbal Seasoning. Dip cheese slices into egg, then flour mixture, coating well to seal in the cheese. Fry in oil in a hot pan until brown on both sides. Serve immediately as an appetizer. Makes six servings.

HICKORY SALT - The delicious smoked flavor of this blend complements meat, poultry, fish, bean, and tofu dishes.
Ingredients: sea salt, nutritional yeast, paprika, hickory smoke (liquid smoke, modified food starch, and silica gel), and silicon dioxide (a naturally-occurring compound which prevents caking).

Smoked Rice Burgers Recipe
2 cups cooked brown rice
1 tablespoon parsley
1/2 teaspoon tamari
1 carrot, grated
1 onion, grated
2 eggs, beaten
whole wheat flour
2 teaspoons Frontier Hickory Salt
In a bowl, combine rice, parsley, tamari, carrot, onion, eggs, and Frontier Hickory Salt. Add flour, beginning with 1/4 cup, until thick enough to form patties. Fry until golden brown on both sides.

ITALIAN SEASONING - Frontier's Italian Seasoning blend is a versatile, salt-free mixture made from fresh and flavorful herbs native to Italian cuisine. Use it in pasta dishes, salad dressings, tomato sauces, and cheese dishes. Sprinkle over pizza during the last five minutes of baking for an extra-special spicy flavor. This blend is available both ground and whole.
Ingredients: oregano, marjoram, thyme, rosemary, basil, and sage.

Broiled Sesame Tomatoes Recipe
4 tomatoes
1/2 cup sesame seeds
2 tablespoons Italian Seasoning
1/2 cup grated Parmesan cheese
Slice tomatoes and place on a shallow baking dish. Sprinkle with sesame seeds and Frontier Italian Seasoning. Top with cheese. Place under broiler for about five minutes, until cheese melts.

LEMON PEPPER - Frontier Lemon Pepper blend adds a vibrant touch to tofu, vegetables, salads, sea foods, sauces, and dips. Try it at the table as a zesty salt substitute.
Ingredients: lemon peel, black pepper, lemon juice powder (corn syrup solids, lemon juice

solids and lemon oil), garlic, onion, and citric acid.

Lemon Pepper Butter Recipe
1/4 pound butter (one stick), softened
1 teaspoon Lemon Pepper
Whip butter with Frontier Lemon Pepper and refrigerate. Serve on any hot vegetable (especially good on boiled new potatoes) or fish.

MEXICAN SEASONING - Frontier's versatile Mexican Seasoning blend can be used to flavor tacos, enchiladas, tamales, and other Mexican dishes. It also spices up potatoes, grains, tofu, dips, sauces, vegetable dishes and cheese dishes.

Ingredients: chili peppers, garlic, onion, paprika, cumin, oregano, celery seed, cayenne, bell peppers, parsley, and bay.

Spicy Nachos Recipe
Line bottom of a shallow baking dish with tortilla chips. Cover with grated cheese and sprinkle generously with Frontier Mexican Seasoning. Broil until cheese melts, about four minutes.

ONION SALT - This is an indispensible blend for those cooks who season almost everything with both onions and salt! It is perfect for seasoning soups, stews, salad dressings, eggs, fish, poultry, meat, and vegetables, and for making your own spice blends. Taste before adding additional salt to your recipe when using this blend.

Ingredients: sea salt, onion powder.

Afternoon Snack Recipe
celery stalks (cleaned)
cream cheese
onion salt
Fill celery with cream cheese. Sprinkle Frontier Onion Salt on top. May be cut into bite-sized pieces.

PEPPERMILL GOURMET BLEND - You'll want to use this colorful blend of peppercorns in a clear peppermill! It will add a gourmet touch to any table.

Ingredients: Tellicherry peppercorns, white peppercorns, green peppercorns, pink peppercorns. (See *Tellicherry peppercorns*, page 35.)

Recipe Suggestions
Use this blend freshly ground in soups, just before serving, or allow guests to grind onto salads at the table.

PICKLING SPICE - Frontier Pickling Spice is a fragrant mixture made up primarily of whole spices. Tie one to two teaspoons into a cheesecloth and simmer in soups, stews, or broths. Use to pickle and preserve meats, and to season vegetables, relishes, and sauces. It is available in both an original and a mild blend.

Ingredients: mustard, cinnamon, allspice, dill, celery, cloves, bay, chili peppers, ginger, and caraway.

Spicy Vinegar Recipe
3 tablespoons Frontier Pickling Spice

1 quart vinegar
1 cup honey
Tie Frontier Pickling Spice in a small piece of cheesecloth. Combine with vinegar and honey. Heat gently for about ten minutes. Remove spices and pour vinegar into bottle. Spicy vinegar is good in vegetable or bean salad dressings.

PIZZA SEASONING - A blend of popular pizza herbs and spices, Frontier Pizza Seasoning can be added to pizza sauce or sprinkled on top of pizza during baking. It also adds a tantalizing pizza flavor to breads, cheese dishes, and vegetables.
Ingredients: bell peppers, onion, fennel, oregano, garlic, basil, parsley, chili peppers, marjoram, celery flakes, and thyme.

Easy Pita Pizzas Recipe
Slice whole wheat pita bread into flat circles. Spread with plain tomato sauce, and sprinkle liberally with Frontier Pizza Seasoning. Top with grated mozzarella cheese and bake until cheese browns, about 20 minutes.

POPCORN SEASONINGS - Frontier sells the following popcorn seasonings:

SPICY CHEESE - This tasty flavoring is great on popcorn (try three teaspoons per quart of popped corn), but also may be used to spice up other foods. Try it on rice!
Ingredients: cheddar cheese flavored powder, nutritional yeast mini-flake, garlic powder, onion powder, red bell pepper powder, cayenne mild.

Recipe Ideas
Use to sprinkle over potatoes, or add to your favorite macaroni and cheese recipe. (Combine Frontier Spicy Cheese Popcorn Seasoning with liquid - such as milk - then add to recipe.)

MAPLE MUNCH - As a popcorn seasoning, use three tablespoons of Maple Munch for one quart of popped corn. The delicious maple flavor is also great sprinkled on cereal, toast, beverages, and baked goods such as cakes, cookies, candies, and quick breads.
Ingredients: maple syrup powder, sweet cream buttermilk powder, nonfat dry milk, vanilla powder, cinnamon ground, nutmeg ground.

Maple Oatmeal Recipe
2 cups milk or water
1 cup water
1 cup oats
1/4 cup raisins
1 tablespoon Maple Munch Popcorn Seasoning
Combine all ingredients in a heavy saucepan. Cook over medium heat until thick and creamy, about ten minutes. Serve with honey and additional milk or cream, if desired. Makes three servings.

POULTRY SEASONING - This ground blend may be used like traditional poultry seasoning - with poultry, in stuffings, gravies, and sauces - but note the special flavor. You'll want to try this seasoning in other dishes, too!
Ingredients: thyme, sage, marjoram, celery seed, black pepper, onion, cayenne.

Baked Chicken Recipe
1 1/2 cup unbleached flour
1 tablespoon Frontier Poultry Seasoning
2 teaspoons paprika
1/8 teaspoon garlic powder
3 pounds chicken pieces
Mix all ingredients except chicken together in a plastic bag. Cut chicken into pieces, wet using either water, milk, or egg. Place one piece of chicken in bag and shake until coated. Repeat until all chicken is seasoned. Bake at 400° until tender and browned, about 50 minutes. Use remaining flour mixture to make gravy. Serves four.

PUMPKIN PIE SPICE - This fragrant combination of sweet spices is famous for the flavor it imparts to pumpkin pies, but it also adds sparkle to spiced desserts such as cakes, cookies, and sweet breads. Sprinkle it on squash and yams when baking.
Ingredients: cinnamon, ginger, cloves, and nutmeg.

Pumpkin Puffs Recipe
3/4 cups honey
1/2 cup butter
2 eggs
1 cup mashed cooked pumpkin
1 teaspoon vanilla
1 1/2 cup whole wheat flour
1 teaspoon baking soda
1/2 teaspoon sea salt
2 teaspoons Frontier Pumpkin Pie Spice
1/2 cup raisins
Blend well: honey, butter, eggs. Add pumpkin and vanilla. Blend. In another bowl, combine flour, baking soda, salt, and Frontier Pumpkin Pie Spice. Add liquid to dry ingredients and mix well. Stir in raisins. Drop by heaping teaspoonfuls onto greased cookie sheets. Bake at 325° for 15 minutes. Makes about 30 cookies.

SALSA GRANDE - For the salsa connoisseur, we have a terrific variety of hot sauces. Try each, in the hotness you prefer. (All are available in hot, medium, and mild.) To prepare Salsa Grande, empty contents (2/3 cups) into one cup warm water and stir. Allow to stand at room temperature for 30 minutes or more before serving. Refrigerate extra sauce in a covered container.

FIESTA ORIENTE - Fiesta Oriente is a sweet and spicy blend made with fresh, flavorful ingredients that tingle your tastebuds. Our all-natural salsa is great with rice, tacos, burritos, tofu, or as a dip for chips.
Ingredients: tomato, pineapple juice powder (pineapple juice concentrate, malto-dextrin), pineapple, onion, vinegar (malto-dextrin, modified food starch, vinegar solids), chili pepper, cumin, cinnamon, soy sauce powder (soy sauce dehydrated, dextrin).

Fiesta Cheese Ball Recipe
1/2 stick butter
8 ounces cream cheese
1/3 cup Frontier Fiesta Oriente blend
parsley
chopped nuts
Cream butter together with cream cheese until very smooth. Fold in dry Frontier Fiesta

Oriente blend. Place in refrigerator overnight. Form into ball and roll in a mixture of parsley and chopped nuts. Serve with crackers or bread.

Picante Mexicana - Picante Mexicana is a traditional salsa recipe with the full flavor of fresh picked vegetables, herbs, and spices. Our all-natural salsa is great with Mexican foods-tacos, enchiladas, burritos, or as a dip for chips. Enjoy its fresh spicy flavor.

Ingredients: tomato, vinegar (malto-dextrin, modified food starch, vinegar solids), onion, jalapeno, celery, parsley, cumin, garlic, oregano.

Picante Cream Dip Recipe

1/3 cup Frontier Picante Mexicana

1 1/4 cup sour cream (or yogurt)

Combine Frontier Picante Mexicana and sour cream (or yogurt). Let stand for one hour minimum before serving. Serve with chips or crackers.

Tex-Mex - When you're hungry for something big on flavor... Our Texas style salsa offers a rich pure flavor that satisfies the strongest cravings. Salsa Grande adds life to Mexican foods - tacos, enchiladas, chili, and burritos. It's a super dip for chips.

Ingredients: tomato, vinegar (malto dextrin, modified food starch, vinegar solids), chili pepper, onion, cumin, bell peppers, garlic, soy sauce powder, soy sauce dehydrated, dextrin, jalapeno, cilantro, celery seed, oregano, bay.

Tex-Mex Casserole Recipe

1 package Frontier Tex-Mex blend

1 1/4 cup boiling water

2 cups cooked lentils

1 pound tofu

3 tablespoons oil

1 1/2 cups grated Mozzarella or Cheddar cheese

Stir Frontier Tex-Mex mix into boiling water. Add cooked lentils. Slice tofu lengthwise into 1/8 inch slices. Brown on both sides in skillet with oil. Place 1/2 of the slices in an eight inch square casserole dish. Cover with 1/2 of the lentil mixture, top with 1/2 of the cheese. Repeat with remaining ingredients. Bake at 350° until bubbly (approximately 20 minutes).

SPIKE - This popular product is not blended by Frontier, but is such an excellent seasoning, we want to offer it to our customers. Spike contains 36 herbs and spices and can be used in cooking and as a table condiment.

Ingredients: earth and sea salt, yeast, hydrolized vegetable protein, orange fructose, soy flour, celery leaf and root, garlic, dill, Pacific sea greens, Indian curry, horseradish, white pepper, orange and lemon peels, summer savory, mustard flour, red and green bell peppers, parsley flakes, tarragon, rosehips, saffron, mushrooms, spinach, tomato, paprika, celery seed, cayenne, oregano, basil, marjoram, rosemary, thyme.

Cooking Suggestions

Use Spike generously on salads, sauces, stews, meats, eggs, cottage cheese, pizzas, popcorn, barbecues, vegetables, tomato drinks, dressings, dips, and hors d'oeuvres.

Cooking & Baking Products

Baking Needs & Edibles

We offer the following selection of fine quality baking items and "edibles," such as natural cheese flavoring powders and food supplements.

APPLE PIECES (potpourri cut) - These 3/8-inch cubes are fun to snack on, and add texture and aroma to potpourris. They are especially effective in simmering potpourris and are processed with calcium chloride and citric acid.

ARROWROOT POWDER - Arrowroot powder is an easily digested, unrefined thickener which contains starch and nutrients (58 mgs. of calcium per 100 gms., for example). It may be substituted for cornstarch in any recipe. An excellent base for cream sauces and clear glazes, it is also a good thickener for very acidic fruits, as it does not lose its thickening ability (as flour does) in the presence of acids. Before adding to hot liquids, mix arrowroot powder with water, or cooking liquid, to form a paste. Add the paste gradually to your recipe. Its bland taste does not affect other flavors, and it is often used in infant foods, salad dressings, pie fillings, and puddings.

Maranta arundinacea is arrowroot's botanical name, and the plant is similar to the cassava. The common name arrowroot is thought to be derived from the fact that a poultice of it was applied to arrow wounds. We carry St. Vincent arrowroot.

BAKING SODA POWDER - Baking soda (Sodium bicarbonate - $NaHCO_3$) is used for its rising action - without the use of eggs or yeast - in quick breads and cakes. The leavening action is produced by the reaction between the alkali soda and acidic substances such as buttermilk, vinegar, fruit juice, yogurt, and molasses. When the soda and acidic ingredients meet, they release carbon dioxide bubbles, resulting in the rising effect. We sell USP #1 grade baking soda.

BEE POLLEN - Bee pollen is currently thought to be an excellent nutritional food. It contains generous amounts of vitamins A, D, E, C, and B complex, as well as calcium, phosphorus, magnesium, iron, manganese, potassium, copper, silicon, sulphur, chlorine, titanium, sodium, essential enzymes, lecithin, inosital, biotin, thiamin, riboflavin, nicotinic acid, folic acid, pantothenic acid, and rutin. A valuable protein source, it contains 20 of the 23 amino acids, including the eight essential aminos. One teaspoon of pollen contains 2.5 billion grains and is produced in 600 bee hours.

Despite the lengthy list above, bee pollen is very digestible. Eat it plain, like candy, or blend with honey to make a spread. It is good on cereals, fruit salads, ice cream, yogurt, or with any blended drink such as eggnog. Store bee pollen in an airtight container. Do not cook it, as valuable nutrients can be destroyed by the heating process.

We sell imported bee pollen from Spain, and domestic bee pollen. The domestic is of especially high quality. It is maintained freezer-fresh by our supplier, who air dries (rather than heat dries) it. This bee pollen is never fumigated, and is guaranteed fresh - rich in vitamins, minerals, amino acids, and protein as they occur naturally in bee pollen.

CAROB RAW (powdered), **ROASTED** (powdered), and **PODS** (kibbled) - Also known as locust bean, or St. John's bread (because it is said to have sustained St. John the Baptist while in the desert), our carob is imported from Cyprus, Portugal, and Spain. It looks, and is used, like cocoa. The benefits of using carob instead are numerous, however! Carob contains three times the calcium of milk, while chocolate actually inhibits calcium absorption. It contains no caffeine (chocolate does), and is 2% fat as compared to chocolate which is 57% fat. In addition, it is naturally sweet, and requires little additional sweetener, while cocoa is naturally bitter. Carob contains B vitamins, calcium, phosphorus, iron, and magnesium.

Roasted carob has more of a chocolate flavor, while the raw carob is very mild and sweet. Raw carob isn't actually raw, as it eases the grinding to have it slightly toasted. Our raw carob is treated for two minutes at 200° F, and the roasted for nine minutes at 450° F.

Kibbled carob pods, which we also sell, air-dried pods which have been cut into pieces smaller than one inch. They are fun to snack on (but be careful of the seeds!), and may be stored for roasting and grinding.

CITRIC ACID - Citric acid ($C_6H_8O_7$) is used in pickling and canning jams and jellies, primarily to acidify or add tartness. Derived from the fermentation of crude sugar, lemons, and/or pineapple, this white crystalline substance dissolves easily in water and is especially good to have on hand during the canning season. It is also used to brighten and hold the color of soups, and to add tartness to recipes (sweet and sour sauce, for example). To use as an antioxidant - in order to prevent browning of fruit - mix one teaspoon of citric acid to one quart of cold water and pour over fruit. It has also been used to prevent cloudiness in winemaking. We sell food grade citric acid, from France.

CORNSTARCH - Cornstarch is used extensively as a thickening agent in sauces, glazes, puddings, and gravies. Like arrowroot, it is recommended for thickening very acidic fruits because it does not lose its thickening power as quickly as flour does in the presence of acid. Unlike arrowroot, it contains no nutrients. To avoid lumps when cooking with cornstarch, make a paste of the cornstarch and liquid, and introduce it gradually into your other liquid. Do not overcook or overbeat cornstarch, as it will lose its thickening ability. Cornstarch is also a good base for homemade baby powder.

CREAM OF TARTAR POWDER - Cream of tartar powder (potassium hydrogen tartrate - $KHC_4H_4O_6$), or tartaric acid, is an effervescent acid. It is used in bath salts, denture powders, nail bleaches, hair grooming aids, hair rinses and coloring, and depilatories. It is widely distributed by nature in many fruits, but is usually obtained as a by-product of wine-making. In strong solutions it many be mildly irritating to the skin.

Cream of tartar is commonly used as a leavening in baking, and to help in beating egg whites. To substitute for one teaspoon of double acting baking powder, use 1/2 teaspoon baking soda and 1/2 teaspoon cream of tartar.

GLYCERIN, VEGETABLE - Vegetable glycerin is used as a solvent, humectant, and emollient in baking and cosmetics. It is primarily used to retain moisture in baked goods and creams, but also improves spreading characteristics of products. Derived completely from vegetable (coconut) oil, we sell it in two ounce, eight ounce, 32 ounce, and gallon jars.

LECITHIN (granulated) - Our lecithin, which is a pure product, without added oil, flours, or extenders, is derived from soybeans. It has a very wide variety of uses. In foods it is used as a stabilizer and emulsifier. In ice creams, margarines, and instant foods, for example, it serves to improve smoothness, decrease graininess, and aid the blending of unlike ingredients. In baked goods, lecithin facilitates mixing, promotes shortening action and fat distribution, eases the handling of yeast doughs, and increases the shelf life of the finished product. (Substitute lecithin for 1/3 the oil in baked goods.) The same properties are appreciated in other kinds of manufacturing - lecithin is used in textiles, plastics, and paints as well.

To use granular lecithin, chew directly, or mix with fruit or vegetable juice in a blender. It does not dissolve readily, but the granules will disintegrate in a couple of minutes. Add it to foods such as cereals, soups, stews, baked goods, yogurt, ice cream, gravies, and sauces. Two tablespoons (15 grams) contains 540 mg. choline, 330 mg. inositol, 300 mg. potassium, 450 mg. phosphorous, 4590 mg. linoleic acid, and 492 mg. linolenic acid. Our lecithin is sugar, salt, and starch free.

LEMON JUICE POWDER - So much easier to keep on hand than a fresh lemon, this powder may be substituted for fresh lemon in salad dressings, baking, beverages, or any recipe calling for lemon juice. To duplicate fresh lemon juice, use 10% powder, 87% water, and 3% citric acid. An excellent lemonade can be made by mixing one cup of Frontier Lemon Juice Powder in one quart of water. Add honey to taste, lemon or lime slices, and ice cubes (or try hot for an unusual winter treat). Our lemon juice contains corn syrup solids, lemon solids, and lemon oil.

MAPLE SYRUP POWDER - This delicious powder may be used as a flavoring in baking, mixes, and beverages. Try it sprinkled on cereal, toast, pancakes, and yogurt. It need not be refrigerated, and is especially convenient for backpacking and camping trips. Our maple syrup powder is 100% pure food grade dehydrated maple syrup.

NIGARI - The ingredients in nigari (tofu solidifier) are: magnesium chloride ($MgCZ_2$), sodium chloride (NaC_{10}), magnesium sulfuric ($MgSo_4$), potassium chloride (KCl), and magnesium bromide ($MgBr_2$). Tofu is a high-protein soybean product which is solidified by the use of nigari. Magnesium chloride, the main active ingredient, causes the tofu to coagulate into curds. The Japanese word "nigari" means "bitter liquid, " and nigari is often referred to as "bittern" in the U.S. We sell unbleached, coarse, grey, granulated nigari from Japan.

NUTRITIONAL YEAST - Nutritional yeast is not a leavening yeast, like baking yeast, but a flavoring. It is grown by introducing pure strain cultures of yeast (*Saccharomyces cerevisiae*) to a sugar medium, typically beet or cane molasses. The yeast ferments, converting the sugar to alcohol and carbon dioxide. After fermentation, the yeast is washed and separated, pasteurized to stop further yeast growth, dried in huge drums, and ground into various textures. We sell a mini-flake texture and a large-flake texture.

Our nutritional yeast contains dried yeast, niacin, pyridoxine hydrochloride (B_6), riboflavin (B_2), thiamine hydrochloride (B_1), and cyanocobalamin (B_{12}). All of the essential amino acids are found in nutritional yeast, which is also very high in protein (40-55%), B vitamins, and many trace minerals. Its golden color is derived from the riboflavin (B_2) content. These dispersable flakes have a mild, pleasant taste, which is delicious in baked goods, casseroles, beverages, cereal, and snacks. (Try it on popcorn!) Stored in a tightly-closed container, nutritional yeast need not be refrigerated, and will last indefinitely.

SOY SAUCE POWDER - This dry soy sauce is convenient for making your own dry mixes (for camping, for example), and in substitution for liquid soy sauce in recipes. It can be added dry to dishes at the rate of one teaspoon dry for every 2 1/2 teaspoons liquid soy sauce called for. It may also be reconstituted by adding 1 1/2 teaspoons of water to one teaspoon soy sauce powder. Substitute the reconstituted form in equal proportions to liquid sauce. The ingredients in this powder are brewed soy sauce and dextrin.

TAPIOCA (whole pearl) - This medium-pearl tapioca is imported from Brazil. Other common names for tapioca include cassava, manioc, and yucca. It is obtained by crushing the starchy tuberous root of cassava with water. After settling, the starch is separated and dried, then crumbled by forcing through a metal sieve or plates. The particles are then tumbled in rotating barrels or cylinders, which results in a round shape and partial gelatinization. They are then sun-dried.

Tapioca is used as a thickener and in desserts. Our tapioca is non-instant, medium pearl. To reduce the cooking time, soak the pearl first by covering with water for about two hours. Drain before using. Four tablespoons of soaked pearl tapioca equals 1 1/2 tablespoon of instant, "minute tapioca."

Tapioca Pudding Recipe
2/3 cup pearl tapioca (soak first for 2 hours)
1/2 cup maple syrup
1/4 teaspoon salt
3 3/4 cups milk
1/2 cup walnuts
1 teaspoon vanilla extract
1 tablespoon arrowroot powder

Combine the first four ingredients in double boiler. Cook while stirring over rapidly boiling water for seven minutes. Remove one cup of the hot liquid and blend with the arrowroot powder. Return liquid to the pot and stir. Cook five more minutes or until tapioca is clear. Remove from heat. Stir in vanilla, coconut, and walnuts. Serves 8.

VITAMIN C BLEND - As a dietary supplement, this powder may be sprinkled over food or dissolved in juice or water. One rounded teaspoon contains 5000% of the U.S. recommended daily allowance of vitamin C. The ingredients are: ascorbic acid, whey, lactose, rutin, hesperidin, boflavonoids, and natural orange oil.

NATURAL CHEESE FLAVORING POWDERS - These delicious flavoring powders may be used in cooking, baking, or dry mixes as a convenient substitute for fresh cheese. Store the powders in airtight containers, away from high heat (keep under 80° F) and humidity for a minimum shelf life of one year. You're sure to find one of your favorite cheese flavors here:

BLUE CHEESE - Contains blue cheese (pasteurized milk, cheese cultures, salt, enzymes), disodium phosphate.

CHEDDAR CHEESE, MILD - Contains aged cheddar cheese (cultured milk, salt, enzymes), buttermilk, cultured buttermilk, salt, lecithin.

CHEDDAR CHEESE - Contains aged cheddar cheese (cultured milk, salt, enzymes), partially hydrogenated soybean oil, buttermilk, salt, sodium phosphate, citric acid, lactic acid, and annatto color.

Parmesan cheese - Contains parmesan cheese (pasteurized milk, cheese cultures, salt, enzymes), disodium phosphate.

Romano cheese - Contains romano cheese (pasteurized milk, cheese cultures, salt, enzymes), disodium phosphate.

Recipes

Parsley Dill Carrots
4 cups sliced carrots
1 tablespoon parsley
2 tablespoons dill weed
6 tablespoons butter
2 tablespoons Frontier Parmesan Cheese Powder
Cook carrots until tender. Melt butter, add Frontier Parmesan Cheese Powder, parsley, and dill. Blend well. Pour over cooked carrots.
*—Recipe by Ruth E. Ohlsen, **The Flavor Connection,** Inc., Glenwood, IL*

Creamy Romano Salad Dressing
1 cup yogurt
1 cup mayonnaise
1/4 cup vinegar
1 tablespoon tarragon
2 tablespoons Frontier Romano Cheese Powder
Mix all ingredients in a bowl. Refrigerate for one hour before serving.

Herbal Cheese Sauce
3 tablespoons butter
2 tablespoons flour
2 cups milk
3 tablespoons Frontier Cheddar Cheese Powder
1/2 teaspoon tarragon
1/8 teaspoon paprika
Melt butter in a heavy saucepan. Sprinkle flour over melted butter, and stir for about one minute. Add milk and mix well. Cook over low heat, stirring occasionally, until mixture begins to thicken. Add Frontier Cheddar Cheese Powder, tarragon, and paprika, and continue cooking until desired thickness. Delicious over vegetables or grains, and in casseroles calling for white sauce.

Broths & Dried Vegetables

Broth powders are convenient, versatile staples to stock in your kitchen. Use them in soups, stews, sauces, gravies, casseroles, or anywhere that stock is required. Add them to grain dishes, especially rice, for a delicious pilaf. As a scasoning, they may be used on both cooked and raw vegetables. Try one teaspoon powder in one cup of hot water for a warming drink. When preparing stock for a recipe, blend the powder with liquid in a blender, or simply stir into the hot ingredients. For a light flavor, mix just a small amount with the liquid; increase the amount of powder used for a strongly-flavored broth. We sell the following variety of broth powders, all meatless. Vegetable broth powder is also available in a no-salt blend, for those on a saltless diet, or those who prefer to add their own salt.

BEEF-FLAVORED BROTH POWDER - Hydrolyzed corn flour, hydrolyzed soy protein, sea salt, onion and garlic powders, pepper and other spices and herbs, celery, carrot, and spinach.

CHICKEN-FLAVORED BROTH POWDER - Hydrolyzed soy protein, sea salt, herbs, yeast, safflower oil, parsley, sea minerals (kelp and dulse), and papaya enzyme (papain).

ONION BROTH POWDER - Salt, onion, yeast, potato flour, garlic, and calcium chloride.

VEGETABLE BROTH POWDER - Soy protein, sea salt, hydrolyzed corn, cereal solids, lecithin, safflower oil, yeast, parsley, Swiss chard, kale, spinach, watercress, celery, carrot, spices, herbs, sea minerals (kelp and dulse), and papaya enzyme (papain).

VEGETABLE BROTH POWDER NO-SALT - Soy protein, hydrolyzed cereal solids, lecithin, safflower oil, yeast, parsley, Swiss chard, kale, spinach, watercress, celery, carrots, spices, herbs, sea minerals (kelp and dulse), and papaya enzyme (papain).

French Onion Soup Recipe
1 quart water
2 tablespoons Frontier Broth Powder (choose your favorite)
2 large onions, sliced (or 1/2 cup dried onion slices)
2 tablespoons butter
4 slices French bread
1 cup grated cheese (Cheddar or Mozzarella)

Saute' onion slices in butter until translucent. Add water, and heat. Add Frontier Broth Powder and stir well. Pour soup into individual, oven-proof soup bowls. Place one slice of bread in each bowl, and top with grated cheese. Bake in 350° F oven until cheese melts, about 15 minutes.

(Note: The following powdered vegetables may also be used to create a flavorful stock.)

Dried Vegetables

We sell a wide variety of dried vegetables. Often used in dried mixes, such as for camping trips, these vegetables are also great to have on hand for everyday cooking. Once you become familiar with the simple cooking techniques, you will enjoy their convenience and versatility.

Some of the following vegetables may be used without rehydrating, as noted. To rehydrate powdered, or granulated vegetables, soak them in three times their volume of water for about ten minutes. Flaked, chopped, sliced, whole, and diced vegetables will rehydrate when simmered for 15-20 minutes in water that has been brought to a boil and then cooled. Without cooking, they may be soaked one to three hours in cold water. Drain only when necessary, to avoid nutrient loss.

Here is a list of the available vegetables, and some tips for cooking with them.

BEANS, GREEN (cut) - Cut to 1/2 inch, these green beans are a rich green color. They are excellent in casseroles, three bean salads, soups, and camping foods. One cup of dried green beans will rehydrate to two cups.

BEET POWDER - For a natural food coloring and slightly sweet taste, beet powder may be added directly (dry) to sauces, jams and jellies, cocktail mixes, tomato recipes, dressings, casseroles, and frostings. Beet powder is high in iron and other minerals. One pound of dehydrated powder yields six pounds of rehydrated coloring.

BELL PEPPERS (diced) - These mixed red and green sweet peppers are diced to 3/8 inch, and offer a pleasing color contrast to many dishes. Use in bean and meat loaves, vegetable pies, potato and macaroni salads, sauces, stir-fries, soups, and as a pizza topping. One cup rehydrates to three cups.

CABBAGE (diced) - For better color and flavor, the core has been removed from these Copenhagen variety green cabbages. Diced to 3/8 inch, one cup of dried cabbage rehydrates to 2 1/2 cups. It is good in green salads, coleslaw, gelatin, potato salad, relishes, soups, sauerkraut, and casseroles.

CARROTS (diced) - Diced to 3/8 inch, these carrots have a full orange color and mild flavor. One cup rehydrates to 2 1/2 cups. Use them in soups, stews, slaws, salads, pot pies, gravies, casseroles, carrot cakes, and mixed vegetables.

CELERY FLAKES (cut) - Dried from a Pascal type head celery, these flakes are cut to 1/2 inch. They are especially good in gelatin salads, casseroles, spreads, stews, soups, tuna salads, tomato dishes, stuffings, and potato and macaroni salads. One cup of dried celery rehydrates to six cups.

CORN (whole) - A good, low-cost protein source, this corn is sweet and colorful. Use it for fritters, scallops, soups and chowders, dip mixes, meat pies, relishes, succotash, puddings, and in Spanish and Mexican foods. One cup of dried corn rehydrates to 2 1/2 cups.

HEARTY STEW BLEND - As the name indicates, this vegetable blend is well suited for your heartiest stocks. It contains corn, potatoes, peas, carrots, onion, green beans, bell peppers, green cabbage, Formosan mushrooms, and celery flakes.

MUSHROOMS, CHILEAN - These dark, sun-dried mushrooms have a strong flavor and are best used finely chopped, in small quantities. They may be substituted for Chinese black mushrooms in egg rolls and wontons. To rehydrate, rinse several times to remove grit and soak in warm water for 1/2 hour.

MUSHROOMS, FORMOSAN - These mushrooms, light in color, are similar to the button mushrooms sold fresh in grocery stores. Sun-dried and mild in flavor, they may be added to soups, stews, or any dish where a mushroom flavor is desired. They are thinly sliced. To rehydrate, soak in warm water until soft, about 1/2 hour.

MUSHROOMS, SHITAKE - Also known as Japanese forest mushrooms, emperor's food, and Japanese black mushrooms, shitake mushrooms are the major edible mushroom in Asia. Valued for their flavor, texture, and nutritive properties, they contain protein, fiber, calcium, phosphorus, iron, B vitamins, and vitamin D2. Shitake mushrooms derive their name from the "shii" trees (Japanese evergreens) on which they were originally gathered wild, and are now cultivated. They are dried whole, and may be rehydrated by soaking in warm water until softened, about 1/2 hour. (The water should be retained for use in cooking.) Their robust flavor is especially good in miso soup. We sell shitake mushrooms in a 1.76 ounce package.

Rice With Shitake Recipe
3 cups of cooked rice seasoned with Frontier Chicken Flavored Broth Powder
1 cup rehydrated shitake mushrooms
1 onion, chopped
1/2 teaspoon sage
garlic powder, black pepper, and sea salt to taste
Saute' onion and shitake in butter for 15 minutes. Add rice. Mix and season to taste.

PEAS (whole) - Just like fresh when rehydrated, these peas are good in mixed vegetables, casseroles, soups, rice mixes, and pea salads.

POTATOES (diced) - Very similar to fresh potatoes when rehydrated, these dried potatoes have excellent color and texture. Use them for hashbrowns, casseroles, soups, and potato salads. One pound of dried potatoes rehydrates to four pounds.

SPINACH (flakes) - These 3/8-inch flakes may be used as a natural green colorant (in noodle-making, for example), and in ravioli fillings, souffles, spinach rings, soups, mixes, casseroles, salad dressings, and vegetable breads. One pound rehydrates to nine pounds.

TOMATO (flakes) - Tomato flakes may be reconstituted to make tomato-base sauces (cocktail sauces, pasta sauces, barbecue sauces, etc.), or used in any recipe calling for tomatoes (casseroles, soups, vegetable dishes).

TOMATO (powdered) - A good thickener for tomato base products such as sauces and juices, this powder may also be used to color and flavor soup stock and grain dishes such as Spanish rice. Contains Silicon dioxide (SiO_2), an anti-caking agent.

VEGETABLE DELUXE SOUP BLEND - This blend consists of the same varieties of these dried vegetables which we sell individually. The ingredients are: carrots, onions, tomato, peas, celery, bell peppers, beans, and parsley. One pound rehydrates to six pounds. As the name implies, this blend is a perfect soup-starter! It also works well in dry camping mixes.

VEGETABLE SOUP BLEND - This blend also consists of the same varieties of dried vegetables which we sell individually. The ingredients are: carrots, celery, tomato, cabbage, white onion, spinach, red and green peppers, and parsley. One pound rehydrates to six pounds. Use for soups, of course, and also for dry camping mixes.

Potato Soup Recipe
1 cup dried potatoes
1/4 cups dried carrots
1/4 cup dried celery
1/2 cup onion slices
3 tablespoons oil
7 cups water
2 tablespoons Frontier Broth Powder
1 teaspoon sea salt
1 tablespoon parsley
1 tablespoon tarragon

Rehydrate vegetables in water. Saute' onions in oil until translucent. Add vegetables and all other ingredients and simmer until all vegetables are tender, about one hour.

Variation: Sprinkle with your favorite Frontier Natural Cheese Flavoring Powder.

Vegie Camping Mix Recipe
Premix: 1/2 cup dried green beans
1/2 cup dried carrots
1/2 cup dried corn
1/4 cup dried tomato flakes

In another pouch, premix: 1/2 teaspoon rosemary, 1/2 teaspoon thyme.

To prepare, soak vegetables in water for two to three hours. Bring to a boil, and simmer until vegies are hot and tender. Drain all but a little liquid. Add seasonings, and cook two more minutes. Serves 4-6.

Sea Vegetables

Seaweeds are ocean vegetables. They have long been traditional staples in the diets of a number of cultures, including Japanese, Irish, Danish, Scottish, Korean, Chinese, and Icelandic. An excellent source of nutrients - especially in winter when fresh greens are unavailable to most of us - seaweeds are high in complex carbohydrates and protein, and low in fat. They contain vitamins A, C, E, and B complex. Their primary nutritional benefit, however, is their outstanding mineral content. Iron, calcium, phosphorus, potassium, and iodine are all abundant in seaweeds.

The taste of seaweeds may be a new experience to many, but it can be a delightful one. You may want to start out slowly by adding small amounts to your meals, and acquaint yourself with the taste before trying main dish seaweed recipes. Use crushed or chopped seaweeds in soups, salads, and casseroles. Most seaweeds are delicious with rice and with fish. Boil or steam strips or sheets and eat as a cooked vegetable. When you're feeling adventurous, sprinkle or crumble a small amount on pizza before baking. Cook seaweed without the use of additional salt, as it is naturally high in sodium. Powdered seaweed may be used as a seasoning in place of salt.

Store seaweeds in a moisture-proof container, and they will keep indefinitely. A wide variety of seaweeds are available.

AGAR AGAR (powdered) - Agar agar is the dried extract from *Gelidium, Cracelaria,* and other related red algae. Although practically indigestible, agar is widely used in food products due to its unique combination of low-gelling and high-melting temperatures. It is a common non-animal substitute for gelatin; the Japanese use it extensively to make candies and sweets, and it is also suitable for jellies, custards, and puddings. The basic proportions are 3 1/2 cups liquid to one tablespoon powder. Heat to simmering, pour into mold and cool.

ARAME - *Eisenia bicyclis* / Arame is dark yellowish-brown when growing and black when dried. Its texture is similar to that of hijiki, but its flavor and aroma are milder. This mild, sweet taste is produced by the mannitol (sugar alcohol) contained in the plant, and it is often used with tamari soy sauce or to flavor miso soups. To prepare, wash well and soak for a few minutes in water to cover. Simmer for 20 minutes and season. Simmer another 15 minutes and serve, or add to other recipes. Arame contains protein, vitamins A, B1, B2 and some minerals. In Japan, it is used fresh or sun dried.

BLADDERWRACK (cut and sifted) - *Fucus versiculosus* / Also known as sea wrack, sea oak, and black tany, bladderwrack is found on submerged rocks on both North American coasts and in Europe north of the Mediterranean. It is often used for its iodine content, and has also been used as a fertilizer, especially for potatoes. Bladderwrack may be sprinkled on the ground and then ploughed under, or dried and burnt into ashes before sprinkling. Kelp is sometimes prepared from several species of *Fucus*, including bladderwrack. Because of its mineral and salt content, bladderwrack is also used in herbal bath preparations.

DULSE (flaked, whole, powdered) - *Rhodymemia palmata* / Dulse is one of the most popular sea vegetables. The best quality dulse grows in crevices away from sunlight. It should be deep red-purple-black. A yellow-pink or light green color means it has been exposed to sun and deteriorated. On the average, a 100 gram sample of dulse contains 25 grams of protein, 550 milligrams of calcium, 100 milligrams of potassium, 150 milligrams of iron, and many other vitamins and minerals. It can be eaten raw or cooked, and has a relatively strong, distinctive taste. The texture is soft and chewy. Dulse flakes may be added to chowder, salads, or sandwiches, or made into fried chips. Whole dulse, which retains more flavor and nutrients than powdered or flaked, is fun to snack on. Powdered dulse can be added to practically any dish, and is a convenient form to use as a table condiment.

Dulse Chowder Recipe

Sauté chopped onion and celery in oil. Add potatoes, corn and chopped dulse. Cook with milk and add arrowroot to thicken.

—from ***Edible Sea Vegetables of the New England Coast****, by Larch and Jan Hanson*

HIJIKI - *Hijikia fusiform* / Hijiki is easy to identify; its mass of shiny curls - brown when fresh, black when dried- adds beautiful texture and drama to meals. It is usually rehydrated in water before using, and will swell to four to five times its dried volume. To prepare, rinse well and soak in enough water to cover for about 20 minutes. It is very popular in Japanese, Chinese, and Korean dishes. This seaweed has a unique and delicious nut-like flavor and a crisp texture. Serve it boiled, parboiled, steamed and sautéed, or simmered with vegetables. Tamari complements it well. Nutritionally it is high in protein, rich in calcium (It contains 14 times the calcium of cow's milk!) and iron, and contains vitamins A, B1, B2, and other trace elements.

Hijiki Sauté Recipe

1 1/2 cups dried hijiki
2 cups carrots, sliced
2 cups onions, chopped
1/4 cup peanut oil
1 tablespoon sesame oil
tamari to taste

Cover the hijiki in cold water and soak for about 30 minutes until tender. Drain well. Chop into bite-sized pieces. Sauté the carrots in hot oil until they are almost cooked. Add the onions and sauté until they are wilted. Add more oil if needed. Add the hijiki. Sauté for five to seven more minutes. Season with tamari. Serve hot. Serves six to eight.

Variations: Substitute or add more vegetables: onions, bean sprouts, garlic, ginger, green pepper, tofu, etc.

IRISH MOSS (flaked, powdered) - *Chondrus crispus* or *Gigartina mamillosa* / Found on the coasts of Ireland, France, the U.S., and Portugal, irish moss is also known as carrageenan. It grows one to three inches tall, and is a deep brown/red. Due to its gelling properties, it is widely used in the food industry as a stabilizer. As an emollient and emulsifying agent it is widely used in cosmetics.

KELP (flaked, powdered) - *Laminaria genus* and *Ascoplayllum nodosum* / Kelp is a dark green seaweed which grows in deep beds. A 100 gram sample contains about seven grams of protein, one gram of fat, 55 grams of carbohydrates, 800 milligrams of calcium, 5,300 milligrams of potassium, 100 milligrams of iron, 150 milligrams of iodine, 400 IUs vitamin A, three grams sodium, 760 milligrams of magnesium, and 240 milligrams of phosphorous. Other minerals and vitamins are found in smaller quantities. Because of its 3% sodium content, kelp enjoys popularity as a salt substitute; it may be substituted for salt in any cooked dish, or used as a table condiment.

Kelp contains glutamic acid, which acts as a natural tenderizer for cooking beans. It cooks quickly, dissolves readily in soups and stews if left to cook 20 minutes or more. Our kelp flakes are chopped pieces of *Ascoplayllum nodosum*, and may contain up to five percent of *Laminaria.* They may be sprinkled on popcorn, cooked grains, soups, and salads. These flakes are as easy to use as the powder, and retain more flavor and texture. Our powdered kelp is finely ground *Laminaria* from the Norwegian coasts. This form is convenient, but does lose some nutrients and flavor from being ground.

Crunchy Kelp Recipe

Heat sesame, safflower, or corn oil in a frying pan and add bite-size pieces of kelp. Stir-fry, pressing down with a pancake turner until it changes color. It can be eaten as is or sprinkled over grains, vegetables, soups, or popcorn.

—from ***Edible Sea Vegetables of the New England Coast*** *by Larch and Jan Hanson*

KOMBU - *Laminaria angustata* / In Japan, kombu is indispensable in everyday cooking. Dark brown with a leather-like texture, it is traditionally used to make soup stock, and boiled and eaten as a vegetable. Try it as a side dish, in salads, or to wrap vegetable hors d'ouevres. To prepare, simply rinse, boil until tender, and cover. Kombu contains natural, taste-enhancing sodium glutamate, and is very rich in iodine, vitamin B2, and calcium. It is also high in protein, and contains various other vitamins and minerals. A small piece cooked with beans helps speed cooking time.

NORI - *Porphyra* spp. / Also known as laver, nori is light pink when young, and dark purple-red when older. The filmy, rubbery plant, which grows on storm beaches, is spread out when harvested and dried into thin sheets. A favorite Japanese lunch food is rice balls and sushi, wrapped in nori sheets. In China it is used to produce a gel in cooking, or as a vegetable in soup. It is also eaten dry or lightly broiled with tamari. The sweet, nutty taste of nori is enhanced by dry roasting. It may then be crushed and sprinkled on grains, popcorn, and salads. Nori has one of the highest protein contents (35%) of all the sea vegetables. It is also very high in vitamin A and iron. We sell nori in packages of ten sheets (.6 ounce)

SPIRULINA (powdered) - Spirulina is a blue-green algae harvested from ponds in California. Dark green when dried, it has a mild taste similar to other sea vegetables. Easy to digest, it has a 60-70% balanced protein content, and is rich in iron, phosphorus, potassium, and magnesium. It also contains the trace elements selenium and chromium. Needing no refrigeration, it is used as a lightweight, no-preparation food by hikers and backpackers, a supplement to a regular diet, and as an aid to fasting. Sprinkle spirulina on foods, or blend into soups, sauces, and dips (it is especially good in guacamole dip and pesto sauce). Try it in juices or kefir, baked goods such as breads and bars, and miso and ramen soups. Our powdered spirulina has been tested to insure purity and freedom from contamination.

WAKAME - *Undaria pinnatifida* / Medium to dark brown, wakame is usually sun dried, but occasionally eaten fresh. It has a soft, delicate texture, and mild taste. In Japan the rehydrated occasionally eaten fresh. It has a soft, delicate texture, and mild taste. In Japan the rehydrated plant is added to miso soup, salads, pork, poultry, fish, and tofu dishes. To prepare, rinse and soak for ten minutes in water to cover. Cook until soft, about 20 minutes. It will rehydrate to seven times its dried size. Wakame is often cooked with rice vinegar and other vegetables for a side dish. Also delicious raw (sprinkle it on salads), it is high in protein, iron, calcium, sodium and magnesium.

Sprouting Seeds

What nutritious, inexpensive, delicious food can you grow yourself, in any weather, in any season, without soil or sun, in one week's time? Sprouts! Sprouting increases the already high nutritional value of seeds, grains, legumes, and nuts. Because its protein is in the form of amino acids, enzymes, chlorophyll, and hormones, it is easily digested by the body. Sprouts are also a good source of vitamins A, C, B, and E, as well as assorted minerals. While most any seed will sprout, it is important to use quality, organic seeds to insure the best results, including maximum nutrition.

Store unsprouted seeds in a tightly covered container in a dry, cool place. Under these conditions, they will stay fresh for about four days.

Easy to grow and economical, one pound of seeds will yield about six pounds of sprouts. They are also an excellent food for dieters. One cup (or 1/4 pound) of mung sprouts, for example, contains only 40 calories.

There are many methods of sprouting, and many special sprouting devices available. All you really need to get started, though, are some quart canning jars and a screen or cheesecloth through which water, but not seeds, will flow. Here's how:

Place the seeds in a clear glass jar and cover with clean water. Stretch the cheesecloth or flexible screen over the mouth of the jar and use the jar rim or a rubber band to secure in place. After soaking for the specified amount of time (usually overnight), rinse the seeds thoroughly. Place the jar in a dark place and tilt it so that all the water will drain out and the seeds will be spread against the sides of the jar. An environment with a temperature of about 60°-70° is ideal. Rinse the sprouts two to four times each day. When they reach the desired length, expose them to sunlight for one day - to turn them green with chlorophyll - then place them in the refrigerator, where they will keep fresh for about four days.

Use sprouts imaginatively and liberally. Try different sprouts with different dishes. Try sprouting combinations of seeds (alfalfa and radish, for example). Add them to rice dishes, omelettes, or bread recipes. Munch sprouts for snacks or in salads. Drop them into soups just before serving, place them in casseroles, or garnish most any dish with them. They are especially good on sandwiches and tacos!

Frontier sells the following sprouting seeds:

ALASKAN PEAS, ORGANIC - When sprouted, these taste like fresh peas, and are best when steamed lightly. They are delicious sprouted in combination with lentils. Use two cups of peas for each quart jar, and soak 10 - 15 hours. Rinse them two to three times each day, and in two to three days, the sprouts will reach the desired length of 1/4 to 1/2 inch.

ALFALFA SEED WHOLE, ORGANIC - Alfalfa seeds are among the easiest to grow and make the most versatile, nutritious sprouts. Their pleasant, light taste, is appreciated in salads and sandwiches. Use two tablespoons of seed in a quart jar. After soaking five to eight hours, rinse them two to three times per day. In four to six days, they will be 1 1/2 to two inches long, and ready to use.

BLACK MUSTARD SEED, ORGANIC - The spicy, tangy taste of these seeds is reminiscent of fresh English mustard. Use three tablespoons of seed per quart jar. Soak six to eight hours, then rinse two to three times per day. They will be ready in four to five days, at one to 1 1/2 inches in length. In addition to sprouting, black mustard seed is used in pickling, sausages, and Indian cooking.

CABBAGE SEED CHINESE WHOLE, ORGANIC - Sprouted cabbage seeds are especially good in salads! Use three tablespoons cabbage seed per quart jar. After soaking six to ten hours, rinse them two to three times each day. In three to five days they will have reached the desired length of one to 1 1/2 inches.

CLOVER RED SEED WHOLE, ORGANIC - Similar to, but lighter in color and sweeter in taste than alfalfa, red clover sprouts are very good in casseroles and sandwiches. Soak two tablespoons in the quart jar for six to eight hours. Rinse them two to three times each day, and in four to six days, they will be ready to use, at 1 1/2 to two inches.

CRESS SEED, ORGANIC - These gelatinous seeds have a strong, peppery taste. They are good sprouted for use in salads and omelets. Soak two tablespoons in the quart jar for eight hours. Rinse them three times each day, and in about four days they will be ready to serve. One tablespoon cress seed will make 1 1/2 cups of sprouts.

MUNG BEANS WHOLE, ORGANIC - Mung beans are used extensively in East Asian countries. Especially good in salads and Oriental dishes, mung beans are easy to sprout. Add 1/3 cup of beans to a quart jar, soak 12 - 16 hours, and rinse three to four times per day. They will be ready (one to three inches long) in three to five days. Wash away the green husks (they will float to the top) before storing.

RADISH SEED WHOLE, ORGANIC - Good when used for flavoring, radish sprouts are a little tangy, like the vegetable. Try them in salads and sandwiches, and in combination with other sprouts. Use three tablespoons per quart jar, soak six to ten hours, and rinse two to three times per day. They will be one to two inches long in four to five days.

SPROUT SPREE, ORGANIC - This is Frontier's own blend of alfalfa seed, red clover seed, mung bean seed, radish seed, and cabbage seed. Try these sprouts on sandwiches, in salads and stir fries, and in casseroles. To sprout, use three tablespoons per quart jar, soak eight hours, and rinse three times each day. In about four days, these sprouts, averaging two inches in length, will be ready to use.

Sautéed Red Cabbage and Sprouts Recipe
2 tablespoons olive oil
3 cups grated red cabbage
1 cup mung bean sprouts
1 tablespoon caraway seeds
tamari to taste
1 tablespoon vinegar

salt and pepper to taste

Heat olive oil in a cast-iron skillet. Saute' the red cabbage for three to five minutes. Add mung bean sprouts and saute' for two more minutes. Add caraway seeds, tamari, vinegar, salt and pepper, and allow to cook gently as you toss together for a few more minutes. Serve piping hot.

*—from **The Green Thumb Cookbook**, edited by Anne Moyer, Rodale Press*

Sprout Omelet Recipe

8 eggs
4 tablespoons water
salt to taste
freshly ground pepper to taste
3 tablespoons butter
1 1/2 cups lentil, alfalfa, or mung bean sprouts
chopped parsley for garnish

Break eggs into a bowl, beat lightly. Add water and beat briefly. Add salt and pepper. Heat butter in a heavy skillet, to medium-high heat. Pour in egg mixture, just enough to cover bottom of the pan. Continue cooking, without stirring, until bottom is golden. Sprinkle with sprouts and parsley. Using spatula, flip over so omelet is a half-moon shape. Carefully turn out onto warm platter; serve immediately.

*—from **The Green Thumb Cookbook**, edited by Anne Moyer, Rodale Press*

Teas

Black & Green Teas

Thea sinensis is an evergreen shrub which ranges from the Mediterranean to the tropics, and from sea level to 8000 feet. The leaves of this shrub are what we commonly refer to as tea. *Thea sinensis* can grow to a height of 25-30 feet but when cultivated is kept pruned to about four feet. This not only makes it easier to harvest, it also keeps the tea plant producing tender new growth.

Tea is harvested every 6-14 days, depending on the area and climate in which the tea is grown. Some areas produce the best tea in the first flush, or growth; others in the second or later growths. Yielding nearly one-quarter pound of leaves per year, each bush produces tea leaves for 25 to 50 years. One harvester can pick about 30,000 leaf shoots, or almost ten pounds of manufactured tea per day.

Black, green, or oolong teas are differentiated by the manner in which their leaves are processed. When tea is harvested the freshly plucked leaves are partially dried and then rolled either by hand or machine to crush the cell structure of the leaf. The partially dried, rolled leaf would then ferment, or oxidize, if left in this state.

In the processing of green tea this fermentation is prevented by first steaming the leaf and then drying it with hot air. In the production of oolongs (which are teas that have been allowed to semi-ferment) and black teas, the partially dried, rolled leaves are spread out on tile, glass, or concrete and fermented until the tea manufacturer decides that the aroma and hence the flavor has blossomed. This takes approximately three hours for black teas, less for oolongs. Then the leaves are steamed and dried. The fermentation process reduces the bitterness of the leaf and develops the color and aroma of the tea. Sometimes black teas are scented by layering fresh blossoms with the tea leaves or by adding bits of spices. Jasmine, orange and licorice spice are examples of *Thea sinensis* which have been scented or flavored.

The nomenclature of teas can be confusing. Names such as Assam, Ceylon, or Darjeeling refer to the country, region, or estate where the tea was grown. Names such as oolong, black, or jasmine refer to how the tea was processed or scented. There are also names which refer to leaf size: broken pekoe, pekoe, orange pekoe, and flowery orange pekoe. Pekoe, which is Chinese for "white hair," originally referred to the leaves of the first picking because of the white down on them. Now it is a reference to a certain size leaf, smaller than the orange pekoe. Orange pekoe was so named because of its association with a Chinese tea scented with orange blossoms. It is the next larger size than pekoe, and the name no longer maintains any reference to scent, flavor, or color. Flowery orange pekoe refers to a tea containing an abundance of tip, or bud leaf, of the plant. Souchong, Chinese for "small kind," referred originally to a tea made from the leaves of a small bush which grew abnormally large leaves. It now refers to any large-leaf black tea. Pouchong means "folded sort" and refers to the Cantonese method of packaging one choice tea plant in a small paper package.

We sell the following black and green teas in bulk:

(All except Kukicha twig contain caffeine.)

ASSAM - The Assam Province in Northeast India produces this high-grade tea. It is a flowering orange pekoe, with a robust, rich, malty taste and a cloudy, amber color.

BANCHA LEAF - A Japanese tea which is picked from the tea plant at the end of the harvest season, bancha leaves contain less caffeine and tannin than other teas and are thus considered of low quality. Graded just above Kukicha, the flavor is milder than that of fermented and fired tea. (Note that while Bancha and Kukicha are considered low grades in Japan, many find them to be truly delicious teas!)

CEYLON - This tea is grown in Sri Lanka, which began tea cultivation in the 1870's only after a leaf disease ruined its coffee industry. Ceylon tea has an intense, flowery aroma and flavor. When available, we offer two grades of this black tea - best (an orange pekoe) and standard (a broken pekoe). Because of political unrest, the availability of Ceylon is spotty. When Ceylon is unavailable, we substitute a South Indian tea of similar taste, aroma and color. The South Indian tea is at least as fine in quality as the Ceylon.

DARJEELING - The finest and most delicately flavored of the black Indian teas, Darjeeling is named after the district in which it grows. It is a dark amber color, with full-bodied, delicate flavor. We carry a flowery orange pekoe.

EARL GREY - A black tea which has been sprayed with French bergamot oil, this is one of our best sellers. It is hearty and aromatic.

ENGLISH BREAKFAST - A Formosan tea of Keemun (fine) quality, Americans imagined this a favorite of the British and named it English Breakfast. It is a rich, mellow, fragrant black tea with Chinese flavor, and is a combination of Assam flowery orange pekoe and Ceylon broken orange pekoe.

FORMOSA BLACK - This inexpensive tea is a broken leaf of standard grade. It is a good base for blending your own flavors. Try it with cinnamon, cloves, or orange.

GUNPOWDER GREEN - This tea is from Formosa. We carry an Imperial type which indicates a round, bold character made from older leaves. It is pungent and rather bitter, and brews to a yellow-green color.

IRISH BREAKFAST - Blended to please the palates of discriminating tea drinkers, this is a combination of Assam flowery orange pekoe and Ceylon orange pekoe. When Ceylon is unavailable *(see Ceylon entry)*, Irish Breakfast consists of a blend of Assam flowery orange pekoe and a South Indian tea.

JASMINE - To make this tea, a base of Pouchong tea from Formosa is scented by adding white jasmine flowers during the final firing. In the highest quality jasmine teas, all flower petals are removed after firing. We sell both "best" and "standard" qualities of jasmine tea.

KEEMUN CONGOU - Similar to our English Breakfast, but of higher quality, this tea comes from the Keemun district of the People's Republic of China. Dark amber in color, it is thought to be the best of China's black teas, comparable in strength to Indian black teas.

KUKICHA TWIG - Comprised of the smallest stems of the tea plant, Kukicha contains less caffeine and acidic oils than the leaves, and is considered the lowest grade of tea. High in calcium, this Japanese tea has a favorable reputation among macrobiotics. Ours has been roasted and cooled four times to eliminate all tannin and caffeine. Simmer at least ten minutes; the flavor is mellow. Although not yet certified, we sell a Kukicha tea which is sold in Japan as organic.

LAPSANG SOUCHONG - From Formosa, this is a fine grade of China Black tea with a strong, distinctive, smoky flavor.

LONG JING - Also known as Dragonwell, this tea is from Dragon Well village deep in the hills behind Hanchow. Terraced rows of tea shrubs are harvested there three times each year. This tea is light and fresh, with a smooth scent.

OOLONG - The word "oolong" is Chinese for "black dragon." Fired in baskets over hot coals, it is a semi-fermented, hand-rolled tea from Formosa. We offer two grades - a standard, inexpensive grade, and a higher-priced, fine grade. It is famous for its delicate, subtle, fruity taste and light color.

YUNNAN - A black tea from the southwestern Yunnan province of the People's Republic of China, this is a flowery orange pekoe grade.

Tea Blends

Blended teas take advantage of the aromas and flavors of many teas - black, green, and herbal. A well-balanced blend is a work of art. You may want to try your hand at blending your own teas to perfectly suit your taste, or you may find a few favorites among those tea blends we sell, listed below:
(Unless noted otherwise, these teas are sold in bulk.)

CINNAMON SPICE - This is a blend of good-grade China Black tea, ginger, cinnamon, and cloves. Prepare as you would any black tea for a highly aromatic and flavorful treat. It does contain caffeine.

FRUIT TEA - Fruity and red-colored, this tea is good hot or iced, and is great when mixed with orange juice! It contains: hibiscus, lemongrass, rosehips, orange peel, and peppermint. Fruit tea does not contain caffeine.

INDIAN SPICE TEA - This rich, warm tea may be served with milk and sweetener, or even simmered in milk rather than steeped in water, for a real Indian treat. It contains: cinnamon chips, fennel, ginger, cardamom, anise, cloves, and black peppercorns. It does not contain caffeine.

JASMINE SPICE - A delicious tea for jasmine lovers, this blend contains: black tea scented with jasmine flowers, orange peel, cinnamon, cloves, and cardamom. It does contain caffeine.

LICORICE SPICE - Because it contains licorice root, children especially enjoy this tea. The other ingredients are: cinnamon, orange peel, cloves, and cardamom. This blend does not contain caffeine.

MU TEA - Japanese Mu tea was formulated by George Oshawa on the macrobiotic principles of yin and yang. It needs to be simmered for at least ten minutes, and it is recommended that you do not destroy its balance by adding cream or sweetener. We sell two blends, neither of which contain caffeine. They are sold in bulk and are also available in teabags.

Mu #9 - This is a blend of: herbaceous peony root, Japanese parsley root, hoelen, cinnamon, licorice root, peach kernels, ginger root, Japanese ginseng, and rehmannia.

Mu #16 - The ingredients of this blend are: mandarin orange peel, hoelen, cnicus, cinnamon, herbaceous peony root, Japanese parsley root, atractylis, ginger root, licorice, peach kernels, rehmannia, cypress, coptis, Japanese ginseng, cloves, and moutan.

ORANGE MINT - This base of Ceylon Black tea is flavored with: orange peel, peppermint, cloves, cinnamon, and licorice. This blend contains caffeine.

ORANGE SPICE - This very popular blend contains black tea, orange peel, natural orange oil, and cloves. It has a definite orange flavor, and does contain caffeine.

SPEARMINT SPICE - This blend of spearmint leaves, cinnamon, orange peel, cloves, and cardamom makes a great iced tea on a hot summer day. It does not contain caffeine.

Tea Tips

Teas easily take on the odor of other foods and seasonings, so proper storage is the first hint to a satisfying cup. Store your bulk tea in a clean, dark, airtight container in a cool, dry place. Many types of strainers are available, both metal and bamboo, as well as the popular tea bag. Reusable cloth tea bags are another choice. Keep your utensils clean and dry so that they do not taint the delicate flavor of your freshly-brewed tea.

Caffeine, tannin, and essential oil are the three principal chemical constituents of black and green teas. Tannin is what gives the tea its strength or body. To minimize the tannin content, pour fresh boiling water over the tea leaves and allow to stand for three to five minutes. A cup of the resulting brew will be robust without being bitter, and contain about one grain of caffeine, 33% less than an equivalent amount of coffee.

Brewed Tea Recipe

Boil fresh water until it is bubbling fiercely. Rinse your cup or teapot with boiling water, then drain it, keeping it warm. Use a clean, dry spoon to remove the bulk leaves from the container. (Use about one teaspoon of tea per cup, plus one for the pot.) Put the tea in your teapot or cup, or use a strainer. Quickly transfer the boiling water to the pot, pouring directly over the leaves. Cover and steep for three to five minutes. If desired, add small quantitites of milk and/or sweetener to your cup of tea; too much of either will spoil the aroma and taste.

Sun Tea Recipe

Large mesh tea infusers are excellent for making big jars of tea for icing. Simply fill the ball with loose tea, place in a clean gallon jar full of cool water, and place in the sun until steeped to desired strength. Strain and ice.

Herbal Teas

A cup of herbal tea can be every bit as satisfying as a cup of the best imported tea. In addition, herbal teas are often inexpensive and healthful. They may be brewed individually or in bouquet mixes to produce a wide range of flavors and aromas. Try them hot or iced, or combined with other beverages such as juice.

Here are just some of the herbs you can successfully brew as teas. All except yerba mate are caffeine free.

ALFALFA LEAF -Good blended with mints; rich in vitamins and minerals.

BASIL LEAF - Faintly clovelike; very aromatic.

CHAMOMILE FLOWERS - Delicate, apple flavor; good alone.

CHICORY ROOT - Used as coffee substitute; slightly bitter; boil 15 minutes and strain.

CINNAMON - Spicy and dark; use to enrich otherwise plain black tea, or with other spices (cloves, for example) to produce a flavorful blend.

CLOVER TOPS - Delicate flavor; good with peppermint or spearmint; simmer for a few minutes to develop flavor.

DANDELION LEAF - Grassy aroma; bland taste, but good with mints; rich in vitamins and minerals.

ELDER FLOWER - Pleasant with mints.

FENNEL SEED - Aromatic and spicy; nutmeg-like flavor.

GINGER - Rich, pungent, warming flavor; use alone or with other spices for a very flavorful blend.

HIBISCUS FLOWER - Tart, lemony flavor; rose color; excellent iced in summer.

HOREHOUND - Mild and pleasant; simmer about 20 minutes to develop flavor.

JASMINE FLOWERS - Fragrant and sweet; good in combination with dark teas.

LEMON PEEL -Fruity and tangy; add to spicy or delicate teas for added flavor.

LEMONGRASS - Fine, lemony taste; best served hot.

LICORICE ROOT - Sweet, good thirst quencher when served cold.

LINDEN FLOWER - Popular continental tea; sweet, pleasant flavor and jasmine-like aroma.

MARJORAM LEAF - Pungent, sage-like flavor; nice with mints.

MINT LEAF - The mints vary slightly in flavor. Spearmint is milder and more fragrant than peppermint. Both make excellent teas served alone, or in combination with other herbs. Both produce a good, clean, green color. An iced mint tea/apple juice combination is delicious.

ORANGE PEEL - Fruity; add to spicy or delicate teas for added flavor.

PARSLEY LEAF - Aromatic; rich in vitamins A, B, C.

ROSEHIPS - Fruity taste; orange color; high in vitamin C.

YERBA MATE LEAF - A favorite beverage in South America; refreshing, grassy taste; does contain caffeine.

YERBA SANTA LEAF - Dry, clean, cinnamic fragrance with peppery aftertaste; clear color.

Potpourris

Craft Ingredients

Potpourri Blends

Potpourris are a delightful way to add the scent of herbs and spices to your home. They are also beautiful - set out in baskets, glass jars, bowls, favorite tins. Consider the color, texture, and scent of a potpourri and select one with a special room or special friend in mind. (Potpourris make lovely gifts!)

Many potpourris may be simmered on the stovetop to more dramatically fill your home with scent. Our Simmer Sacks have been developed with just this purpose in mind, and most of our regular potpourris may also be used for this purpose.

We have blended a wonderful variety of potpourris for you to try. These are all available by the pound, and refresher oils are available for all of the following except the Dream Pillow and Herbal Moth blends. (See *Essential Oils*, page 100.)

Caution: All of our potpourris contain oils and herbs which are dangerous if consumed. Keep out of reach of small children.

***BLUE MOON** - *New*- The white bouganvillier, blue cornflowers and fresh breezy scent remind you of the full moon in a star-filled sky on a clear summer night. It's a natural for any room in your home.

CHOCOLATE DREAM - Rich shades of chocolate brown with white flowers, a hint of spice, and a deep chocolate aroma. This potpourri contains: cinnamon chips, cracked nutmeg, Roman chamomile, pine cones, star anise, guarana seed, cloves, peeled orris root, white globe amaranth, tilia star flower, and chocolate fragrance.

***CINNAMON STIX** - *New*- This bright and lively visual potpourri also doubles as a spicy simmering potpourri. The tiny cinnamon sticks, when simmered with orange peel, produce a spicy scent that delightfully fills any room.

COOL MINT ICE - Bits of purple in a bed of oak moss and cool, refreshing mint leaves. Cool Mint Ice contains: oak moss, blue malva flowers, corn flowers, uva ursi leaf, purple glove amaranth, spearmint leaf, peppermint leaf, peppermint oil, spearmint oil, and pennyroyal oil.

***ELFIN CHRISTMAS** - Berries, needles and moss combine as a simmering or visual potpourri to bring the magical spirit of the Holidays into your home. This blend contains: rosehips, juniper berries, rosemary, uva ursi, allspice, pine cones, oak moss, Roman chamomile, and fragrance oils.

FAIRIES-N-FLOWERS - This soothing blend combines red rosebuds, orris root, lemon thyme, oak moss, and uva ursi to creat a delicate scent.

FLOWER FANTASIA - Blossoms of blue malva, red and pink rosebuds, and purple globe amaranth nestled in a bed of ten colorful flowers and leaves place this fragrance in a class of its own. It also contains: orris root, tilia star, uva ursi, spina cristi, oak moss, calcatrippae, life everlasting, feverfew, calendula, broom flowers, cedar chips, and fragrance oils.

FOREST FANTASIA - A warm, arousing blend rich in texture and fragrance. The ingredients in this potpourri are: rosehips, star anise, hibiscus, tonka beans, saw palmetto, balm of Gilead buds, tilia star flowers, cinnamon chips, pine cones, spina cristi, sage, oak moss, and fragrance oils.

HAPPY HOLIDAYS - *New-* This decorative blend of frosty silver and white flowers and moss is highly accented by red rosehips and green olive leaves. A fresh, crisp bayberry fragrance makes this potpourri an excellent natural room freshener.

HARVEST APPLE SPICE - This simmering potpourri with apples and spices creates a warm, homey feeling. It contains: rosehips, calamus, star anise, cracked nutmeg, cinnamon chips, orange peel potpourri, apple potpourri, cloves, and fragrance oils.

INDIAN SUMMER - *New-* Sure to be one of your favorites. Includes all autumn colors in a combination of strawflowers, leaves, pods, and grasses. You'll smell the sweet scent of those lazy end-of-the-summer days.

MARMALADE - This party blend with its sweet, fruity aroma is dominated by berries and citrus peels. It contains: orange peel potpourri, saw palmetto berries, frankincense tears, buchu leaf, rosehips, juniper berries, hawthorne berries, chamomile flowers, red sandalwood chips, kesu flowers, cornflowers, calamus root, and fragrance oils.

RASPBERRY RIPPLE - *New-* A scrumptious fun and fruity potpourri. This red and white medley with its real fruit pieces and fresh raspberry scent add excitement to the room of your choice.

SPICE OF PARADISE - A warm, spicy recipe. Enjoy the stimulating aroma of clove, frankincense, cinnamon, and juniper in your favorite container, or as a simmering potpourri. This blend also contains: orange peel, rosehips, star anise, orris root, uva ursi, calendula, allspice, annatto seed, lemon peel, pine cones, hops flowers, and fragrance oils.

SUMMER BREEZE - *New-* Shows off the light, airy qualities of both purple and white bouganvillier. This potpourri is a soft mixture of pinks and purples with an appealing baby powder fragrance.

VANILLA SPICE - This textured, mellow vanilla potpourri with hues of gold, red, brown, white, and green is perfect for the kitchen. Set it on your table, or simmer it on your stove. The ingredients are: mace, roman chamomile, star anise, cinnamon chips, cracked nutmeg, cloves, vanilla beans, ginger root, red sandalwood chips, tonka beans, calamus root, uva ursi, spina cristi, and fragrance oils.

VICTORIAN LACE - A traditional blend of lavender, roses and other aromatic flowers reminiscent of grandma's perfume. Victorian Lace contains: blue malva flowers, peony flowers, red rosebuds, poppy flowers, calcatrippae flowers, oak moss, lavender flowers, pink rosebuds, vetiver, and fragrance oils.

WOODLAND GATHERINGS - This stimulating and spicy potpourri is a unique mix of tilia star flowers, uva ursi, broom flowers, vetiver roots, pine cones, feverfew flowers, tonka beans, and fragrance oils. Makes you feel like you've been tromping through the woods gathering flowers.

* *Denotes blends that can also be used as a simmering potpourri.*

Simmer Sacks

Simmer Sacks are mixtures of fragrant flowers, seeds, leaves, roots, barks, spices, pure essential oils, and unique fragrances. Neat and convenient, they are sold in packages of two cotton bags. (Each sack contains 1/2 cup.) Simmer Sacks are easily simmered in water to release nature-fresh scents that gently float through your home. To simmer, set aside a special pot. Fill it with two to four cups of water and bring to a simmer. Place one Simmer Sack directly into the pot. Simmer for as long as the scent continues, adding water as needed. Simmer Sacks contain an abundance of fragrant material, allowing for hours of aromatic pleasure.

Our simmering potpourris are available in six aromatic varieties:

CINNAMON SUNSET - A tantalizing blend with cinnamon, orange, and bay.

FRUIT PUNCH - A party blend with berries and citrus.

HARVEST APPLE - A warm, homey recipe with apples and spices.

HOLIDAY SPIRIT - A festive blend of needles, berries, and moss.

PATCHOULI ROSE - An old-fashioned blend with rose and patchouli.

WOODLAND SPICE - A spicy mixture with anise, cinnamon, and clove.

Cosmetic/Craft Ingredients

To help you with your herbal craft projects, and in creating your own natural cosmetics, we offer the following items:

BEESWAX - We sell pure beeswax in one pound blocks. Practically insoluble in water, it is used cosmetically as an emulsifier, and is found in many creams, salves, depilatories, lotions, and hairdressings. It may be substituted for paraffin in craft and cooking recipes (candle-making and candy-making, for example), and is generally recognized as safe for human consumption.

BENZOIN GUM POWDER - This balsamic resin is obtained from *Styrax paralleloneurus*, known commercially as Benzoin Sumatra. Before grinding, it is made up of blocks or lumps of various sizes, compacted together with a gray resinous mash. The scent is balsamic and vanilla-like, the taste aromatic and slightly acrid. Cosmetically it is used to retard darkening and as a preservative. It is found in various lotions, creams, and soaps. It is also used as a fixative in sachets, incense, and potpourris. Benzoin gum powder contains celite and triacalcium phosphate.

GUAR GUM POWDER - This powder is ground from the seeds of the guar plant, *Cyamopsis tetragondolobus*, from India, Pakistan, and the southwestern U.S. It is a white to yellowish-white, nearly odorless, tasteless powder. Used as a natural thickener, guar gum powder will disperse and swell in cool liquids (no heating is required). It is used commercially in ice creams, fruit drinks, cheese, jams, toothpastes, lotions, pie fillings, and salad dressings. With five to eight times the thickening power of starch, it is also useful cosmetically in various lotions and creams.

TRAGACANTH GUM POWDER - Native to the Middle East and Turkey, this product is ground from the tap root and branches of several species of the genus *Astragalus*. The powder is creamy white and very fine. It swells in cold water to serve as a thickener; no heating is required. When possible, blend with other dry ingredients before adding liquids. This will prevent lumping. In commercial food products, it is used as a thickener, binder, suspending and emulsifying agent. Cosmetically it is used as an emollient, and is especially useful in vegetable-base cosmetics such as lotions and creams. It also serves as a binder in incense making.

Oils

Essential Oil Uses

Essential oils are intriguing. Most often found in small, colored bottles, they beckon the shopper to open them and sniff. Wonderfully aromatic and enticing! But what exactly are essential oils and what can be done with them?

Essential oils are the concentrated aromatic oils of plant leaves, flowers, seeds, barks, roots, and the rinds of some fruits. Generally obtained by a lengthy distillation process, essential oils vary in strength, but are always very potent, and often smell best when diluted (as in other oils, colognes, shampoos, etc.). While there are hundreds of aromatic plants, not all are used to produce commercial essences. We offer a variety of 52 essential oils, available in 1/2 ounce and 2 ounce bottles, and for some oils, 8 ounce, 32 ounce, and 5 gallon containers.

Essential oils should be stored so that they remain unexposed to air, light, heat, and heavy metals. If allowed to deteriorate, they become less fragrant, more viscous, and darker. Because they have no fatty acids, rancidity is not a problem. Citrus oils are more susceptible to spoilage because of their high terpine content, and should not be stored over six months. Properly stored and tightly sealed, however, other oils may last for years. Some, like patchouli, vetiver, and sandalwood, reputedly improve with age.

Extremely versatile, these aromatic oils may be used to add flavor when cooking, in the production of body care items, and to add fragrance to any room. They are easy to use, and with just a few guidelines, you'll be ready to use them yourself.

Cooking

Essential oils are quite popular in the production of commercially prepared foods. Beer makers use oil of hops instead of hops flowers so that they need not wait for the flavor of the hops to be absorbed by the beer, and need not test each batch of hops flowers for oil content to determine how much needs to be used to obtain a uniform effect from batch to batch. Pickle makers use dill oil for similar reasons. Herbal tea makers are turning to oils to standardize the oil content of their teas. Candies and gums have long contained oils for flavoring. Oils are an easy method of obtaining a desired taste, and they are easy to store. Many home cooks enjoy similar advantages when cooking with essential oils. The characteristic flavor and odor of most cooking spices is found in their essential oil content. While ground spices may oxidize and loose potency over a period of time, properly stored essential oils will retain a uniform quality for longer periods. Some cooks prefer oils to dried flavorings because they are more consistent (spices may vary in their essential oil content) and disperse more evenly into liquid ingredients. Use an eye dropper for easy measurement, and, whenever possible, add to liquid rather than dry ingredients.

Essential oils are extremely potent, containing the equivalent of 50 pounds to several tons of plant material per quart of essential oil. Always use them sparingly, and always check to be sure of the suitability of an oil for cooking. Please note that not all essential oils are safe for consumption.

Here is a list of some of the oils used in cooking. Use them when you would use the dried spice; as a very rough guideline, substitute two drops of essential oil for each teaspoon of spice called for in your favorite recipe.

Essential Oils Used In Cooking:

Allspice	Anise
Basil	Bay
Caraway	Celery Seed
Cinnamon Bark	Clove Bud
Fennel	Garlic
Ginger	Grapefruit
Lemon	Lime
Nutmeg	Onion
Orange Sweet	Peppermint
Rosemary	Sage
Spearmint	Tangerine
Tarragon	Thyme

Bodycare Products

A fun way to use essential oils is in concocting your own body care products. Experiment to discover your favorite scents and combinations, and you'll be eager to develop your own colognes, skin care products, massage oils, hair rinses and treatments, herbal baths...

In addition to essential oils, "fragrance" oils are often used in the blending of body care products. This term is used to describe oils which are generally comprised of blends of natural essential oils and synthetics. Their uses vary from delicate colognes to industrial strength floor cleaners! Jasmine, musk, rose, and violet are some examples of fragrance oils.

Colognes

Experiment to find a combination of essential oils which pleases you. It is often best to stick to one fragrance "family" when starting your cologne (herbal scents, floral scents, spicy scents, for example), and then add a "blender" which may or may not be a contrasting aroma. Mix a few drops of oil together and allow odors to mingle for some time before smelling. Little strips of blotting paper work well for testing. Use one drop of oil on each strip. Eventually you will want to test blends on your own skin (scents smell differently on different people), but wait until you have something you think is right, or you'll wear out your wrist washing between applications. Experiment for only short time periods - your nose will tire quickly, too!

Common combinations are jasmine and orange sweet, rose and musk, patchouli and lavender. Sandalwood and cinnamon or musk blend nicely for a men's cologne. Carefully note the amounts you use, measuring with glass eyedroppers. To make a simple cologne, use one part oil to six parts perfume diluent (available in scent shops and some pharmacies), and one part fixative (powdered orris root works fine). For an after-bath splash, increase the perfume diluent to ten parts. Why pay for expensive perfumes and colognes when you can blend your very own individual scent inexpensively?

Skin Care Products

While essential oils should not be applied alone directly to the skin, they may be easily incorporated into any cream, lotion, or ointment. Add to your home-concocted facial mask or lotion, and to make a simple bath powder, simply add arrowroot or cornstarch to a few drops of your favorite scent.

A facial sauna will really treat your face: boil some water and remove from heat. Add a few drops of essential oil and steam your clean face by leaning over the pot, with a towel draped over your head, tent fashion. Steam for 10 minutes. Rinse with warm, then cool water. Good oils for skin care include: lavender, sage, rosemary, chamomile, ylang ylang, peppermint, and geranium.

Massage Oils

Enhance your massages by incorporating aroma. The essences penetrate the skin, and the psychological, sensual effect of scent helps relieve stress and tension. Simply add a drop or two of essential oil to your massage oil (olive, sweet almond, or other non-scented vegetable oils). Gently warm your oil over a candle - it's worth the wait!

Hair Rinses and Treatments

Essential oils can add a new dimension to your hair care routine. Here are just a few suggestions:

-Add 1/4 ounce of oil to 4 ounces of shampoo and wash hair as usual.

-Coat the bristles of your brush with rosemary oil before starting your 100 strokes.

-Combine 1/3 ounce of oil in 4 ounces of sweet almond or coconut oil. Massage into scalp. Shampoo and rinse well.

-Experiment with rosemary, sage, chamomile, and cedarwood to determine beneficial results on your hair.

Herbal Baths

Perhaps the simplest way to introduce the fragrance of oils to your daily routine is in your bath. Add 15 drops of oil to your bath water to turn an ordinary bath into one to suit your mood each morning or evening - energizing, relaxing, or sensuous. Keep a stock in your bathroom cupboard. To increase the moisturizing effect and make it easier to clean out of the tub, dilute first with bath oil or unscented bubble bath. Try chamomile, sage, rosemary, juniper, lavender, marjoram, and thyme.

The opportunities for introducing fragrance to your home are abundant. Some are very simple, others more involved craft projects.

Potpourri

Many excellent books and articles are available on the popular subject of potpourri. Please refer to one early in your venture into this craft. You may get started by placing appropriate dried petals, flowers, leaves, and herbs in a large stainless steel bowl. Add a fixative, and stir well, turning over and over. Add spices and any special "blenders." Lastly, one drop at a time, add fragrant or essential oils. Because the oils quickly become overpowering, add sparingly and slowly.

Oils are essential (no pun intended) to good potpourri crafting. You may want to develop potpourri based on your favorite oils rather than determining which oil to add to an already blended potpourri, which is the more common approach.

The list of essential and fragrance oils which may be used for potpourri is very long! Here are just a few **essential** and ***fragrance*** oils used in potpourri crafting:

PATCHOULI	***MUSK***
ROSE	**ROSE GERANIUM**
VIOLET	**HEATHER**
VANILLA	**BALSAM**
PINE	***ORIENTAL BLEND***
VETIVER	**SANDALWOOD**
JASMINE	**LILAC**
LILY OF THE VALLEY	**GARDENIA**
MAGNOLIA	**HONEYSUCKLE**
FRAGIPANI	**APPLE**
AMBERGRIS	**THUJA**

Other Crafts

Introduce essential oils to other craft projects for an aromatic touch. Strings of paper beads may be dipped into paste containing some oil; kitchen witches may hold scented cotton balls under their scarves; dried flower arrangements and wreaths may be scented with oils; and scented candles may be made by adding some fragrance oils to the heated wax. If you are a craftsperson, you will invent a myriad of ways to successfully involve scent in your projects.

Even if you are not an especially "craftsy" person, you can easily use essential oils to scent your home or work area. Try some of these ideas:

-Add a few drops of oil to your water-based vacuum cleaner to scent each room as you clean. For non water-based cleaners, place a scented cotton ball inside the vacuum cleaner bag.

-Aromatic diffusers, used to clean and revivify the air, are now on the market, and work especially well with oils. A few drops of oil added to your humidifier also disperses the scent nicely.

-If you don't want to sew sachets, scent cotton balls with lavender, sandalwood, cedar, or patchouli oils and place in drawers and closets to add aroma.

-Rub fragrant oils into wooden closets, shelves, and cupboards.

-A drop of oil on a light bulb will release its aroma when the bulb is lit.

-A drop of your favorite oil in the rinse water of hand-washables will keep the scent with you through the day.

The list goes on and on! Start your own list. If you are intrigued by those little bottles of essential oil in the store where you shop, take a few home and enjoy them!

Essential Oils

The following is a list of the essential oils sold by Frontier. The format for our entries is: Botanical name / Part(s) of the plant from which the oil is distilled / Primary chemical constituent(s) of the essential oil in proportion to the whole essential oil (when available) / Country or area of origin / Uses, other pertinent information / Legal status with reference to the specific FDA regulation.

Caution: *All essential oils are extremely potent. One-half ounce of an essential oil is the equivalent of five pounds of plant material! Use them with care and the recommendations of a reliable cookbook or other reference source. Note in the following entries which oils are not suited for human consumption. Those suited for consumption should be used very sparingly - all can cause an upset stomach and/or other physiological reactions (some are lethally poisonous) if used in excessive quantities. Please store out of the reach of anyone not responsible for their own actions.*

GRAS: Generally Regarded As Safe.

ALLSPICE - *Pimenta officinalis* / leaf / eugenol 65-95% / Central and South America, especially Jamaica / Allspice oil is used as a flavoring in culinary preparations such as baked goods, catsups, soups, sauces, pickles, canned meats and sausage. / *GRAS.*

ALMOND BITTER - *Prunus spp.* / kernels of the pits of apricots, cherries, peaches, and plums / benzaldehyde 80-95% / Sweden / Almond bitter oil is an important flavoring agent in baked goods such as cakes, confectioneries, and candies. It is also used to scent cosmetics and soaps. This oil was originally derived from a bitter almond (*Amygdalus amara*), which is not the common eating almond. The kernels mentioned above provide the same volatile distillate. Synthetically produced benzaldehyde may be sold as artificial oil of bitter almond. Almond extract is bitter almond oil diluted with water and alcohol, containing at least 1% oil of bitter almond. Almond bitter oil is distilled to remove the very toxic hydrocyanic acid (prussic acid), to which many cosmetic users are allergic. / *GRAS.*

ANISE - *Pimpinella anisum* / seed / anethole 80-90% / Near East, Egypt, India, North Africa, and South America / Anise oil is used as a flavoring in beverages, confectioneries, toothpastes, and mouthwashes. Good quality anise oil is indicated by a high anethole content, which can be found by determining the melting point. The fact that our anise oil often congeals during the winter is a sign of its high anethole content. Anise extract is 2% oil of anise. / *FDA approved as a spice and for flavoring foods.*

BASIL - *Ocimum* spp. / herb / methyl chavicol 67.8% / Reunion Islands / Basil oil is used as a flavoring in baked goods, condiments, spiced meats, sausages, dental products, and in the scenting of some perfumes and soaps. / *FDA approved as a spice and for flavoring foods.*

BAY - *Pimenta racemosa* / leaves / eugenol 73-85% / West Indies / Bay oil's pleasing, spicy odor is used in perfumes and toilet waters, and to flavor table sauces. This product is derived from the leaf of the bay or bay rum tree, not the bay laurel leaf which is used in cooking. / *FDA approved as a spice and for flavoring foods.*

BERGAMOT - *Citrus aurantium* / flavedo / l-linalyl-acetate 36-45% / Italy is the principal source, but it may be grown anywhere citrus is grown / One of the all-time classic perfume materials, bergamot oil is also used in creams, powders, and soaps. Bergamot oil is a photosensitizer; brown skin stains or dermatitis may result if skin with bergamot oil on it is exposed to sunlight. / *FDA approved as a spice and for flavoring foods.*

BIRCH SWEET - *Betula lenta* / bark / methyl salicylate 97-99% / northeast U.S., especially eastern Pennsylvania / Birch sweet is used similarly to wintergreen oil. This tree is also known as the cherry birch. Although the essential oil is in the bark, it is so inefficient to peel the trees that the whole tree is cut into chips and distilled. This is the same process that occurs in the production of wintergreen oil. / The FDA has not provided any explicit decision on the suitability of this oil for use in products for human consumption. We do not sell birch sweet oil for human consumption. Methyl salicylate is a strong irritant to the skin and mucous membranes and may be absorbed readily through the skin. / *No FDA designation for safe use in food.*

CAJEPUT - *Melaleuca* spp. / leaves / cineole 50-60% / Malaysia, Indonesia / In Malaya, cajeput is employed as a room spray. Our cajeput oil is redistilled. / *FDA approved for flavoring foods.*

CAMPHOR - *Cinnamomum camphora* / wood / terpene alcohols 43%, cineole 15% / China / Camphor oil is most commonly used in pharmaceutical preparations, soaps, and perfumes. / Camphor oil is approved for human consumption if used according to the conditions of 21CFR 172.510, with the restriction that it be safrole free. Chinese camphor contains .2% safrole. / *FDA approved for flavoring foods.*

CARAWAY - *Carum carvi* / seed / carvone 50%, d-limonene / Europe, Asia / Caraway oil is used in scenting soaps and to overcome unpleasant odors or tastes in oral preparations. / *FDA approved as a spice and for flavoring foods.*

CEDARWOOD- *Juniperus virginiana* / lumber by-product / cedrene 80% / southeast U.S. / Cedarwood oil is used to scent soaps, room sprays, deodorants, insecticides, moth-proof bags, floor polishes, and janitorial supplies. It is produced entirely by distilling the waste shavings, sawdust, etc. of the lumber mills where red cedarwood is being processed. Cedarwood oil can be a photosenstizer (see bergamot oil). / *No FDA designation for safe use in food.*

CELERY - *Apium graveolens* / seed / d-limonene 60% / India / This oil, with its warm, aromatic, pleasing fragrance and taste, is used as a flavoring in canned soups and meats, celery salts, tonics, and sauces. / *FDA approved as a spice and for flavoring foods.*

CINNAMON BARK - *Cinnamomum cassia* / leaves, twigs, bark / cinnamic aldehyde 80-95% / China / This is one of the most valuable flavoring ingredients and is used extensively in baked goods and confections, as well as soft drinks, table sauces, and meats. It is also used sparingly in oriental type perfumes. The oil of the twigs and leaves of the *C. cassia* is the same composition as the bark oil. Cinnamic aldehyde can be irritating to the skin and mucous membranes, especially if undiluted. / *FDA approved as a spice and for flavoring foods.*

CITRONELLA - *Cymbopogon nardus* / grass / geraniol 55-65% / Ceylon / One of the most important essential oils, citronella is used to scent soaps and technical preparations. This oil is distilled from the Ceylon type of citronella. The other popular type, the Java type, is a related species with a similar essential oil. / *FDA approved as a spice and for flavoring foods.*

CLARY SAGE - *Salvia sclarea* / leaves and flowering tops / linalylacetate 40%, linalool 35% / Mediterranean, USSR / Clary sage oil is valuable in perfumery. It blends well with lavender, bergamot, and jasmine. It is also used to flavor wines. / *FDA approved as a spice and for flavoring foods.*

CLOVE BUD - *Eugenia caryphyllata* / unopened flower bud / eugenol 70-95% / Zanzibar, Madagascar / This oil is used extensively as a flavoring in meats, baked goods, candies, table sauces, pickles, and chewing gums. It is also found in perfumes, and oriental, spicy, soaps. The oils of the leaf and stem are sometimes used but are considered inferior to bud oil. Clove extract may be made with 2% clove oil. / *FDA approved as a spice and for flavoring foods.*

EUCALYPTUS - *Eucalyptus globulus* / leaves / cineole 70-80% / Australia, China / This oil is used in clothes cleaners, spot and stain removers, and in perfumery. / *FDA approved for flavoring foods.*

FENNEL - *Foeniculum vulgare* / seed / anethole 50-60% / France, Italy, Greece / Fennel oil is used as a flavoring agent in bread, pastry, liqueurs, and for correcting unpleasant odors in oral preparations. This is the sweet (or Roman) fennel. / *FDA approved as a spice and for flavoring foods.*

FIR SIBERIAN - *Abies sibirica* / needles / bornyl acetate 29-45% / USSR / Fir Siberian oil is the most important of all pine, fir, and spruce needle oils, and is widely used for scenting soaps, bath preparations, room sprays, deodorants, and disinfectants. / *FDA approved for flavoring foods.*

FRANKINCENSE - *Boswellia* spp. / bark / France / Frankincense oil is an excellent perfume fixative and is used in perfumes and soaps. / *FDA approved for flavoring foods.*

GINGER - *Zingiber officinale* / rhizomes / zingiberene / Jamaica, India / Ginger oil is used to flavor food products, particularly baked goods and spicy table sauces. It also has limited use in perfumery. Oil of ginger contains the aroma but not the pungency of ginger. / *FDA approved as a spice and for flavoring foods.*

GRAPEFRUIT - *Citrus paradisi* / flavedo / d-limonene 90% or more / Florida, California, Texas / Grapefruit oil is used primarily as a flavoring, particularly in beverages. Our grapefruit oil is cold pressed. Grapefruit oil is a photosensitizer (see *Bergamot*, page 101). / *FDA approved as a spice and for flavoring foods.*

JUNIPER - *Juniperus communis* / berries / Yugoslavia / This is the popular flavoring used in gin and other alcoholic beverages. It is also used to flavor sausages, and non-alcoholic beverages. / *FDA approved as a spice and for flavoring foods..*

LAVENDER - *Lavandula officinalis* / leaves / l-linalyl acetate 30-60% / France, southern Europe / The clean, fresh, sweet odor of lavender is used in perfumes, toilet waters, and soaps, and blends well with other essential oils. Lavender's cousins, lavandin and spike lavender, are hardier, but do not produce such a fine oil. There are widespread accusations that the genetic standards of true lavender has been debased by breeding with these two oils. / *FDA approved as a spice and for flavoring foods.*

LEMON - *Citrus limon* / flavedo / d-limonene 90% / Florida, California, Brazil / Lemon oil is an important flavoring for beverages, baked goods, candies, ice creams, perfumes, colognes, and cosmetics. It is a photosensitizer (see bergamot oil). Lemon extract may be made with only 5% oil of lemon. Our lemon oil is cold pressed. / *FDA approved as a spice and for flavoring foods.*

LEMONGRASS - *Cymbopogon citratus* / grass / citral 75-82% / Caribbean, India, southeast Asia / Because of its strong lemon scent, this oil is used to scent soaps, detergents, and other domestic products. It is also used in the production of citral, which is used in flavoring, cosmetics, and perfumery. The quality of lemongrass oil is determined by its citral content, which decreases gradually with storage and aging. In order to maintain the citral content, it is important that the oil be stored away from light, and be minimally exposed to air. / *FDA approved as a spice and for flavoring foods.*

LIME - *Citrus aurantifolia* / flavedo / d-limonene 90% / Florida, Caribbean / Lime oil is a chief flavoring ingredient of carbonated, nonalcoholic beverages, baked goods, and candies. Our lime oil is distilled, not pressed. Lime oil is a photosensitizer (See *Bergamot*, page 101). / *FDA approved as a spice and for flavoring foods.*

MARJORAM - *Thymus mastichina* / whole flowering plant above ground / cineole 63-65% / Spain / Used as a seasoning in table sauces, meats, and soups, this oil is distilled from the wild Spanish marjoram, not the same species normally sold as a spice. / *No FDA designation for safe use in food.*

MYRRH - *Commiphora* spp. / tree gum / resins, 25-45%, gums 30-40% / France / Used extensively in oriental-type perfumes, the heavy, balsamic odor of myrrh blends well with sandalwood, vetiver, patchouli, and geranium oils. / *FDA approved for flavoring foods.*

MYRTLE - *Myrtus communis* / Mediterranean / leaves and flowers / Myrtle oil is used to flavor table sauces, and to add a spicy note to toilet waters. / *FDA approved only for flavoring alcoholic beverages.*

NUTMEG - *Myristica fragrans* / seed / d-pinene and d-camphene 80% total / West Indies / Nutmeg oil is used to flavor baked goods, custards, puddings, pickles, table sauces, and catsup. It is also found in perfumes and dentrifices. Nutmeg extract must contain at least 2% oil of nutmeg. / *FDA approved as a spice and for flavoring foods.*

ORANGE SWEET - *Citrus sinensis* / flavedo / d-limonene / California, Florida / This oil is used to flavor confectionery, alcoholic and non-alcoholic beverages, and in perfumes, lotions, colognes, creams, soaps, and other cosmetics. It is also used to cover objectionable odors in pharmaceutical and oral preparations. Orange extract must contain at least 5% of the expressed oil. Our orange oil is cold pressed. Orange oil is a photosensitizer (see bergamot oil). / *FDA approved as a spice and for flavoring foods.*

PATCHOULI - *Pogostemon cablin* / leaf / Indonesia, Malaya / Patchouli is an important perfume oil, and is also used in soaps, incense, and cosmetics. It is best if aged up to a few years. / *FDA approved for flavoring foods.*

PENNYROYAL - *Mentha pulegium* / whole herb / pulegone 85-96% / Spain, Morocco / Pennyroyal is used to scent soaps, and for manufacturing synthetic menthol. This oil is distilled from the European species, not the American species (*Hedeoma pulegoides*). The American pennyroyal has one-third the pulegone of the European. / *FDA approved for flavoring foods.*

PEPPERMINT - *Mentha piperita* / whole plant above ground / menthol 45-65% / U.S. and northern Europe / Peppermint oil is a flavoring used in oral preparations, gums, confectionery and alcoholic liqueurs. It is one of the most widely used oils. Extract of peppermint must contain 3% oil of peppermint. Our peppermint oil is redistilled. Peppermint oil can be irritating to the skin, especially if a dressing is applied over the oil. / *FDA approved as a spice and for flavoring foods.*

PERU BALSAM - *Myroxylon pereiraa* / trunk exudation / cinnamein / El Salvador / This oil is popular for use in perfumes, soaps, and cosmetics. / *FDA approved as a spice and for flavoring foods.*

PETITGRAIN - *Citrus aurantium* / leaves and petioles / France, northern Africa / This product is petitgrain bigarade oil. Its strong, pleasing odor is often used in conjunction with much higher priced oil of neroli bigarade, to reduct the cost of perfume compounds. / *FDA approved as a spice and for flavoring foods.*

ROSE GERANIUM - *Pelargonium graveolens* / flowers, leaves, stalks / geraniol 35-60%, citronellol 20-35% / Egypt, Reunion Island, many other places in the Indian Ocean / This oil is used extensively to scent soaps and cosmetics. It is distilled from geranium plants and is called rose geranium because of its strong similarity to the scent of rose oil. Because it is about a hundreth the price of true oil of roses, it is often used as a substitute for rose oil, a constituent of synthetic rose scents, and an adulterant of true rose oil. / *FDA approved as a spice and for flavoring foods.*

ROSEMARY - *Rosmarinus officinalis* / leaf / cineole 41% / Mediterranean coast / Rosemary oil is used for scenting soaps and room sprays and in the flavoring of table sauces and meats. / *FDA approved as a spice and for flavoring foods.*

SAGE - *Salvia officinalis* / leaf / thujone / Yugoslavia, some other Mediterranean countries / Sage is used to flavor table sauces, canned foods, soups, and meats, especially sausage. / *FDA approved as a spice and for flavoring foods.*

SANDALWOOD - *Santalum album* / root and heartwood / santalol 90% / southern India, Malaya, Indonesia / Sandalwood oil is used in cosmetics and perfumes, and as a perfume fixative. It takes at least thirty years to grow a tree with enough heartwood to make an extraction of sufficient sandalwood oil to make the process worth the cost. India has government regulation of the trade and only allows use of dead or diseased trees. The disease does not affect the oil. / *FDA approved for flavoring foods.*

SASSAFRAS - *Sassafras albidum* / bark of the root / safrole 80% / eastern U.S., mainly the southeast / Sassafras oil is used for scenting soaps. / Sassafras oil contains a carcinogen, safrole. *FDA prohibited for use in food due to naturally occurring toxins.*

FDA prohibited for use in food due to naturally occurring toxins.

SPEARMINT - *Mentha spicata* / whole herb / carvone / midwest and northwest U.S. / Spearmint oil is used to flavor chewing gums and toothpastes. Extract of spearmint need contain only 3% oil of spearmint. / *FDA approved as a spice and for flavoring foods.*

SPRUCE - *Picea* spp. / young branches and adherent leaves / northwest U.S., principally New York and Vermont / Spruce has a pleasant, pine needle odor, and is a major constituent in pine and cedar blends such as sprays, deodorants, soaps, and disinfectants. It is derived from black and white spruce, common (or eastern) hemlock an western hemlock, all used indiscriminately together. / *FDA approved for flavoring foods.*

TANGERINE - *Citrus reticulata* / flavedo / d-limonene 96% / Florida / Tangerine oil is used to flavor juices and to scent perfumes. It is a photosensitizer (see *Bergamot*, page 101). / *FDA approved as a spice and for flavoring foods.*

TARRAGON - *Artemisia dracunculus* / herb / methyl chavicol 65% / France / methyl chavicol 65% / Tarragon oil is used to flavor vinegars, table sauces, salad dressings, canned soups, and liqueurs. It is also used in some perfumes. / *FDA approved as a spice and for flavoring foods.*

THUJA CEDAR LEAF - *Thuja occidentalis* / ends of branches and adherent leaves / thujone / northeast U.S. and eastern Canada, especially New York and Vermont / This oil is a common ingredient in pine and cedar blends which are used to scent room sprays and other technical preparations. The odor is said to be reminiscent of sage. The tree is more commonly known as the Eastern Arborvitae. This oil contains thujone. / *FDA prohibited for use in food due to naturally occurring toxins.*

THYME - *Thymus zygis* / leaf and stem / Spain, Morocco, Mediterranean / Thyme is a powerful germicide, and is used in disinfectants and antiseptics. It is found in mouthwashes and other oral preparations, and soaps. It is also used to flavor meats, sausage, sauces, and canned foods. / *FDA approved as a spice and for flavoring foods.*

VETIVER - *Vetiveria zizanoides* / root / Indonesia / An important constituent in many perfumes, vetiver oil blends well with sandalwood, patchouli, and rose oils. It is also used for scent in cosmetics and soaps. / *FDA approved only for flavoring alcoholic beverages.*

WINTERGREEN - *Gaultheria procumbens* / leaf / methyl salicylate 96-99% / Canada, and northeast U.S., especially eastern Pennsylvania / Wintergreen oil is used as a flavoring agent in candies, chewing gums, soft drinks, toothpastes, and mouthwashes. Methyl salicylate occurs in this product as a result of the fermentation of the crushed leaves. Synthetic methyl salicylate may be sold as artificial oil of wintergreen. Wintergreen extract need only contain 3% oil of wintergreen. / *No FDA designation for safe use in food.*

YLANG-YLANG - *Cananga odorata* / flowers / Indian Ocean Islands, Indonesia, Malaya / The ylang ylang is a flowering tree from which this oil, popular for use in perfumes, is distilled. Its floral scent blends well with jasmine, lilac, gardenia, lily of the valley, bergamot, and rose. It is also found in cosmetics and soaps. / *FDA approved as a spice and for flavoring foods.*

Fragrance & Other Oils

The term fragrance is used to describe oils which are generally comprised of blends of natural essential oils or synthetics. There are several reasons why fragrances are sometimes used in place of pure essential oils.

One reason is the prohibitive cost of some essential oils. This often occurs with perfumery oils, such as jasmine, rose, and violet oils, which cost about $2,000 per pound. Formulas are closely guarded secrets, but fragrances attempt to duplicate the same chemical composition of the pure essential oil with the use of less expensive essential oils and synthetic scents.

Fragrances are sometimes used instead of pure animal essences such as musk and ambergris. The reason in this case is two-fold. The cost of these oils is prohibitive, and the methods of harvest are considered by many to be unethical. For example, genuine musk oil is harvested from the musk glands of the Siberian musk deer. Fifteen deer are required to yield one pound of oil. As with other fragrances, the chemical composition is copied through the use of other essential oils and synthetic aromas.

The final and simplest reason for the use of fragrances instead of pure essential oils is that, for some scents, no natural essential oils exists. This is true for strawberry, chocolate and blueberry, for example.

Like essential oils, fragrances are used to scent perfumes, colognes, soaps, cosmetic ingredients, crafts such as potpourri, as well as domestic supplies. They are not used for cooking purposes.

Caution: *These fragrances have not been determined safe by the FDA for internal consumption. We sell them for aromatic purposes only and not for food use.*

ALMOND
APPLE
APRICOT
BAY RUM
CARNATION
CHOCOLATE
COCONUT
CYCLAMEN
TONKA SCENT
FRENCH VANILLA
GREEN FOREST
HELIOTROPE
HONEYSUCKLE
JASMINE
LILY OF THE VALLEY

AMBERGRIS
APPLE BLOSSOM
BAYBERRY
BLUEBERRY
CHERRY
CLOVER MEADOW
CRANBERRY
ORRIS SCENT
FRANGIPANI
GARDENIA
HEATHER
HERBAL ESSENCE
HYACINTH
LILAC
LOTUS BLOSSOM

MAGNOLIA
MUSK
ORIENTAL EVENING
PINE
ROSE
SPRING FLORAL
VANILLA
MIMOSA
ORANGE BLOSSOM
PEONY
RASPBERRY
SPICY APPLE
STRAWBERRY
VIOLET

Fixed Oils

Fixed oils are non-volatile and are obtained by a means other than distillation (such as cold-pressing). Oils are generally labelled fixed when they do not evaporate on simple exposure to the atmosphere. They do not have the aromatic characteristics of essential oils. These are the fixed oils we sell:

ALMOND SWEET - Often found in combination with essential oils and fragrances, almond sweet is used for its excellent emolliency in cosmetics, creams, lotions, and salves. Our almond sweet is USP grade. *FDA approved for food use.*

APRICOT KERNEL - This oil is prepared by pressing the apricot kernel. National Formulary grade, it can be used as an eating oil, and is popular for use in massage ointments, creams, lotions, salves, pomades, cosmetics, soaps, and cold creams. *FDA approved for food use.*

CASTOR - This pure, undiluted oil is pressed out of the seed produced by the *Ricinus communis* plant. The seed contains an extremely toxic substance, ricin, which is not present in the oil. Our castor oil is cold pressed and USP grade. We sell castor oil for external use only. It is commonly used as a lotion, and in the making of transparent soaps.

JOJOBA OIL - The seeds of the jojoba shrub yield this oil, used as a skin lubricant by natives of the southwestern U.S. Chemically similar to sperm whale oil, jojoba offers industry a humane, high-quality substitute. It will store well for several years without preservatives, and is used as a skin moisturizer and hair conditioner.

Other Oils

ALOE VERA EXTRACT IN VEGETABLE OIL - This oil is comprised of 40% aloe extract, derived from the leaf and stem of the aloe vera plant, and 60% soybean oil. Although it is an edible grade, and contains no preservatives, we do not sell this product for human consumption. Aloe vera oil is used in cosmetic preparations such as lotions, creams, lip balms, hair products, anti-perspirants, and soaps.

VITAMIN E - (d-alpha tocopherol acetate, 544 iu/gram) - Our Vitamin E oil is made up of tocopherols derived from vegetable oils, primarily soybean oil. As a supplement, the recommended daily allowance of Vitamin E oil is 15 iu's. It is commonly used as an anti-oxidant in the preparation of lotions, baby preparations, deodorants, hair grooming aids, massage oils, and other oil blends. Our Vitamin E oil is certified by the Natural Source Vitamin E Association as being 100% natural source Vitamin E.

Potpourri Refresher Oils

These oils are used to "refresh" Frontier potpourris or sachets as they lose their aroma. Add just a few drops at a time, to determine the amount needed, then cover the mixture and allow the scent to meld. You might also try them as pre-mixed scents for your own potpourri blends. We have a refresher oil for each potpourri sold by Frontier. (See *Potpourri Blending*, page 171.)

Essential Oil Recipes

lease note that the strength of oils varies with quality; whenever possible, add one drop at a time and taste.

Culinary Recipes

Toddy

1 cup milk
1 Tablespoon honey
1/4 teaspoon vanilla
1 drop cinnamon oil, 1 drop nutmeg oil.
In a small saucepan, warm above ingredients. Drink warm. Serves 1.

Gingerbread

Combine in a bowl:
2 cups whole wheat flour
1 teaspoon baking soda
2 teaspoons baking powder
1 teaspoon salt

In a separate bowl, mix:
2 beaten eggs
1/2 cup melted butter
1 cup molasses
1/2 cup hot water, 3 drops ginger oil

Combine liquid and dry mixtures and stir. Place in oiled 9"x 9" pan and bake at 325° until done (about 30 minutes).

Carob Chip Mint Cookies

Mix together:
2 cups whole wheat flour
1 teaspoon baking powder
1/2 cup carob powder
1 teaspoon baking soda
1 teaspoon sea salt

In another bowl, mix together:
1 cup milk
1/2 cup softened butter or margarine
1 cup honey
2 eggs
1 teaspoon vanilla, 3 drops peppermint oil

Combine dry and wet ingredients and beat well. Stir in 1 cup unsweetened carob chips. Add more flour if needed for drop-cookie consistency. Drop onto greased cookie sheet. Bake at 350° for about 18 minutes. Makes about 3 dozen.

Potato Soup

Saute' in a large pot:
2 onions, chopped

1 carrot, diced
2 sticks celery, chopped
Add:
6 cooked, diced potatoes
1 quart water or other stock
2 drops marjoram oil
1 drop garlic oil
1 drop celery seed oil
4 Tablespoons butter.

Warm through and sprinkle with parsley and grated cheddar cheese. Serve immediately. Serves 4.

Guacamole

2 ripe avocadoes, mashed	*1 teaspoon tamari*
1 drop onion oil	*1 cup mayonnaise*
1 drop garlic oil	*2 drops lemon oil*
1/4 teaspoon cayenne	*2 drops lime oil.*

Mix ingredients together. Chill and serve with chips or raw vegetables. Makes about 1 1/2 cups.

Body Care Recipes

Hair Lotion

Combine: 1 ounce olive or coconut oil, 8 drops nutmeg oil, 1 ounce rosemary or lavender oil. Massage into scalp. Cover head with plastic, then towel. Leave on one hour. Shampoo well and rinse.

Men's Cologne

1 ounce musk oil, 1 ounce sandalwood oil, 12 ounces perfume diluent (or vodka), 2 ounces orris root powder. Mix and store in a colored glass bottle in a cool place.

Yogurt Apricot Mask

Mash 1 apricot and combine with 1/4 cup yogurt and 1 drop lemon grass oil. Apply to clean face. Rest, preferably with feet up, for 20 minutes. Rinse well and pat dry.

Bath Oil

Mix 1 cup sesame or safflower oil with 1/2 cup wheat germ oil, 1/2 ounce rose oil, 1/4 ounce violet. Shake well.

Massage Oil

Combine 1/4 cup of unscented massage oil (olive, sweet almond or other non-scented vegetable oil) with 2 drops birch, rosemary, juniper, or lavender oil.

Toothpaste

Combine: 4 ounces arrowroot powder, one ounce orris root powder, 10 drops lemon oil, 5 drops peppermint oil.

Craft Recipes

Refer to the *Herbal Crafting* section of this handbook for potpourri and sachet recipes, as well as directions for a pomander and straw wreath.

Miscellaneous

Listed below are two miscellaneous products available through Frontier:

GELATIN CAPSULES - An easy way to ingest powdered herbs, gelatin caps are available in two sizes - "OO" and "O." The "OO" is slightly larger than the "O." Gelatin is obtained by the hydrolysis of collagen, the main organic constituent of bones, tendons, cartilage, and skin. In manufacturing these caps, our supplier uses a blend of 1/2 USP type A gelatin (made from pork skins) and 1/2 USP type B gelatin (made from bones). They contain no artificial colorings or preservatives. We sell them in 1/4 pound packages of approximately 1,000.

AMBER SPICE JARS - These square glass jars are tinted amber to protect your herbs and spices from direct sunlight. Use them to store your herbs and spices. Frontier "consumer pack" pouches are designed to nicely fill a four ounce jar. Available in cases of 12, they come in two convenient sizes - four ounce (4 1/4" x 2 7/8") and eight ounce (5 1/8" x 2 1/8") - and are fitted with white plastic screw-on caps. Labels for these jars are also available.

Printed Matter

The distribution of accurate, informative product information is important to us. In an effort to provide you with such information, we print the following publications:

Publications

FRONTIER FACTS - A bi-monthly newsletter, it is filled with information about the herb & spice industry and Frontier products. In addition, its articles cover store profiles, marketing tips and reviews of the latest technology.

PEPPERMINT SAGE - This publication explores cooking, craft, and natural body care uses for herbs, spices, oils, teas, and other Frontier products. Published bimonthly, it is four pages long, and regularly includes a book review and recipes.

HERB & SPICE HANDBOOK - This annual publication presents an in-depth look at Frontier's products and offers a wealth of tips and ideas showing you how to use our products.

POTPOURRI, THE ART OF FRAGRANCE CRAFTING - An attractive book of 131 pages, this is an in-depth guide with complete base formulas for blending potpourris, perfumes, sachets, and more.

Informational Handouts

These are one to four page flyers which provide information on different aspects of cooking and crafting with herbs, spices, oils, and teas. Examples of the informational handouts currently available are:

HERBAL SKIN AND HAIR CARE
COOKING WITH HERBS AND SPICES
POTPOURRI BLENDING
BLACK AND GREEN TEAS
ESSENTIAL OIL USES
STORAGE OF HERBS & SPICES

New handouts are published regularly.

Posters

Appealing and creative, these posters by artist Margo Davis depict the inherent properties of herbs in a unique way to complement any living space. These posters feature pen and ink renderings of traditional herbs, culinary herbs, and perennial flowers. Hand-printed in a calligraphic style, these works of art are packed with useful information. The following beautiful herb posters are available in full color:

TRADITIONAL HEALING HERBS POSTER - Designed in French country motif, this poster shows 24 herbs with their specific properties and uses. It measures 19.5" x 25.25".

CULINARY HERBS POSTER - Carefully designed to suit both rural and urban kitchens, this posters shows 20 culinary herbs with several appetizing uses for each. It measures 18" x 22".

PERENNIAL FLOWERS POSTER - A blend of modern and traditional botanical design, this poster features 20 perennial flowers with heights and blooming times. It measures 18" x 22".

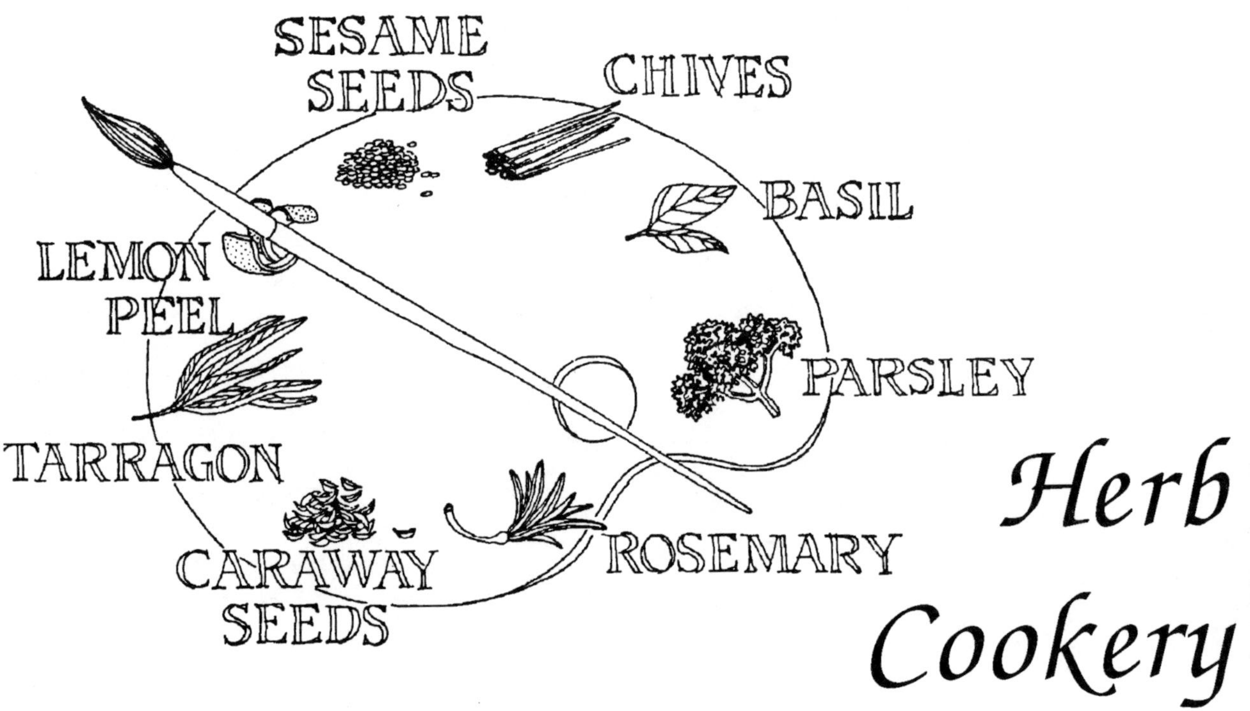

Herb Cookery

Cooking With Herbs

Learning to cook with herbs and spices is fun and rewarding. As a result, you'll be making more interesting, delicious meals, and enjoy cooking as a creative endeavor. While you're at it, why not let herbs and spices help you cook more healthful meals?

Although current cooking trends are supportive of more healthful eating, the transition is not always an easy one. Learning to season your food with herbs and spices can be a tremendous help, paricularly in cutting salt from your diet. Other seasonings may simply be substituted for the salt in your favorite dishes. Even if you've never been much of a cook in the past, you can learn to create meals to suit your individual needs and tastes by practicing the art of seasoning.

It isn't necessary to spend a great deal of time over the stove, either. In fact, raw or simply prepared foods are often most desirable. Simply experiment with different herbs and spices until you become familiar with them, distinguish your favorites, and build on those. Even the simplest dish becomes special and elegant with the addition of some favorite herbs and spices.

Here are some guidelines and cooking tips to help you get started:

—Prepare a culinary palette. Have on hand a good assortment of quality herbs and spices from which to choose, and be sure to store them properly. (See *Storing Herbs & Spices*, page 118.)

—Pre-blended, salt-free seasonings are wonderful to have in place of a salt shaker. Don't stop there. Create a blend using your favorite seasonings, and use individual herbs and spices to season each dish.

—Although salt sometimes functions as a flavor enhancer, delicate flavors are much more noticeable without the use of salt. In addition, when vegetables are cooked in salted water, the water leaches the vitamins and much flavor out of the food. Try herbs and spices, vinegar, or garlic in place of salt, and taste food that is really enhanced!

—Use dried mushrooms in a sauce in place of cream. Rehydrated and pureed into the sauce, they produce a creamy smoothness.

—While many standard low-fat, salt-free recipes tend to be flat and tasteless, the skillful addition of herbs and spices can transform them into delicacies. Herbs and spices are generally low in salt, but read labels carefully. (Some herbal blends do contain salt.)

—Grind unsalted nuts and seeds and add them to recipes (casseroles, grain, fish, or vegetable dishes, sauces, baked goods), or sprinkle them on salads. They add wonderful taste and texture.

—Sauces and soups in particular should be well-seasoned, not heavily salted. Make a stock using broth powders (chicken, beef, or vegetable flavored). Use the stock as a base for soups, glazes, or for cooking liquid.

—Marinate fish in lemon juice and herbs several hours before cooking. As an alternative to marinating, herbs may simply be laid across fish before steaming. Basil, fennel, dill, tarragon and thyme work well with fish.

—It is usually best to add whole spices during cooking to allow their flavor to permeate the food. Add ground spices midway or at the end of cooking. When preparing salad dressings, blend a few hours before needed and refrigerate, allowing the flavors to meld.

—To reduce your sugar intake, substitute one of the following spices for 50% of the sugar in fruit-dessert recipes: cinnamon, cloves, allspice, ginger, anise, fennel.

—For reduction of salt intake, substitute strong, flavorful spices such as black pepper, curry, cumin, basil, oregano, onion, and garlic.

—An easy way to season vegetables is with herb butters. Simply add herbs or spices to melted butter and pour over vegetables, or refrigerate for later use. To reduce fat intake, the butter may be mixed with an equal quantity of oil, cooled, whipped, and then refrigerated. Good herb butter seasonings include parsley, lemon pepper, thyme, marjoram, garlic, basil, oregano, chervil, tarragon, and dill weed.

—When browing meat and herbs, brown the meat before adding the herbs, to prevent overcooking the herbs.

—To release the flavor of dried herbs, crumble them before adding to your dish.

—When using red pepper or spice blends containing red pepper, allow for buildup of pungency. First taste tests often seem mild.

—When using curry powder, especially a ready-made one, the flavor will be improved if the powder is heated on a heatproof plate in a low oven before using.

—Bouquet garni is a fancy name for a bunch of herbs - most often parsley, thyme, and bay leaf. Held together in cheesecloth, or a metal ball, it is used to add flavor to stews, soups, and when braising meat.

—Use your imagination for ways to incorporate herbs into your cooking. Try herb jellies, herb ice cubes, herb sugars, mulled ale spices...

—With a few exceptions, use herbs and spices sparingly - to enhance other flavors rather than dominate them. On the average, for a dish with four to six servings, use about 1/2 teaspoon of any spice, and for herbs use 1/2 teaspoon powdered, 1 1/2 teaspoon dried, chopped, and 1 tablespoon fresh chopped. About half the quantity of dried herbs is required as fresh because dried are more concentrated and have a less delicate flavor. Some herbs and spices are stronger and should be used more sparingly.

Choosing which herbs and spices to use when cooking can be confusing if you are a beginner. Here are some hints to help you flavor your dishes with confidence and a touch of creativity. As you familiarize yourself with tastes and textures, you will become more adept at choosing the the best additions, in just the right proportions!

Always remember that the herbs and spices you add to your food must combine to enhance the flavors already present, as well as complement each other. Some herbs and spices easily form flavor families. These combinations can often be purchased as a blend or they can be made at home.

Below are some common flavor families:

BOUQUET GARNIS — basil, bay, oregano, parsley.
HERBAL — basil, marjoram, rosemary, thyme.
HOT — chili peppers, cilantro, cumin, garlic, onion.
PUNGENT — celery, chili peppers, cumin, curry, ginger, peppercorns.
SPICY — cinnamon, ginger, pepper, star anise.
SWEET — allspice, anise, cinnamon, cloves, nutmeg.

An easy and tasty method for testing herb and spice combinations is to mix several blends into small proportions of cream cheese or other mild cheeses. After allowing them to sit for at least one hour, sample your combinations noting which flavors you like least and which ones are overpowering. Be sure to label the samples so that you will know how to duplicate or modify each seasoning to your taste.

Following is a list of foods and suggested seasonings. We recommend using one flavor family at a time, otherwise the flavors will become muddled. We also encourage you to try some of the combinations that are new to you. A dash of cinnamon to your spaghetti sauce or a sprinkle of horseradish in a salad will liven up "old stand-bys" and have your friends asking about your secret ingredients!

BEANS (dried) - cumin, cayenne, chili, onion, parsley, pepper, sage, savory, thyme.

BREADS - anise, basil, caraway, cardamom, cinnamon, coriander, cumin, dill, garlic, lemon peel, onion, orange peel, oregano, poppy seeds, rosemary, saffron, sage, sesame seeds, thyme.

CHEESE - basil, caraway, celery seed, chervil, chili peppers, chives, coriander, cumin, dill, garlic, horseradish, lemon peel, marjoram, mint, mustard, nutmeg, paprika, parsley, pepper, sage, tarragon, thyme.

EGGS - basil, chervil, chili peppers, chives, curry, dill, fennel, ginger, lemon peel, marjoram, oregano, paprika, parsley, pepper, sage, tarragon, thyme.

FRUITS - allspice, anise, cardamom, cinnamon, cloves, coriander, ginger, mint.

MEATS:

Beef - basil, bay, chili pepper, cilantro, cumin, garlic, marjoram, mustard, oregano, parsley, pepper, rosemary, sage, savory, tarragon, thyme.

Chicken - allspice, basil, bay, cinnamon, curry, dill, garlic, ginger, lemongrass, paprika, saffron, sage, savory, tarragon.

Lamb - basil, bay, cinnamon, coriander, cumin, curry, dill, garlic, mint, parsley, rosemary, tarragon, thyme.

Fish - basil, bay, chives, curry, dill, fennel, garlic, ginger, mustard, oregano, parsley, savory, tarragon.

POTATOES - basil, caraway, chervil, chives, dill, marjoram, oregano, paprika, parsley, rosemary, tarragon, thyme.

SALADS - basil, caraway, chives, dill, garlic, lemon peel, lovage, marjoram, mints, oregano, parsley, rosemary, tarragon, thyme.

SALAD DRESSINGS - basil, celery seed, chives, dill, fennel, garlic, horseradish, marjoram, mustard, oregano, paprika, parsley, pepper, rosemary, saffron, tarragon, thyme.

SOUPS - basil, bay, chervil, chili peppers, chives, cumin, dill, fennel, garlic, marjoram, parsley, pepper, rosemary, sage, savory, thyme.

SWEETS - allspice, angelica, anise, cardamom, cinnamon, cloves, fennel, ginger, lemon peel, mace, nutmeg, mint, orange peel, rosemary.

TOMATOES - basil, bay, cinnamon, chili peppers, fennel, ginger, gumbo filé, lemongrass, marjoram, oregano, parsley, tarragon, thyme.

*(The above list was adapted from **Cooking With The Healthful Herbs** by Jean Rogers.)*

We hope you're now eager to try your hand at cooking with herbs and spices. Don't expect instant perfection, but be ready for some very satisfying results. Enjoy yourself. As with many art forms, appreciate the process and you are more likely to appreciate the results. Take this opportunity to let herbs and spices help you cook more thoughtfully and eat more healthfully.

Storing Herbs & Spices

The question is frequently raised as to the best way to store herbs, spices, and teas. The answer is quite simple. Store them in glass containers with air-tight lids in a cool, dry, dark place.

Spices are dried agricultural products. Although seemingly more exotic, they are prone to all the same problems of the crops grown around us. They can be too dry, too wet, and even insect infested. By controlling environmental variables we can prevent some of these problems. Have you ever reached for parsley flakes to garnish a soup only to find them faded and flat-tasting? When this happens the best solution is to replace your old stock of parsley with new and store them according to the following guidelines.

The first step is to *buy quality spices*. Check to see how they are packaged or stored. Closed containers protected from direct sunlight or extreme heat are the best. Examine the spice. Does it look fresh or faded? When permitted, open the container and smell. Spices can lose their aroma as well as absorb odors of other products. Check for dirt, webs, eggs, and any damage which may indicate insect infestation.

Once you have the spices home, store them in clean, airtight containers. This prevents oxidation which deteriorates the flavor, color, and aroma. Air sealed in the container can also cause deterioration. Therefore, use containers comparable in size to the quantity of the spice to be stored. For long-term storage, including freezing, use glass jars with airtight lids.

Light causes fading. When possible, store spices in opaque containers such as amber glass or in a cupboard or drawer. If your only choice is to set your jars in the light, cover the jars with large opaque labels to reduce the light's penetration or hang a curtain or any covering over your spice rack when you are not using it.

Storage temperature is best if kept below 70° F. Whenever possible, store your spices away from the furnace, stove, or direct sunlight. Temperature fluctuations can cause condensation. Excessive moisture will, initially, cause the flavor to taste "off." Eventually, it will mold. When using spices that have been stored in the freezer, promptly return the containers to the freezer to reduce condensation and any damage.

Time's effect on spices is known as "shelf life." The shelf life is different for each herb, spice, and tea you store. This is because much of the flavor comes from the plants' volatile oils. As the name implies, volatile oils evaporate or oxidize. The form of the spice is also a factor in storage. Spices that have been cut or powdered will lose their flavor more rapidly than those in whole form. The chart below provides some general timelines for storing spices under optimum conditions. Don't hesitate to replace spices that are faded. The pleasure found in using fresh spices, herbs, and teas will far outweigh this cost.

WHOLE SPICES AND HERBS	
Leaves and flowers	1 year

Seeds and barks	2+ years
Roots	3+ years
GROUND SPICES AND HERBS	
Leaves	6 months
Seeds and barks	6 months
Roots	1 year
TEAS	
Black and green	1 year
COFFEE	
Whole beans and roasted	3 months
Ground (not vacuum packed)	2 weeks

Finally, handle your spices with care. Always use clean, dry utensils and containers. Breakage of fragile herbs, spices, and teas can be prevented by carefully placing or pouring them into your utensils, rather than using a scoop.

Cajun Cooking

Interest in the cuisines of other cultures - Mexican, Oriental, French, Italian - has been strong in the recent past. Lately however, interest in American regional cooking has also blossomed. Perhaps the most distinctive and popular ethnic cuisine of interest today is "Cajun cooking."

What is "Cajun?" In the 1700's, French Canadians, under political pressure, migrated to the Louisiana bayous. While they were "common" rather than wealthy people, they found their new environment an abundant food source. Excellent seafood, fresh produce, and meats were available. Appreciative of the bounty, the new arrivals liberally seasoned and slowly simmered the foods, and "Cajun cooking" in this country was born.

Sometimes called "Louisiana cooking," along with Creole cooking, Cajun is actually quite different, and less complex than Creole. Creole cooking, developed by rich New Orlean planters, is much more refined, while Cajun has been described as "country fare." In fact, Cajun is not only a cuisine, but a culture as well. Cajuns are family-oriented people, fond of rituals and dancing (particularly after meals!).

Spicy and robust, Cajun food is often cooked in one pot, and sometimes utilizes such unusual ingredients as alligator and frog's legs (both of which taste much like chicken). A variety of hot peppers is used, and there is an art to preparing a dish with just the right hotness. Paul Prudhomme, Cajun cook, says, "Stay just this side of the threshold between pleasure and pain. If you cross that threshold, people won't enjoy the food. If you stay this side of it, each bite leaves an aftertaste, and you want one more bite."

When cooking your own Cajun food, you might tone down the traditional recipes and serve hot, cayenne-based sauces on the side. The most popular dish in Cajun restaurants today is blackened fish, prepared by dipping fish in a spicy mixture of garlic powder, cayenne, and white pepper, and then charring it in a hot, greased skillet.

A major Cajun cooking ingredient is fish, especially crawfish; 90% of the world's crawfish comes from the bayous. Other fish commonly used include swamp shrimp, catfish, crab, redfish, and oysters. "Cajun popcorn" is made with pieces of shrimp, crawfish, or crabmeat that are rolled in cornmeal and deep fried.

Other popular ingredients are "boudin" or blood sausage which is stuffed with rice, and gumbo, a stew concocted with a wide variety of ingredients. In a town called Mamon a huge gumbo is made during the Louisiana Mardi Gras. The men of the town, costumed and on horseback, ride through the countryside and, throughout the day, stop at houses to collect contributions for the gumbo. Cajuns thicken their gumbo with filé powder, while Creoles imported okra for the same purpose.

One of the very many seasonings used, file powder, is made of ground sassafras leaves which were originally obtained from the Choctaw Indians. (Sassafras trees grow wild along the Gulf Coast.) The filé is added at the end of cooking, because boiling makes it stringy.

To give you a better image of the taste of Cajun food, here is a list of other commonly used seasonings:

bay leaves	red hot chilies
cayenne	allspice
paprika	dill seed
cloves	Tabasco sauce
garlic	peppercorns
onion	thyme
lemon	oregano
mustard seed	

In addition, cinnamon and nutmeg are used in desserts such as bread pudding and sweet potato pie.

Recipes

Because of the number of ingredients used, authentic Cajun food does take time to prepare, but the time is well spent! Here are some recipes for you to try. If you enjoy them, you might buy one of the excellent books now available on the subject, or use similar ingredients and cooking techniques to develop your own "Cajun" recipes.

Cajun Rice
1 cup brown rice, raw
3 cups water
3 tablespoons oil
1 teaspoon garlic flakes, rehydrated
1/4 cup onion flakes, rehydrated
1 green pepper, chopped
1 cup mushrooms, sliced
1 dried red jalapeno pepper, rehydrated and finely chopped
2 tomatoes, chopped
1/4 teaspoon allspice
1/2 cup grated cheese

In a heavy skillet, saute' the rice and garlic flakes in 1 tablespoon of the oil. Pour boiling water into the skillet and cover. Simmer 30 minutes.

Meanwhile, in another skillet, saute' the onion flakes, peppers, and mushrooms in the remaining oil.

Add the vegetables to the rice. Add the tomatoes and allspice and stir.

Top with grated cheese and cover until melted.

Serves 3-4.

Cajun Cakes
1 1/2 cups cooked black-eyed peas
3 tablespoons minced fresh parsley (1 1/2 tablespoons dried parsley)
2 tablespoons finely minced bell pepper
2 tablespoons finely minced onion
generous dash freshly ground pepper
1/4 teaspoon thyme

2 tablespoons olive oil
2 tablespoons yogurt
2 tablespoons tomato sauce

Pureé black-eyed peas in a food processor, or use a potato masher. Add parsley, pepper, onion, ground pepper and thyme. Mix by hand until well combined.

Heat a large non-stick skillet, and brush with a small amount of olive oil. Then form the pea mixture into 10 balls, each the size of a well-rounded tablespoon. Flatten the balls between your hands and set four or five in the skillet. When brown, flip them gently and brown the other side. Repeat with remaining cakes.

Combine yogurt and tomato sauce and serve with the warm cakes.

Makes 10 small cakes.

—from ***Rodale's Organic Gardening Magazine****, January 1987*

Parsley-Garlic Fresh New Potatoes

16 small fresh new potatoes
1 tablespoon olive oil
4 cloves garlic, minced (3/4 teaspoon garlic flakes)
1/2 teaspoon salt
1/2 teaspoon freshly ground black pepper
1/4 teaspoon white pepper
1/2 teaspoon basil
1 bay leaf, crushed
1 tablespoon unsalted butter
1/2 cup minced fresh parsley
1/2 teaspoon Tabasco sauce

Wash the potatoes well under cold water. If any spots need to be cut off, cut them as thinly as possible. In a very heavy skillet that has a cover, heat the olive oil over high heat until very hot, but do not let it smoke. Add the potatoes and cook over high heat for 3 minutes, constantly stirring to be sure the potatoes don't stick. This will lightly brown the potatoes and help to hold in all their natural juices.

Reduce the heat to medium-low. Add the garlic, salt, black pepper, white pepper, basil, and bay leaf. Saute', stirring constantly, for 6 minutes. The potatoes will be browned well on all sides. Add the butter, parsley, and Tabasco sauce. Reduce the heat to low, cover the skillet, and simmer for 10 minutes, shaking the skillet every few minutes. Serve at once. Serves 4.

—from ***La Cuisine Cajun*** *by Jude W. Theriot, copyright 1986 by Jude Theriot, reprinted with permission of the publisher, Pelican Publishing Company, Inc.*

Cajun Boiled Shrimp

1 gallon of cold tap water
1/3 cup salt
2 large unpeeled onions, washed and cut into fourths
2 cayenne peppers or 1 jalapeno pepper
3 stalks of celery, cut into 2 inch pieces
2 lemons, sliced into circles
1/4 bunch of parsley with stems (1 tablespoon dried parsley)
10 black peppercorns
1 small bell pepper, cut into fourths

3 bay leaves
1/2 teaspoon basil
3 whole cloves
2 unpeeled cloves of garlic, crushed (1 teaspoon garlic powder)
3 whole allspice
2 tablespoons sugar
2 tablespoons Worcestershire sauce
4 1/2 pounds unpeeled large shrimp, heads removed
1/2 teaspoon Tabasco sauce

In a large gumbo or stockpot, place the cold water, salt, and onions. Bring the pot to a hard boil over high heat. Cut one of the cayenne peppers into fifths and place it in the pot with the remaining whole cayenne pepper. (If you are using a jalapeno, just cut it in half.) Add the celery, lemons, parsley, peppercorns, bell pepper, bay leaves, and basil. Once the water is at a hard boil again, reduce the heat and let the pot stay at a slow boil for 15 minutes.

Add the cloves, garlic, allspice, sugar, and Worcestershire sauce. Return the heat to high and add the shrimp. When the water begins to boil again, add the Tabasco sauce and boil for exactly 3 minutes, then remove the pot from the heat and scoop the shrimp out of the water. Serve hot right from the pot or chill and serve later.

Serves 6.

—from ***La Cuisine Cajun*** *by Jude W. Theriot, copyright 1986 by Jude Theriot, reprinted with permission of the publisher, Pelican Publishing Company, Inc.*

Chicken Gumbo

1 cup finely chopped onions (1/4 cup onion flakes)
1 green bell pepper, chopped
1 clove garlic, minced (3/4 teaspoon garlic flakes)
2 stalks of celery, chopped
2 cups chopped cooked chicken
1 bay leaf
2 quarts stock
1/4 teaspoon basil
1/4 teaspoon garlic powder
1/8 teaspoon white pepper
1/8 teaspoon cayenne pepper
1/4 teaspoon black pepper ground
1/4 teaspoon Tabasco
1 teaspoon filé powder
1/8 cup parsley
1/4 cup chives
2 cups corn

Saute' the onions in a large heavy pot. Add the peppers, garlic and celery and sauté until tender. Add stock, chicken, corn and seasonings (except filé powder). Heat to a boil, then reduce the heat to low. Add the chives and parsley, and stir in the filé powder. Serve immediately.

Serves 8.

Indian Cooking

Indian cuisine is beautiful, delicious, and healthful. A wide range of fruits, nuts, vegetables, legumes and spices contribute to the variety of traditional dishes, each suited to the environment of its people. In the North, where wheat is grown, very rich dishes are created. In the South, rice is a staple and coconuts are used in abundance. Dishes there are spicy hot. Rice also predominates in East Indian food, while West Indian cooks prefer sweeter foods and other grains.

Are you surprised at the use of hot spices in a land with such warm climate? The reason is that eating such spicy foods heats the body and makes the surrounding air seem cooler. Nevertheless, cooling yogurt dishes are often welcomed at the end of these spicy meals!

Indian meals are not difficult to prepare. A basic knowledge of ingredients and a few good recipes will have you well on your way. To familiarize you, we've included here some background information on the types of Indian foods typically served. Refer to one of the many excellent cookbooks available on Indian cooking as you become more experienced and interested.

Basic Foods

VEGETABLES - Vegetables are cooked in a variety of ways, depending upon locale. In the North, for example, vegetables are served with a thick gravy, while in the South they are spicy hot and served with coconut and curry leaves. Eastern Indians use mustard oil and asafetida on their vegetables, resulting in a pungent taste, while in the West cooks prefer spices which yield a sweeter taste.

***DALS* AND CURRIES** - Simply defined, *dals* are cooked legumes. When spices are added to the *dal*, a curry is the result. *Dals* look like thick soups and may be served over rice or thinned and served in soup bowls.

To prepare a *dal*, some recipes suggest boiling, others soaking overnight. Lentils, chickpeas, black-eyed peas, mung beans, and pigeon peas are commonly used legumes. A pressure cooker speeds the process. Dry *dals* are prepared by cooking in a small amount of water, covered, until mushy. Then seasonings are added. A wet *dal* is cooked in more water, just until tender. It may be served with gravy. (The gravy is prepared by using the water from the dal plus spices.)

EGGS - Although previously forbidden to vegetarian Hindus, egg dishes are becoming more popular in India today. Many of the recipes are adaptations of Western recipes, with the addition of Indian spices.

RICE - White rice is a staple in much of India and is prepared in a variety of ways— boiled in water or coconut milk, steamed, or curried. It may be placed in a mound, garnished with parsley or mint leaves, served in small bowls, or out of fancy molds with a curried dish in the center.

BREADS - In the North where wheat is grown, bread is eaten three times a day, prepared fresh each time. Fried breads, spicy breads, and stuffed breads are common.

RAITAS - *Raitas*, or yogurt salads, are a perfect accompaniment to Indian meals because of their cooling effect. Unflavored natural yogurt is used, and roasted cumin powder is kept on hand to sprinkle on these salads.

CHATNI - These fresh chutneys are not pickles, but spicy hot relishes served in small quantities along with deep-fried food. Coconut and mangoes are commonly used as bases for chutneys.

ACHAARS - Hot, sweet, sour, or salty, pickles are served as a substitute for, or alongside curries. They are an excellent way for the Indian cook to preserve foods safely, without refrigeration. Oil, vinegar, lemon juice, hot red peppers, and salt are used as preservatives.

MITHAI - Sweets are generally limited to festive occasions, and are often exchanged at celebrations and rituals. Milk balls, puddings, breads in syrup, yogurt dishes, and sweet drinks are commonly served desserts.

Spices

ALLSPICE - Allspice imparts a bitter, hot taste, and is sometimes substituted for *garam masala*. The taste of allspice is similar to a blend of cloves, cinnamon, and pepper.

ANISE SEED - With its sweet, pungent taste, anise seed is used in curries. The seeds are also roasted and served as a condiment.

ASAFETIDA - This spice is used in small amounts, for a richly-flavored curry.

CARDAMOM - Many Indians chew cardamom seeds plain. The seeds of this plant are also used in *garam masala* and the whole pods by North Indian cooks.

CHILIES, GREEN - These are used to add heat and zest to curries and in pickles, chutneys, and *raitas*. The smaller the chilies, the hotter.

CHILIES, RED - Used as a preservative in pickles, these chilies determine the range of hotness of a curry, and add a red color.

CINNAMON STICK - This dried young bark has a sweet, aromatic effect. It is used in broken pieces to flavor rice and lentils, and in *garam masala*.

CORIANDER - Reminiscent of orange peel and honey, coriander is a basic spice in curry powders, pickles, chutneys, and vegetables.

CUMIN - The seeds of this plant are sometimes roasted and ground, to be used as a condiment, or fried in oil to release flavor before adding to other ingredients. It is also used whole or powdered to flavor curries.

CURRY POWDER - Curry powder is simply a blend of Indian spices, and is prepared by each cook to suit a particular dish, climate, or guest. The ingredients most often used (fresh or dried) include: onions, ginger, garlic, turmeric, coriander, red chili, cumin, cloves, cayenne, and cinnamon. You may want to try a pre-blended curry powder in your beginning efforts at Indian cooking, and experiment later to develop your own array of curry powders.

FENUGREEK SEED - The whole seeds are used in small quantities to flavor vegetables, soups, legumes, and pickles. Ground, the seeds thicken curries.

GARAM MASALA - This spicy mixture, used to flavor curries, may be ground or whole. The ground variety often consists of: black peppercorns, cloves, cardamom seeds, cinnamon stick, cumin seeds, and bay leaves, all ground together. A pre-blended *garam masala* is available. The whole variety may be blended by mixing equal parts of the same ingredients whole.

GARLIC - A basic ingredient in curries, Indians grind fresh garlic daily. Powdered garlic is an acceptable substitute.

GINGER - Fresh ginger, with its pungent flavor, is used peeled, or ground into a paste, or chopped in legumes and vegetables. Dried ginger may be substituted.

MACE - This warm flavoring is used sparingly in Indian cooking.

NUTMEG - Similar to mace (found on the same plant), the flavor of nutmeg is slightly more bitter and is also used sparingly in Indian cooking.

MUSTARD SEED - In South India, black, brown, and yellow mustard seeds are used in curries, pickles, and chutneys.

PEPPERCORNS - Most often used freshly ground, but sometimes as a whole, uncrushed condiment, peppercorns are grown as a cash crop in India. Indians often use chilies instead.

POPPY SEEDS - The nutty flavor of these seeds is released by roasting and grinding. For special occasions, they are used to thicken curries.

SESAME SEEDS - Used as a substitute for poppy seeds, to thicken and flavor curries. Usually roasted and ground, they are also used in pickles and chutneys.

SPICED SALT - Spiced salt, which actually contains no salt at all, is comprised of: roasted ground cumin seeds, black pepper, coriander, and red chili.

TURMERIC - A basic ingredient in all curries, yielding the characteristic yellow color. In sweet dishes, saffron is sometimes substituted for turmeric.

Recipes

All this sounds colorful and tasty doesn't it? Mix some of these ingredients together by trying a few of the following recipes, and you'll be eager to learn more!

East Indian-Style Black-eyed Peas

1 cup dried black-eyed peas
1 chopped onion
2 tablespoons coconut
1/4 teaspoon turmeric
1 teaspoon honey
1/4 teaspoon cumin
3 cups water
sea salt to taste

Add ingredients except salt to boiling water and simmer until liquid is absorbed and beans are tender. Salt to taste.

Makes 4 servings

—from ***Stocking Up*** *by Carol Hupping Stoner*

Indian Pudding

Preheat oven to 325° F.

1/4 cup soy grits
1/2 cup water
1 1/2 cups skim milk powder
3 3/4 cups water
1 cup corn meal
1/4 cup oil
1/4 cup honey
2/3 cup molasses
3/4 teaspoon sea salt
1/2 teaspoon cinnamon
1/4 teaspoon cloves
1/4 teaspoon ginger
1/8 teaspoon allspice
2 eggs
yogurt, served separately

Soak soy grits in 1/2 cup water.

Combine skim milk powder with 3 3/4 cups water using wire whisk.

Scald milk, add corn meal and soaked soy grits gradually.

Lower heat and beat with wire whisk to make a smooth mixture. When mixture begins to thicken, remove from heat.

Add remaining ingredients, except eggs, and allow mixture to cool.

Beat eggs and add to cooled mixture; blend thoroughly.

Pour into oiled dish, and bake 45 to 60 minutes in a preheated oven, or until pudding is firm.

Pudding can be served hot or cold. Yogurt can be used as a topping for the pudding.

Makes 4-6 servings.

—from ***The Rodale Cookbook*** *by Nancy Albright*

Indian Rice and Peanuts

2 tablespoons oil
1 onion, finely chopped
2 cups brown rice
1/4 teaspoon cloves

1/2 teaspoon cinnamon
1/4 teaspoon cardamom
5 cups soup stock
1 cup peanuts
2 cups green peas
2 tablespoons oil or butter

Saute' 2 tablespoons oil and onion in a large pot for 5 minutes. Add the brown rice and stir until browned, 3 to 5 minutes. Add the spices and stock. Simmer until rice is tender and and liquid absorbed, 30 to 40 minutes.

In a separate pan, saute' the peanuts and green peas in 2 tablespoons oil for 3 to 5 minutes. Mix the peanut mixture into the rice mixture. Serve. Makes 6 servings.

*—from **Preparing Nature's Bounty** by M.A.F.A. in Ames, Iowa*

*The following recipes were taken from **The Spice Box, Vegetarian Indian Cookbook** by Manju Shivraj Singh.*

Egg Fritters

1 dozen eggs, hard-cooked, peeled and halved
(Fritter Batter, Traditional):
1 cup chickpea flour
1/4 teaspoon turmeric powder
1/4 teaspoon sea salt
dash cayenne pepper
1 teaspoon cumin seeds
1/4 teaspoon baking soda
1/2 cup water (approximately)
2 cups oil for frying

Mix batter with your hand or a wooden spoon. Add liquid slowly to get the consistency of a pancake batter. Dip the egg halves in batter, and deep-fry, one at a time.

Makes 24.

Variations: Instead of eggs, use 1/4 lb. cheese cut in 1-inch cubes, or pieces of raw vegetables. Or you may incorporate 1/4 cup roasted peanuts and 3/4 cup cooked, drained, chopped spinach into the batter.

An "Americanized Fritter Batter" is prepared by mixing:
1 1/2 cups all-purpose flour
1/4 teaspoon sea salt
dash of cayenne pepper
1/2 teaspoon baking powder
1/2 cup milk
1 egg

Mulligatawny Dal

1 tablespoon oil
1 teaspoon cumin seeds
2 medium onions, sliced (or 1/2 cup onion flakes)
1/2 teaspoon turmeric powder
1 cup yellow split peas or 1 cup red lentils, washed
6 cups water
sea salt to taste
1/4 teaspoon cayenne pepper

1/2 teaspoon ground black pepper
1 tablespoon lemon juice
12 tablespoons boiled white rice
a few chopped mint leaves, for garnish

Heat the oil. Add cumin seeds and onions and fry until the cumin changes color. Add the turmeric powder and yellow split peas. Fry 1 minute. Add the water, salt, cayenne, and black pepper. Bring to a boil and simmer for 30 minutes or until the yellow split peas are tender. Strain them. Add lemon juice to the strained fluid. Use the strained lentils for another dish or discard them.

To serve, put 2 tablespoons of rice in each bowl and pour the soup over the rice. Garnish with chopped mint leaves.

Serves 6.

Fried Eggplant

2 medium eggplants
sea salt and black pepper
(Batter):
1/2 cup chickpea flour
1/2 cup yogurt
sea salt to taste
1 teaspoon cayenne pepper
1 teaspoon garlic powder or paste
1 teaspoon cumin seeds
2 cups oil for frying

Slice the eggplant 1/4 inch thick, sprinkle with salt and pepper and set aside. Make a batter with the chickpea flour, yogurt, salt, cayenne, garlic and cumin seeds. Dip the eggplant slices in the batter and deep-fry. Serve with mint chutney and chappatis.

Serves 4-6.

Italian Cooking

Good Italian food is a treat, one that many people reserve for dining out. Although Italian cuisine has a long, rich tradition and can be elaborate and rather involved to prepare, any cook can learn the basics and enjoy excellent, simple Italian meals at home. Formal Italian dinners are fun to learn about, and to prepare occasionally. But another way to approach this study is to learn about each of the courses so that you can prepare a wide variety of delicious, one-course meals based on your knowledge of the many aspects of Italian cooking.

Here's an introduction to some of the basic ingredients:

Herbs and Spices

Italian cooking is especially fun for those who enjoy cooking with herbs and spices, as these are the primary ingredients in Italian dishes. Italians use the aromatic herbs that grow there in abundance - basil, rosemary, garlic, and fennel. Parsley and sage are also used, particularly in Tuscan cooking (northwestern coast of Italy), while oregano is more popular in the cooking of southern Italy. Tarragon, marjoram, thyme, chives, dill, and bay leaf are also widely used, as are fennel seed and anise seed in specialty dishes. To add hotness to dishes, cayenne, crushed red pepper, curry powder, Tabasco, ginger, and various chili peppers are used, and dry mustard is sometimes substituted for prepared Dijon mustard. Garlic and onions are primary cooking ingredients. Garlic is used extensively to accent sauces and dressings, vegetables, and soups. The favorite onion is the shallot, which is enjoyed for its intense but delicate flavor. White and yellow onions are also used. In older Italian recipes, cinnamon, ginger, cardamom, coriander, and cumin may be found, and at one time saffron was used as much as salt and pepper are today.

Other Ingredients

Lemon juice brings out the tastes of other ingredients, and is used by Italian cooks for chicken, lamb, veal, fish, vegetables, salads, appetizers, and desserts.

Ground almonds are used as a thickening agent, and to make almond milk. Bitter almonds, as found in the Italian *amaretti* cookie, are also used.

A wide variety of cheeses grace the Italian table: Parmesan, Pecorino (sheep's cheese), Groviera (Swiss cheese), Gorgonzola, Mozzarella, and Ricotta are the most popular.

Oils are selected for specific uses. Olive oil is used for dressings, while butter is used for cooking some sauces, and a special mixed-seed oil known as *olio di semi* is used for other cooking.

Cold meats such as prosciutto (unsmoked, uncooked ham that has been cured in salt), salami (especially fennel-flavored *finocchiona*), and pancetta (salted pork) are popular. They are available in Italian cooking shops and some Italian delicatessens.

Wines are used for cooking, for dressings (wine vinegar), and for accompanying the meal. One could spend a great deal of time learning about the varieties of Italian wines. It is a fascinating subject, one you may want to explore as an "Italian cook" or lover of Italian food.

Some of the other ingredients you'll need to stock before you become proficient in Italian cooking include: mushrooms, truffles, anchovies, beans, rice, tomatoes, eggs, olives, fruits, and fresh vegetables.

Background Information

Various regional styles of Italian cooking developed because cooks in Italy use the produce at hand, particular to the location, and always in season. The delicious taste of true Italian cooking comes from the natural taste of the ingredients, which are enhanced, rather than camouflaged, by the cooking techniques. Italians appreciate the tradition and ritual of food - its preparation, presentation, and taste. A formal Italian dinner is based on an appetizer plus four or five courses: pasta; fish, poultry, or meat with a vegetable; salad; fruit and cheese; dessert. An informal, one-course meal is perhaps more appropriate for today's American cook, and any of the following dishes could serve as the focus of an excellent Italian meal.

The Dishes

ANTIPASTO - Served "before the pasta" this appetizer tray includes fruit, prosciutto, cheese, salami, raw vegetables with light dips, and seafoods with light dressings or lemon sauce. Such a tray would make an excellent centerpiece for a light lunch.

SOUPS - Soups may be served by Italians as a light first course or a hearty main course. Minestrone is a thick vegetable soup, and *zuppa di pesche* , a thick fish soup. Clear soups are made with beef or chicken stock, sometimes with pasta added. Some soups are made with pureéd vegetables, and many are topped with grated Parmesan cheese before serving. Any Italian soup would make an excellent lunch or light dinner, served with salad and homemade bread.

PASTA - One of the most popular dishes in the world, pasta is served in Italy as a separate course, in small amounts, with delicate sauces. A wide variety of pastas is available, in a variety of colors (white, yellow, light brown, green), and shapes (tiny circles, squares, shells, stars, flat ribbons...). Although the Italians typically serve it as part of a many-course meal, you can serve pasta as a main course with salad, cheese, fruit, and a good Italian wine. You might also want to try one of the many pasta salads to accompany another meal.

RICE - In northern Italy, rice is chosen over pasta, and it is the strong second choice elsewhere in Italy. Italians prefer their rice not sticky, with a recognizable texture and good flavor. Creamy, sweet, hot, and spicy versions are made, and served with seafood, meat, wine, herbs, or vegetables. Rice is often shaped or molded.

FISH - Fresh fish is readily available in Italy, and simply and quickly prepared by Italian cooks. The flavoring ingredients are varied rather than the cooking techniques. The fish most often used are sole, turbot, and flounder.

CHICKEN AND GAME - Chicken, quail, and rabbit are popular in Italy, and Italian cooks take advantage of the affinity of chicken for wines, herbs and spices.

RED MEAT - Not as readily available as it is in America, beef does not play a major role in

Italian cooking. When it is prepared, thin steaks are sautéed or pan-fried, with lemon juice, herbs, and wine. Veal is the most popular meat because of the limited grazing area available. Italians appreciate its delicate, light taste. Lamb is cooked with a variety of sauces and accompaniments. It is most often found enhanced by rosemary, garlic, and onions, and basted in white wine.

EGGS - In Italy, eggs are not served for breakfast, but for lunch or dinner, often as a first course or light main course. They are prepared poached, scrambled, fried, baked, boiled, and with a variety of fillings. Most popular is the *frittata*, a flattened omelet combined with vegetables, cheese, herbs, and sometimes seafood or ham. *Tortina*, an Italian egg pie, is also popular. Serve a *frittata* or *tortina* with a salad and fruit for a lovely meal in itself.

VEGETABLES - High-quality produce is found in abundance in Italy, and is always served in season. Careful thought goes into each vegetable as an accompaniment to another dish, or as a salad ingredient. Antipasi includes a variety of raw vegetables, and they are also the chief ingredient of salads. Vegetable main dishes such as tomatoes stuffed with spinach and mushrooms are also found.

SALADS - Italians serve salads after the main course rather than as an appetizer. The purpose is to help digest the heavy part of the meal, to take away the taste of the main course, and to prepare the palette for fruit, cheese, and sweets. Consisting of a variety of fresh greens and raw vegetables, Italian salads are traditionally simple. Dill is used as a seasoning, and eggs, seafood and pasta are also used. A similar salad might be served as a main lunch course, or after the main part of any meal.

SAUCES AND DRESSINGS - Italian cooks prepare classic, light sauces to enhance, not overpower their dishes. Herbs are combined with various liquids - wine, stock, tomatoes, and milk.

DESSERTS - Fruit and cheese most often end an Italian meal, but for special occasions, sweets are served. The favorites are a dish similar to ice cream, tortas (layered cakes), and pastries.

Recipes

Perhaps you're not yet ready to invite guests to a five course Italian meal, but hopefully you're eager to try your hand at an Italian dish or two! Here are some recipes to get you started. If you enjoy yourself and want to learn more, visit your library - most stock an abundance of books on Italian cooking. Keep track of all your favorite recipes, and you'll soon be enjoying true Italian fare in your own home on a regular basis!

Italian Fish and Pasta Salad
1 pound haddock fillets
3/4 cup whole wheat pasta shells
1 cup cherry tomatoes
2 tablespoons dillweed
2 tablespoons parsley
1/2 small red onion, thinly sliced into rings
1/4 teaspoon garlic powder
2 tablespoons olive oil

2 tablespoons lemon juice

Place a large saucepan half filled with water over high heat. Place water in a large skillet to a depth of 1 inch, and set the skillet over high heat.

Meanwhile, cut the haddock into bite-size pieces. When the water in the large skillet is just below boiling, add the haddock. Poach about 5 minutes.

When the water in the large saucepan is boiling, stir in the pasta. Let the water return to a boil, then stir and turn down the heat. Boil pasta until firm-tender, about 7 to 9 minutes.

When the haddock is poached, remove it to a large plate where it can be spread out to cool. Drain the cooked pasta and run under cold water to cool.

Halve the cherry tomatoes and place them in a serving bowl with the dill, parsley and onion rings. Add the garlic.

Add the cooled fish cubes and pasta shells. Toss all together with the oil and lemon juice, and chill before serving.

Makes four servings.

—adapted from ***The 20-Minute Natural Foods Cookbook*** *by Sharon Claessens*

Rosemary Minestrone

1/2 cup dried kidney beans or black beans
2 cups water or unsalted stock (Chicken-flavored broth powder works well for this soup)
1 medium-size onion, coarsely chopped
1 tablespoon garlic flakes, rehydrated
2 tablespoons rosemary
1 tablespoon olive oil
2 ripe tomatoes, peeled and chopped
2 or 3 celery leaves, chopped
1 small carrot, cut into chunks
1 scant cup chopped cabbage
freshly ground pepper to taste
1 cup fresh green beans, broken into 1 inch pieces
1 tablespoon whole wheat macaroni
grated Parmesan or Romano cheese for garnish

Wash and soak beans about 8 hours. Drain. Add water or stock, bring to a boil, and simmer, covered, 20 minutes.

Meanwhile, in a 3 or 4 quart saucepan, saute' onion, garlic, and rosemary gently in oil about 5 minutes. Add tomatoes, celery leaves, carrot, cabbage, and some of the liquid from the beans. Bring to a gentle boil.

Add pepper and hot beans. Simmer 15 minutes. Add green beans and simmer 15 minutes more. Add hot water if needed. Five minutes before serving, add macaroni. Serve topped with grated Romano or Parmesan cheese.

Serves 4.

—adapted from ***No Salt Needed Cookbook*** *by the editors of Rodale Books.*

Italian Cheese Pie

pastry for one pie crust
1 1/2 pounds ricotta cheese
1/4 cup chopped roasted almonds
4 eggs
1/4 cup honey
1 teaspoon vanilla extract
ground cinnamon

Roll out pastry on a flat surface and line a 9 inch pie plate.

Preheat oven to 375°.F.

Put ricotta through a sieve into a large bowl. Add almonds. Set aside.

Beat eggs and honey until foamy. Add vanilla. Blend with ricotta mixture until smooth. Pour mixture into pastry.

Bake for about 45 minutes, or until filling is firm. Cool on a wire rack. Decorate with cinnamon just before serving.

Makes 1 pie.

—from ***Rodale's Basic Natural Foods Cookbook*** *by Charles Gerras, editor*

Italian Meatballs and Noodles

1 pound lean ground beef
1/8 teaspoon ground black pepper
1 tablespoon parsley
1/4 cup grated Parmesan cheese
1/2 cup whole grain bread crumbs
2 cups beef stock (Beef-flavored broth powder works well here)
1 egg, beaten
2 tablespoons wheat germ (optional)
1/4 cup olive oil, or more as needed
1 clove garlic, minced
1/2 pound mushrooms, sliced
2 cups chopped canned tomatoes
1 teaspoon oregano
1/2 teaspoon basil
2 cups uncooked whole wheat noodles
2 tablespoons cornstarch, dissolved in 1/4 cup cold water

In a large bowl , mix together beef, pepper, parsley, cheese, bread crumbs slightly moistened with a little of the stock, egg, and wheat germ. Form into balls about 1 inch in diameter.

Heat oil in a Dutch oven and saute' garlic. Add meatballs and brown on all sides, adding more oil if needed. Remove meatballs and reserve. Saute' mushrooms in the same pot, adding more oil if needed. Add tomatoes, remaining stock, oregano, and basil. Return meatballs to pot, cover, and simmer for 20 minutes.

While meatballs are simmering, cook noodles until tender. Drain.

When meatballs are done, add cornstarch mixture to pot and cook until liquid thickens, stirring constantly. Gently mix in drained noodles and serve.

Makes 6 servings.

—from ***Rodale's Basic Natural Food Cookbook*** *by Charles Gerras, editor*

Panettone (Italian Holiday Bread)

1/2 cup raisins
2 tablespoons orange peel cut and sifted, rehydrated
1 tablespoon active dry yeast
1/2 cup warm water
1/2 cup melted butter
1/4 cup honey
3 eggs
2 egg yolks

1 teaspoon sea salt
1 tablespoon lemon peel cut and sifted, rehydrated
1 teaspoon vanilla extract
5 cups unbleached white flour
melted butter
chopped almonds

Combine raisins and orange peel and set aside. Sprinkle yeast over the warm water, stir well. In a large bowl, combine butter, honey, eggs, egg yolks, and sea salt. Mix. Add the yeast and water mixture, lemon peel, and vanilla. Stir in 2 cups of flour, then enough flour to make a stiff dough.

Turn out onto a lightly floured surface and knead until the dough is smooth and silky (about 8 to 10 minutes). Cover with a towel and let rest for 10 minutes. Then knead the fruits into the dough.

Return to bowl, cover and allow to rise in a warm spot until doubled in bulk (about 45 minutes to 1 hour). When doubled, turn out onto lightly floured surface and punch down. Divide the dough in half and place each part in a buttered, 9 inch round cake pan. (If you have smaller cake pans, the recipe will make 3 breads.)

Brush tops with melted butter and sprinkle with chopped almonds (optional). Lightly cover and let rise for about 1 hour. Brush tops with melted butter again and bake for 40 to 50 minutes in a 350° F oven.

Makes 2 or 3 breads depending upon size of cake pans.

—from ***Bread Winners*** *by Mel London*

Mexican Cooking

Lively and full of spice, Mexican cooking is becoming increasingly popular throughout the world. In Mexico, the cuisine is a colorful reflection of the markets one finds there. In addition to both ordinary and exotic produce, vendors also sell tacos, coconuts with straws inserted for drinking, and fruitades.

Some vendors are stationary, some are moving peddlers. Goat milk is even sold by peddlers who walk their nanny goats in the streets and milk to order! Fresh and dried herbs are sold alongside vegetables, and special booths with only herbs and spices can also be found. Ceramic bowls filled with earthy and vibrant colors make quite a display. Sometimes prepared pastes are available - green mounds of pumpkin seed paste, red *achiote* paste, dark brown pepper paste and jet-black paste of burned, dried chilies. Small bundles of dried herbs - *hierbas de olor* or "fragrant herbs" - are often sold to be used as bouquet garni. Most often this bundle consists of bay leaves, thyme, and marjoram.

After a trip to the market, many Mexican cooks prepare their own blends and pastes, adding seasonings to suit their individual tastes. Exact measurements are seldom used, but are replaced by "a little of this" and "a touch of that." Not all Mexican food is spicy hot. Many dishes are subtly flavored, and the spicier dishes may vary greatly in degrees of hotness.

While some good recipes will be indispensable to those interested in learning to cook Mexican cuisine, experimentation, a sense of adventure, and familiarity with ingredients will help you enjoy the process of developing authentic Mexican dishes. This article will outline the herbs and spices most distinctive in Mexican cooking, and provide some information regarding their properties and uses.

Herbs & Spices

ANNATTO SEED - Known in Mexico as *achoite,* these small, reddish-brown seeds of the annatto tree are used to impart a rich yellow color and mild, distinctive flavor to foods such as rice and sauces. To use, cover seeds with water and simmer for five minutes. Soak in water for an hour and cool before crushing with a mortar and pestle or blender. Commercially prepared (ground) *recado rojo* or "red seasoning" is available in the Yucatan and southern Mexico, where it is used primarily for seasoning pastes for meats and fish.

AZAFRAN - This is Mexican saffron, a plant only slightly different from the saffron grown in Europe and Asia. A member of the crocus family, the small, dried threads are hand-picked and thus expensive. They impart a pleasantly bitter flavor, and most dishes require only a small amount. To use, dissolve first by crumbling a small amount in hot water. (Frontier carries European saffron, an acceptable substitute.)

BASIL - A pungent member of the mint family, basil turns a brown/olive color when dried, and is used either fresh or dried, most often in tomato dishes.

CAYENNE - An orange-colored powder, cayenne is simply a variety of very hot, ground chili peppers. It is used sparingly, to add extra hotness to dishes.

CHAMOMILE - This herb resembles a tiny white daisy and is traditionally considered the perfect tea to end a Mexican meal.

CHILIES - Known for their spicy hotness, in the correct amounts chili peppers may also add mild and subtle flavor to dishes. A very wide variety of chilies are cultivated, and range greatly in size as well as hotness. When cooking, it is useful to know that the smallest peppers are generally the hottest, and that the seeds and stems (the hottest parts of the peppers) are usually removed during preparation. To increase hotness, add a touch of cayenne, crushed red pepper, or some seed and stem of the chili to your recipe. When preparing chilies, always wear rubber gloves as the volatile oils are capable of burning your skin. To prepare dried chilies, rinse well in cold water. Slice open, discard the stems and seeds, and cut or tear into small pieces. Cover with boiling water and let soak one hour. Drain and use the chili water in your recipe if a liquid is called for. Directions for preparing chilies after this point vary depending upon the recipe. They may be lightly toasted, ground, fried, or burnt black.

Crushed red pepper, often found on the table in Italian restaurants, is a good substitute for chili peppers. It is simply a dried and crushed chili pepper. Use 1/2 teaspoon for each chili pepper required. Chili powder may also be substituted for chili peppers. In Mexico, chili powder is a powdered form of a red pepper such as *Ancha*. Domestic chili powder contains extra seasonings such as cumin, garlic, oregano, salt, and coriander. Mexican cooks make a paste by mixing one tablespoon chili powder, one teaspoon flour, and two tablespoons of cold water. To yield the correct flavor, the paste should reach a boil sometime during cooking. Chili is perhaps Mexican cooking's most indispensable spice. To learn about the tastes of different chili products, choose one sauce and make it using different chilies each time. Chili sauce is found on every Mexican table during mealtime.

CINNAMON - Cinnamon was first introduced to Mexican cooking by the Spanish. Much milder and softer than the dark, hard "cassia" bark from Malabar, Mexican or "true cinnamon" is light brown and sold as bark or in sticks. The sticks are thin layers of rolled bark rather than one thick piece of bark, and are most often used in beverages.

CORIANDER - Coriander leaves and seeds are both used extensively, though not interchangeably, in Mexican cooking. The fresh leaf, which looks like parsley but tastes very different, is known as cilantro, fresh coriander, or Chinese parsley. Used both as a garnish and seasoning, it is a main ingredient in the dish *Mole Verde*. There is no known substitute for cilantro, which should be used dried only in recipes where it is to be cooked.

Coriander seed is the dried seed of the same plant, but yields a very different taste, resembling somewhat a combination of lemon peel and sage. Its mild flavor is used both in main dishes and sweets.

CUMIN SEED - Known as *comino* seed, this spice is used extensively in Mexican cooking. Its taste is similar to caraway and it is the predominant flavor in many chili powder blends. Found often in combination with chilies, its flavor is used to balance the hotness of other spices.

MEXICAN SEASONING - A potpourri of many spices used in Mexican cooking, this blend may be conveniently used in most Mexican main dishes. Frontier's Mexican seasoning contains: mild chilies, garlic, onion, paprika, cumin, chilies crushed mild, oregano, celery seed, cayenne mild, ground bell peppers (red and green), parsley, and bay.

MINT - Mints are sparingly used in some Mexican recipes for meatballs, soups, and beans.

NUTMEG - The fruit of a tropical evergreen tree, this oval, brown seed has a warm, sweet, spicy flavor and is most often used in beverages and desserts.

OREGANO - There are 13 varieties of Mexican oregano. Its strong, aromatic, pleasantly bitter taste is very popular in Mexican cuisine. Used fresh or dried, the leaf is more desirable than powdered, and in some places is lightly toasted before adding to dishes.

SAGE - Used whole, rubbed, or ground, sage has a strong, aromatic, slightly bitter taste. It is often used in soups and stews.

THYME - A member of the mint family, thyme has a dry and pungent flavor and is used in Mexican soups and sauces.

Recipes

While the herbs and spices used in authentic Mexican cooking are quite distinctive, most are readily available. Experiment with amounts and use seasoning to enhance dishes rather than overwhelm them. Start with some of the following recipes. Adapt each dish you cook to suit your own culinary tastes, and in time you will be creating your own Mexican cuisine!

Tofu Chili
4 cups cooked pinto beans
2 10 oz. cans whole tomatoes
2 tablespoons onion flakes
2 tablespoons oil
1 clove garlic, minced
3 tablespoons Mexican Seasoning
1 pound tofu, cubed
1 tablespoon tamari

Saute' tofu, onion and garlic in saucepan. Add remaining ingredients. Simmer for 30 minutes.

Makes 6 servings.

Mexican Omelet
6 eggs
1/4 cup cream
2 tablespoons Mexican Seasoning
1 small onion, chopped (or 1/4 cup onion flakes)
3 sweet banana peppers (or 1 large green bell pepper)
1 sliced red chili pepper, seeds and stem removed
1 cup grated cheese (cheddar, Swiss, or other favorite)
2 tablespoons oil
2 tablespoons butter
1/4 cup picante or tomato-chili sauce

1/4 cup plain yogurt

Blend together eggs, cream, and Mexican Seasoning. In small skillet, melt 1 tablespoon oil and 1 tablespoon butter. Saute' onions and sweet peppers until soft. Remove from heat. In a large skillet, melt remaining oil and butter. Pour egg mixture into large skillet and cook over low heat. With spatula, loosen edge of omelet and let uncooked egg run under. When nearly cooked through, sprinkle onions, sweet peppers, chili peppers, and cheese on half of the eggs. Fold in half and cover until cheese is melted. Top with sauce and yogurt.

Makes 2 servings

Mexican Pan-Bread

Preheat oven to 350° F.

1 onion, chopped (or 1/4 cup onion flakes)
1 clove garlic, minced (or 3/4 teaspoon garlic flakes)
1 tablespoon oil
1/2 cup dried kidney beans, cooked
3/4 cup bean liquid (reserved from cooking the beans)
1 egg, beaten
1 cup cornmeal
1 tablespoon chili powder
1/2 teaspoon cumin, ground
1/2 teaspoon salt
1/3 cup grated cheese

In a heavy-bottom skillet, saute' onion and garlic in oil.

In a medium-sized mixing bowl, mix together all the remaining ingredients except the cheese. Pour this mixture into the skillet and stir to mix well.

Sprinkle grated cheese on top and bake in preheated oven for about 10 minutes.

Makes 4 servings.

*—from **The Rodale Cookbook** by Nancy Albright*

Mexican Bean Dip

1 cup dried, red kidney beans
water to cover
1/2 teaspoon sea salt
1/4 cup oil
1 cup shredded cheddar cheese
1/2 teaspoon kelp powder
1 teaspoon chili powder

Wash kidney beans, remove any foreign particles. Place them in a medium-size bowl and cover with water. Allow to stand at room temperature about one hour. Add more water, cover and place in refrigerator overnight.

The following day, transfer kidney beans with liquid to medium-size saucepan. Add more water to cover kidney beans. Place over medium heat and bring to boil; reduce heat, add one-half teaspoon salt, cover, and simmer over low heat until tender.

Remove from heat and drain kidney beans, reserve liquid.

In a medium-size skillet, heat 1/4 cup oil. Add drained kidney beans and mash with potato masher until smooth. Add 1/3 cup of reserved bean liquid to help make a smoother mixture, adding more liquid if beans appear to be too dry. Stir constantly.

Add shredded cheddar cheese, kelp, and chili powder, stirring constantly until cheese melts. Taste and adjust seasoning.

Pour mixture into a chafing dish or heated casserole and serve hot with corn pone or corn crackers. If mixture gets too stiff for dipping, thin with a little more of the bean liquid.

Makes 3 cups.

South of the Border Bulgur

1 1/2 cups stock
1 1/2 cups uncooked bulgur
2 large onions, diced (or 1/2 cup onion flakes, rehydrated)
1 cup thinly sliced celery
3 cloves garlic, minced (or 1 tablespoon garlic flakes, rehydrated)
2 tablespoons butter
1/2 cup stock
1-2 tablespoons chili powder
1 teaspoon ground cumin
dash of cayenne pepper
1/4 cup minced parsley
1 cup shredded Cheddar or Monterey Jack cheese
2 cups yogurt
1 cup alfalfa sprouts
1 cup chopped roasted peanuts
1 pepper, diced
2 tomatoes, chopped
1/2 cup sliced scallions

Bring the 1 1/2 cups of stock to a boil in a small saucepan. Stir in the bulgur, cover, remove from the heat, and let the mixture stand for 20 minutes.

In a large frying pan combine the onions, celery, garlic, butter and 1/2 cup stock. Cover and cook over low heat until the onions are very soft, about 20 minutes. Stir in the chili powder, cumin, cayenne and parsley.

Fluff the bulgur with two forks, and stir it into the onion mixture.

Place the cheese, yogurt, sprouts, peanuts, pepper, tomatoes, and scallions into separate bowls and serve as toppings for the bulgur.

Serves 4.

—from **Cooking With the Healthful Herbs** *by Jean Rogers*

Oriental Cooking

An old Japanese saying states that "if you have the pleasant experience of eating something that you have not tasted before, your life will be lengthened by 75 days."

Oriental cooking - beautiful in color, taste, and design - gives many of us a chance to broaden our culinary horizons, enabling us to taste entirely new foods or familiar foods prepared in unique ways. Well balanced, high in nutrients and low in calories, Oriental cuisine emphasizes grains and vegetables, and is thought by some to represent the diet of the future.

There is much for a student of Oriental cooking to consider - a deep and rich history, a wide range of regional styles of cooking, extensive preparation and cooking techniques, intricate menu planning, and an appreciation of each dish as a highly creative expression of its cook. You needn't study this art for years in order to experience its rewards in your own kitchen, however. Some familiarity with basic ingredients and a few good recipes are all you need to get started. And don't be afraid to dabble - the Chinese, in particular, value innovation and creativity in cooking.

About the Seasonings

Oriental dishes may be subtly or boldly spiced, often depending upon the guidelines of the regional cuisine. For example, meat or fish curries in coconut milk and moderately-seasoned rice and noodle dishes are typically Southeast Asian, while Indochinese cooking is known for its spicy hot dishes. Indonesia and Malaysia, whose ports were once stopping points along the China-India spice trade route, use cinnamon, cloves, anise, and cardamom extensively.

All Oriental cuisine, however, strives to preserve the intrinsic properties of each main ingredient. The yin and yang of tastes are juxtaposed by combining salty and sour, salty and bitter, and sweet and sour, while spices and herbs are used to unify and enhance the tastes of the combined ingredients. Strong-tasting garnishes or seasonings are often added at the last minute, preventing permeation of the other ingredients.

While emphasis is on preparation, little time is spent actually cooking the ingredients. For this reason, it is a good idea to familiarize yourself with the ingredients needed and assemble them beforehand. The following section will acquaint you with some of the seasonings used in Oriental cooking:

AGAR-AGAR - This flavorless seaweed is used as a thickener in aspics and sweet dishes. Use cold water to soften, and chill to quicken jelling. Although it acts like unflavored gelatin, it need not be refrigerated.

ANISE - Ground cloves of star anise are sometimes used (sparingly) in place of whole star anise.

CHICKEN BROTH - A concentrated stock may be made from scratch, although vegetarian chicken-flavored broth powder works perfectly well. Many Oriental soup and stew recipes call for chicken broth.

CHILI PEPPERS - Dried whole chili peppers are used in Chinese and Southeast Asian cooking. They are small and very hot. (Use with the seeds for full hotness.) Crushed red peppers may be substituted at the rate of 1/4 teaspoon per chili pepper.

A very hot Chinese chili sauce is used to season fish, pickled vegetables, and salted cabbage. It is made with small red chili peppers, apricots, lemon, and garlic.

Chili pepper oil, used in salads, dip sauces, or for cooking spicy food, may be made by heating one cup of oil until very hot. Add 10 to 12 whole dried chili peppers (or 3 tablespoons chili powder) and stir for one minute. Turn off the heat and cool. Stir and strain into a bottle. Store for up to one month.

Green chili peppers are used as a hot seasoning as well, primarily in Szechwanese cooking.

CHIVES - A member of the onion family, chives add a sharp, pungent flavor to noodle, egg, or stir-fried dishes.

CINNAMON - Cinnamon bark is used in slow cooking meats, and ground cinnamon is used in blends to impart a sweet taste to dishes.

CORNSTARCH - This powder provides a glistening, bright appearance and thickness to gravies, soups, and sauces. It is also used to coat fish and meat, smoothing the surface and encouraging tenderness by sealing in the juices. When adding to sauces, dilute beforehand and add slowly, to very hot liquid.

CURRY - Introduced centuries ago from India, curry powder is used in many seafood and meat dishes. Oriental cooks prepare their own small batches of curry daily. Typically it contains turmeric, coriander, cloves, cardamom, ginger, mace, and red and black pepper. Often it is cooked over low heat in a dry pan before other ingredients are added. Stir constantly to prevent burning!

FIVE SPICE - Also known as five-flavored powder or five-fragrance spice powder, this cocoa-colored blend is a combination of star anise, anise pepper (or licorice root), fennel, cloves, and cinnamon. (Slightly different ingredients are sometimes substituted for each of these.) Used sparingly in meat and poultry, it is pungent, fragrant, and slightly sweet. Allspice is sometimes used as a substitute for five spice.

GARLIC - Garlic is a commonly used seasoning, particularly in "northern-style" Chinese cooking. It is often cooked directly in hot oil to enhance its flavor, but be careful - burnt garlic adds a bitter taste. Garlic is used with meat, seafood, poultry and vegetables. Dried garlic may be substituted for fresh at the rate of 3/4 teaspoon garlic flakes per clove of garlic.

GINGER - Ginger has a pungent, fresh, spicy taste and is used in small quantities to season soups, meats, vegetables, sweet dishes, and seafood. It is also used to subdue undesirable tastes such as fishiness. To use, lightly scrape the skin and slice. Then mince or prepare according to the recipe directions. Dried ginger root may be substituted for fresh, and when neither is available, ginger powder may be used at the rate of 1/8 teaspoon powder per 1 tablespoon of fresh ginger.

Pickled ginger is a popular Chinese and Japanese condiment, and for a good dipping sauce, mix minced ginger with soy sauce and scallions or crushed garlic.

GINSENG - Known as the "root of life," ginseng is an aromatic, sweet, licorice-tasting plant, used in soups and as a medicinal tonic. It is also exported in spirits and tea.

KELP - Kelp is a sweet seaweed, rich in calcium and minerals, and used primarily for making stock and fish rolls. Store at room temperature in an airtight container.

KOMBU - Harvested in northern Japan, this dried tangle seaweed forms the base of dashi (basic soup stock).

LEMON GRASS - Often used as a tea or in broths, this citrus-scented herb is found in Indonesian, Malaysian, Indochinese and Thailand cooking.

LICORICE ROOT - Licorice root is sometimes used in place of anise pepper in the blending of five spice powder.

MUSHROOMS - Many Oriental recipes use dried mushrooms to add color, texture, and flavor. Before using, discard the stems and rinse the mushrooms in cold water to remove any sand. Then soak in hot water for at least thirty minutes; they should resume their original size and become soft. The soaking water may be reserved and used in the recipe, in place of water. Dried mushrooms are strong and should be used sparingly. Six dried mushrooms equals a six-ounce can of mushrooms.

MUSTARD - Chinese hot mustard, much hotter than the mustard we are accustomed to, is served as a condiment with Oriental meals. To make, moisten mustard powder with warm water to form a thin paste. Allow to stand for 10 minutes to develop hotness and pungency. Because the pungency dissipates within a few hours unless vinegar or other acidic liquid is added, plan to use within an hour.

NORI - This dark brown dried laver seaweed is used as a garnish, or as sushi wrapper.

PARSLEY - Chinese parsley is cilantro, stronger and more aromatic than American parsley. Its Chinese name means "fragrant vegetables" and it is used sparingly as a garnish and in soups, poultry, seafood, and chopped meats.

SALT - In much of China, salt is a scarce and treasured commodity. In certain regions, cooks bring out the flavor of foods by substituting vinegar and hot peppers for salt. The Chinese say that there are seven items required to begin housekeeping: oil, salt, soy sauce, vinegar, fuel, rice, and tea.

SESAME SEEDS - These tiny seeds are used for flavoring cold dishes and sweets, and as a garnish. Store in an airtight container in the refrigerator.

STAR ANISE - This spice, the dried seed cluster plus the pod of the anise shrub, is hard and star-shaped. It is used in simmering meats and poultry, and will stay fresh indefinitely in an airtight container.

WAKAME - Rich in calcium and vitamin A, this sweet-tasting seaweed is used coarsely chopped in soups and salads. Dusty and dark when dried, it returns to its vibrant green color when soaked.

About Oriental Teas

Entire books have been devoted to the topic of tea in Oriental cuisine, and indeed it is an integral part of both the ceremony of eating and the culinary appreciation of the meal. It has been said that the Chinese will use any excuse to drink tea — before, during, or after a meal, for conversation, relaxation, day's beginning or end — and there are more than 250 kinds from which to choose! Basically, they fall into these categories: unfermented or green tea such as Gunpowder; semi-fermented or oolong tea; fermented or black tea such as Keemun; scented tea (green, black, or oolong teas to which scent has been added); and smoky tea, such as Lapsang Souchong, made from black tea by allowing the smoke of the firing process to flavor the tea.

Tea drinking is a lovely custom, and may add much authenticity to an Oriental meal you have prepared. Experiment with the many Chinese teas available to find your favorites.

Recipes

Oriental cooks state that a well-prepared dish must "appeal to the eye by its coloring; to the nose by its aroma; to the ear by its sounds (when eaten); and, of course, to the mouth by its flavor." The rewards of a beautifully prepared Oriental meal are even greater for Western cooks. We experience the adventure of exploring another culture through one of its most basic activities - the preparation of food.

Spicy Peanuts
1 cup water
2 teaspoons sea salt
1/2 teaspoon five spice powder
2 pounds raw shelled peanuts
Preheat oven to 250° F.

Combine water, salt and powder. Heat until very hot. Add peanuts and mix well. Spread entire mixture into a roasting pan and gently toast (50-70 minutes), stirring often.

Curried Stir Fry
1 pound tofu
1 onion (or 1/4 cup onion flakes)
2 teaspoons cornstarch or arrowroot powder
2 tablespoons water
1/2 teaspoon honey
dash of black pepper
2-3 tablespoons oil
1/2 teaspoon sherry
2-3 tablespoons curry powder
1/2 cup chicken broth powder stock
Cube tofu. Thinly slice onion.
Blend cornstarch, water, honey, and pepper to a paste.

Heat oil. Add salt, then tofu, and stir-fry for one minute. Sprinkle tofu with sherry, stir-fry for one minute, then remove from heat.

In another pan, stir curry powder over low heat for a few seconds. Add onion and stir-fry for one more minute. Combine tofu and onions, and heat gently for one minute.

Stir in stock and heat quickly. Cook until onion is soft. Stir in cornstarch paste to thicken. Serve immediately.

Makes 6 servings

Egg Drop Soup

6 cups broth made from chicken-flavored broth powder
2 teaspoons peanut oil
2 teaspoons sea salt
2 eggs
2 teaspoons minced scallions
4 sheets nori, torn into small squares

In a saucepan combine the stock, oil, and salt. Bring to a boil.

Beat the eggs well and slowly pour into the soup, gently stirring. Remove the pot from the heat and garnish with scallions and nori.

Makes 8 servings.

Green Bean Salad

1 pound of green beans, cooked until tender
2 teaspoons mustard powder
2 teaspoons cold water
1 teaspoon sea salt
1/4 teaspoon ginger root powder
1 teaspoon honey
1 tablespoon tamari
1 1/2 tablespoons white vinegar
1 tablespoon peanut oil

Blend together well the mustard powder and water. Add the salt, honey, ginger, tamari, vinegar, and oil. Add the beans and toss well. Chill and serve.

Makes 8 servings.

Peppers and Sprouts

1 pound bean sprouts, blanched
3 stalks celery
2 green peppers
2 red chili peppers (or 1/2 teaspoon crushed red peppers)
1/4 teaspoon ginger root powder
2 tablespoons oil
1/2 teaspoon tamari
1/4 cup chicken-flavored broth powder stock
1/2 teaspoon honey
1 teaspoon cooking sherry

Seed and slice peppers. Chop celery.

Heat oil in fry pan or wok. Add peppers, celery, tamari and ginger.

Saute' 2 minutes. Add bean sprouts and stir fry 1 more minute.

Add stock and cook 2 minutes over medium heat. Stir in honey and sherry and serve immediately. Makes 4 servings.

Almond Cookies

50 almonds, blanched
1 cup butter

3/4 cup honey
1 egg, beaten
1/2 teaspoon almond extract
1/2 teaspoon vanilla extract
2 1/2 cups flour
1 1/2 teaspoons baking powder
1/8 teaspoon sea salt

Preheat oven to 350° F.

Grind 12 of the almonds to a fine powder.

Cream honey and butter together. Add egg, ground almonds, and extracts.

In another bowl, sift flour, baking powder, and salt. Add gradually to wet ingredients. Knead into a dough. (Add a drop of water or flour at a time if necessary to make a kneadable consistency.)

Pinch off small balls of dough and place on greased cookie sheet. Press flat into 1/2 inch thicknesses. Make an indentation in top of each cookie and place a whole almond in each. Bake for 15 minutes.

Makes about 3 dozen cookies.

Baking

What images come to mind when someone mentions baking? A warm, fragrant kitchen? Loaves of freshly-baked bread, cookies, pies, and cakes? Make the scene a healthful, nutritious one by learning to bake your own goodies, using wholesome ingredients. Through the use of carefully selected herbs and spices, overly sweet baked goods can be replaced with interesting, flavorful, and distinctive treats. "Fortifiers" such as nutritional yeast and wheat germ can give your culinary creations extra nutritional value. In addition, carefully choosing the best baking items (sweeteners, thickeners, etc.) will maximize wholesomeness.

Imagine: Gingerbread made with iron-rich molasses, whole wheat flour, wheat germ, spicy ginger and cloves. Whole wheat coffee cake with plump raisins, cardamom, honey, nutmeg, and vanilla. A wide loaf of rye bread dotted with caraway seeds, and a tall loaf of dark wheat bread full of aromatic herbs and spices.

While some baked goods take hours from start to finish, most actually require much less actual preparation time and many can be ready to pop in the oven in just minutes.

Interested? Familiarize yourself with the following ingredients to make your creations the best they can be. Then try some of the recipes at the end of this article. If you're a beginning baker, follow them exactly for perfect results. Improvise as your confidence grows!

Standard Baking Items

ARROWROOT POWDER - Arrowroot is an easily digested, unrefined thickener containing both vitamins and minerals (58 mgs. of calcium per 100 gms., for example). It may be substituted for cornstarch in any recipe.

BAKING POWDER - Often used in "quick breads" (no rising before baking), baking powder contains both baking soda and tartaric acid. These two ingredients interact when moistened. Use only one teaspoon per cup of flour - any more baking powder results in the loss of thiamine, a B vitamin.

BAKING SODA POWDER - Used for its rising action (without the use of eggs or yeast) in cakes and breads. It reacts with acidic ingredients such as buttermilk, vinegar, fruit juice, yogurt and molasses to release carbon dioxide bubbles which result in the rising effect.

LECITHIN - Derived from soybeans, lecithin is used as a stabilizer and emulsifier. In baked goods it facilitates mixing, promotes shortening action and fat distribution, eases the handling of yeast doughs, and increases the shelf life of the finished products. To use, substitute lecithin for 1/3 the oil in baked goods.

CAROB POWDER - This looks like, and is used like cocoa. It contains three times the calcium of milk, while chocolate actually inhibits calcium absorption. It contains no caffeine (chocolate does), and is 2% fat as compared to chocolate which is 57% fat. In addition, it is naturally sweet, and requires little additional sweetener, while cocoa is naturally bitter. Carob contains B vitamins, calcium, phosphorus, iron, and magnesium.

CORNSTARCH - A thickening agent with very little nutritive value. (See *Arrowroot Powder*, page 147.)

CREAM OF TARTAR POWDER - Used as a leavening agent in baking, and to help in beating egg whites. To substitute for one teaspoon of double acting baking powder, use 1/2 teaspoon baking soda and 1/2 teaspoon cream of tartar.

FLOURS - There is much to learn about the wide variety of available flours. Basically, whole wheat flour is ground whole wheat berries and contains high-quality protein. It may be substituted, cup for cup, for white flours. Whole wheat pastry flour is more finely milled whole wheat flour, used for pies and pastries that require a lighter texture. White flour is a processed flour which has been stripped of the protein-rich germ and is often bleached.

GLYCERIN, VEGETABLE - Primarily used to retain moisture in baked goods, and to improve spreading characteristics of many food items. A few drops added to cookie batter will produce a softer cookie.

SEA SALT - Contains trace minerals not found in salt purchased at the supermarket. In addition, supermarket salt usually contains sodium silico aluminate and dextrose.

Fortifiers

Why not add fortifiers to your baked products to increase their nutritive value? Once you know the possibilites, it's easy to give your baked goods a boost.

MILK POWDER - To increase the protein content of your baked goods, add milk powder as a dry ingredient, or blend one cup of milk with 1/4 cup milk powder and use in place of one cup of water or milk in your recipe. Non-instant milk powder can easily be stirred into dry ingredients.

NUTRITIONAL YEAST - Full of B vitamins, mineral, and protein (2 grams per tablespoon), nutritional yeast does not rise like active dry yeast, but may be added to any baked items. Use sparingly, mixing with dry ingredients, until you develop a taste for it.

WHEAT GERM - The germ is the embryo of the wheat and contains most of the vitamins, minerals, and protein. (Two tablespoons of wheat germ contains two grams of usable protein.) Refrigerate and use in place of some of the flour in baked goods for an added boost.

Sweeteners

The average American now consumes a startling one pound of sugar every three days. We should be very aware of the quality, as well as the quanitity, of the sweeteners we use in cooking. While some experts argue that all sugars are harmful and should, therefore, be avoided, others assert that unrefined, unprocessed sugars which contain trace minerals and are naturally sweeter (thus requiring less per recipe) are certainly preferable.

To substitute honey for sugar in your favorite recipes, use 1/2 cup honey in place of each cup of refined sugar. Then decrease the liquid ingredients by 1/2 cup or increase dry ingredients by 1/2 cup. Because honey makes goods brown faster than sugar does, lower your oven temperature 25°. For a brown sugar taste, mix honey and molasses together.

Date sugar, another natural sweetener, is made from ground dried dates. It is a good sweetener, but has limited use because it does not dissolve. Brown sugar is not raw sugar but rather refined white sugar with a bit of molasses added. Since molasses does contain some minerals, brown sugar may be slightly preferable to white, but some brown sugar manufacturers use carmelized refined sugar as an additive instead.

Molasses, the residue of the last refinement stage of white sugar, does contain some minerals from the original sugar cane, plus calcium and iron from processing.

Seasonings

The choice of herbs and spices is what makes a baked item distinctive. Glance at the recipes at the end of this section. If you are an inexperienced cook, follow the recipes verbatim. But by all means experiment as soon as your confidence is bolstered by some success! Here are a few guidelines for using the most common baking and dessert seasonings:

ALLSPICE - pumpkin and mincemeat pies, carrot cake

ANISE - rye bread, cookies, apple pies

CARAWAY - rye bread, apple pie, cookies, cakes

CARDAMOM - fruits, pastries, cakes, custards

CINNAMON - apple dishes, blueberries, pears, fruit compotes, rice pudding, cakes, nut breads

CLOVES - applesauce, puddings, gingerbread, cakes, nut breads, stewed fruits

CORIANDER - carrot cake, pies, breads, biscuits

DILL - breads

GINGER - breads, cakes, cookies, puddings, fruit salad dressings, fruit compotes

MACE - baked goods, custards, stewed apricots, cherries, peaches

MARJORAM - cooked fruits

NUTMEG - apple, cherry, pear and pumpkin pies, custards, cakes, cookies, nut breads

POPPY SEED - breads and rolls, fruit salads, cakes and pastries. Heat or crush the seeds to release full nutty flavor.

SESAME SEED - breads, rolls, cakes. Heat or toast the seeds to release full flavor.

VANILLA - fruit, custards, puddings, preserves, compotes, pies, cookies, cakes. Experiment with other extracts in place of vanilla in your recipes. For example, try lemon, orange and almond extracts.

—suggested uses adapted from ***Cooking With the Healthful Herbs*** *by Jean Rogers*

Recipes

By now we hope you're eager to get to the kitchen and whip up one of the following recipes or adapt one of your old favorites to meet good nutritional guidelines! You'll delight in serving your family and friends a special treat that also promotes good health.

Pumpkin Chiffon Pie

1 9-inch, baked pie shell
1/4 cup skim milk powder
1/2 cup water
3 egg yolks
6 tablespoons honey
2 tablespoons molasses
1 1/2 cups pumpkin purée
1/2 teaspoon sea salt
1 teaspoon cinnamon
1/2 teaspoon ginger
1/2 teaspoon mace
3 teaspoons unflavored gelatin
1/2 cup cold water
3 stiffly-beaten egg whites
chopped walnuts to garnish

Mix skim milk powder with water, using wire whisk. Set aside.

Beat egg yolks until thick and lemon-colored; add honey, molasses, pumpkin purée, milk mixture, salt and spices. Cook in double boiler until thick, stirring constantly.

Soften gelatin in cold water, then stir into hot mixture. Chill until partially set.

Beat egg whites until stiff. Fold into gelatin mixture.

Pour into a baked 9-inch pie shell. Chill until set. Sprinkle with chopped walnut meats.

—from ***The Rodale Cookbook*** *by Nancy Albright*

Spice Bread

1 package dry yeast (1 tablespoon active dry yeast)
1/2 cup warm water
1/2 cup mashed potatoes
1/4 cup honey
1 cup milk
5 cups whole wheat flour
2/3 cup unsulphured molasses
1/2 teaspoon allspice
2 teaspoons anise seed
2 eggs, beaten
1/2 teaspoon cloves

Dissolve the yeast in the warm water. Let stand for a few minutes, then add the mashed potatoes, honey, and milk. Add 3 cups of the flour, 1 cup at a time, stirring after each addition. Cover the bowl and let rise in a warm place for 1 hour.

Then add the molasses, allspice, anise seed, and the 2 beaten eggs. Add the cloves and then beat together, gradually adding more flour as needed, up to 2 additional cups. Mix well, cover and let rise in a warm spot for 1 hour.

When dough has risen, turn out onto a lightly floured board and shape into 2 loaves or 12 buns. Place on a greased baking sheet, cover lightly and let rest for 15 minutes.

Bake for 30 minutes at 350° F or until breads test done.

Cool on wire racks.

*—from **Bread Winners** by Mel London*

Soft Gingerbread

1/2 cup butter
1/2 cup honey
1 cup molasses
1 teaspoon ginger
1 teaspoon cinnamon
2 1/2 cups unbleached white flour
1 teaspoon baking soda
1 cup boiling water
2 eggs, well beaten

Stir together the butter and the honey. Add the molasses, ginger, and cinnamon. Beat in the flour and then mix the baking soda with the boiling water to dissolve it and add to the batter. Add the eggs. Mix well.

Take 2 square (7"x 7") cake pans and line them with ordinary brown bag paper, cut to fit the pans. Butter the paper with softened butter. Pour batter into lined pans and bake at 350° for 40 to 60 minutes.

*—from **Bread Winners** by Mel London*

Carob Nut Brownies

2 eggs, beaten
1/2 cup honey
1 tablespoon molasses
1/4 cup melted butter
1/4 teaspoon almond extract
1 cup whole wheat pastry flour
1 cup carob, sifted
1/2 teaspoon sea salt
2/3 cup chopped walnuts

Combine eggs, honey, molasses, butter and almond extract.

Mix flour, carob, and salt, then combine the wet and dry mixtures.

Mix thoroughly, add nuts and turn into an oiled 8"x 8" baking pan.

Bake in preheated 350° F oven for 25 minutes.

Remove from oven and cut while warm. Cool on rack.

Makes 16 brownies.

*—from **The Natural Foods Epicure** by Nancy Albright*

Lemon Caraway Bread

2 1/4 cups whole wheat pastry flour
1 1/2 teaspoons baking soda
2 tablespoons poppy seeds
1 tablespoons caraway seeds
2 eggs

1 cup buttermilk
3 tablespoons honey
3 tablespoons corn oil
1 tablespoon lemon juice
2 teaspoons finely grated lemon rind (or 1 teaspoon cut and sifted lemon peel)
1 teaspoon vanilla extract

Combine the flour, baking soda, poppy seeds and caraway seeds in a large bowl.

In a medium bowl, beat the eggs and add the buttermilk, honey, oil, lemon juice, lemon rind and vanilla. Stir into the dry ingredients.

Pour the batter into a lightly oiled 8 1/2" x 4 1/2 " bread pan. Bake in a preheated 350° F oven for 1 hour or until a cake tester inserted in the center comes out clean.

—from ***The 20-Minute Natural Foods Cookbook*** *by Sharon Claessens*

Soups & Stews

There is something special about homemade soup. Hot mugs of a favorite soup on cold days and steaming ladles of vegetables and broth nourish both body and spirit. Soups are versatile, serving as appetizers, hearty main dishes, nutritious snacks, or refreshing desserts (fruit soups!). A soup can be light and simple as a lovely vegetable broth, or thick and hearty as a beef stew. Making good soup is an art - one that may be mastered with careful attention, experimentation, and a little inspiration.

It's a good idea to keep good soup ingredients on hand at all times. Then you can mix up a quick batch for unexpected guests, a big batch to freeze for the coming months, or a special favorite to simmer in the crockpot while at work or play. While fresh and garden-canned vegetables are almost always included in the soup pot, dehydrated vegetables, broth powders, and prepared blended seasonings also have become important staples. Here are some of the ingredients you might like to try, and some tips for successful soup cookery!

BROTH POWDERS - Available in a variety of flavors, these powders are simply added to water to form a tasty broth on which to build your soup. Start with one teaspoon of broth per cup of water; increase the amount for a strongly-flavored stock. When your recipe calls for a soup base such as water or potato broth, these will substitute perfectly.

DEHYDRATED VEGETABLES - Any dried vegetable may be used in soup making. Onion and garlic flakes, celery flakes, and diced carrots are perhaps the dried vegetables most commonly used. Others well worth trying are green beans, bell peppers, cabbage, corn, mushrooms, peas, potatoes, spinach flakes, tomato flakes, carrots, and celery flakes. Special vegetable blends have also been developed with the soup cook in mind. Hearty Stew Blend, Vegetables Soup Blend, and Vegetables Deluxe Soup Blend are three varieties which provide a nice shortcut when it comes time to add vegetables to your stock!

When cooking with dried vegetables, remember that vegetables which are cut very small (flakes or small cubes, for example) will best contribute flavor to your soup stock if allowed to cook for a long period. Larger vegetables - added for bulk, color, and their own individual flavors - may be added closer to serving time. Generally, dried vegetables are reconstituted before use. Soupmaking simplifies this process, as you may simply allow the vegetables to reconstitute while cooking. An added bonus is that the great nutritional value of the liquid used to reconstitute is included in your final meal.

Allow the dried vegetables in your soup to reconstitute before adding sweeteners, salt, or spices, as they will hinder the absorption process. Experiment with various ingredients, and make note of the results. For example, cabbages and carrots tend to slightly sweeten a soup, and potatoes are great for making any soup or chowder heartier.

When substituting dried vegetables for the fresh ones called for in a recipe, 1/2 cup of dried generally equals one cup of fresh. Dried vegetables, even when reconstituted, do not look or taste exactly like fresh. They can contribute their own unique qualities, however, particularly for a creative and resourceful cook.

Herbs, Spices And Other Seasonings

Herbs and spices are essential to the art of soupmaking. In a few soups, they are the central theme. Generally, however, they serve to enhance and complement the other soup ingredients. Almost any available spice and many herbs can be used in seasoning soups.

Some of the most commonly used are:

BASIL - good with tomato-base soups and many vegetables.

BAY LEAF - used in stews and with beans and vegetables. Remove the leaves before serving!

CAYENNE - adds spicy hotness, and may be used in place of black pepper.

CELERY SEED - a strong, distinctive flavor, to be used sparingly. Whole seeds should be cooked for at least an hour, while ground seed may be added towards the end of cooking.

CHERVIL - a pungent addition to many thin soups, sometimes substituted for parsley.

CHILI POWDER - most often found in chili stews, but also delicious in some other soups.

CUMIN - good in vegetable soups, chili, and other bean soups, as well as Mexican and Indian soups.

CURRY - a mild curry tastes great in soups containing grains, vegetables, lentils, or split peas.

DILL - fragrant and delicious in potato or onion soups. Dill weed is best added near the end of cooking while the seed needs to cook for a long period and is best used ground.

FENNEL - strong tasting, small amounts are good in squash soup and beef stew.

GARLIC - used in small amounts, garlic adds wonderful flavor to most any soup. It is available in a variety of forms— fresh, powdered, granulated, and flaked. Granulated is easy to measure and dissolves nicely if allowed to cook a few minutes before serving. Powdered is less strong than granulated.

MARJORAM - flavorful in minestrone, onion, chicken, and potato soups.

ONION - many soups start with the sauteéing of onions, and for good reason! Onion is available in the same forms as garlic.

PARSLEY - may be added to almost any soup. It adds lovely color and a refreshing taste. While fresh parsley is sometimes tough in soups, dried parsley is consistently tasty, easy to measure, colorful, and delicate.

ROSEMARY - strong-flavored, to be used very sparingly.

THYME - good with vegetable and rice soups

SEA SALT - If you choose to salt soup, do so very sparingly. It should serve to bring out, not dominate the other flavors. Sea salt contains trace minerals and is free of additives sometimes found in table salt.

Spice Blends

Several spice blends are now available, each with its own unique flavor. Try them in small amounts to determine which contain combinations that are pleasing to you. Blends which might be suitable for soup cookery include All-Seasons Salt, Celery Salt, Garlic Salt, Herbal Seasoning (no salt), Italian Seasoning, Mexican Seasoning, Onion Salt, and Spike.

With the help of seasoning, the possible results in soupmaking are endless. Try different combinations, but remember not to overseason. Take a small amount of soup from your pot and season it lightly. When you like the results, season the contents in your soup pot similarly. Remember that some herbs such as bay leaves, celery seed, rosemary, and thyme require longer cooking times for best results.

Even the most experienced cook sometimes ruins a soup. There are times when it will be salvageable. For a burnt soup, use small amounts of different seasonings to mask the flavor, or add potatoes to absorb some of the burnt taste (dehydrated potatoes work fine). Potatoes will also absorb the strong flavor of a soup which has been oversalted, as will dairy products such as milk or yogurt. If all else fails, compost it, but make note of where you went wrong— a good homemade soup is worth the practice!

Recipes

Bean Soup With Swiss Chard

1 onion, finely minced (or 1/4 cup onion flakes)
1 small clove garlic, minced (or 3/4 teaspoon garlic flakes)
3 tablespoons olive or corn oil
1/4 cup tomato purée
1/4 cup water
2 cups cooked navy or kidney beans
3 cups vegetable stock or water
1 carrot, diced (or 1/4 cup dried carrots, diced)
1/2 cup celery leaves, chopped (or 1/4 cup dried celery flakes)
2 cups Swiss chard, shredded
1/2 teaspoon sea salt
dash of black pepper
1/4 teaspoon basil
1 teaspoon oregano or marjoram
chopped parsley for garnish

In a saucepan, saute' onion and garlic in oil until lightly browned. Add tomato purée and water, and let this basic sauce simmer about 15 minutes, or until it has cooked down and needs water.

Add beans, stock, carrot, celery leaves, chard and seasonings. Cover and cook over medium heat until vegetables are soft.

Put soup through a food mill or strain through a colander, and put all vegetables in a blender to liquefy. You will have a thick, creamy soup that can be thinned if desired and seasoned to individual taste. Garnish with chopped parsley.

For a hearty supper dish, try this soup thinned down with brown rice or egg noodles cooked in it.

Makes 4 servings.

—adapted from **The Green Thumb Cookbook** *by Anne Moyer*

Curried Carrot Soup

1 medium onion, chopped (or 1/4 cup onion flakes)
2 tablespoons butter
4 carrots, thinly sliced (or 1 cup dried carrots, diced)
4 cups chicken broth (made from chicken-flavored broth powder)
1/4 teaspoon lemon juice
1 teaspoon curry powder
sea salt and black pepper to taste
1/4 cup sprouts, chopped

Saute' onion in the butter in a saucepan until golden.

Add carrots, broth, lemon juice and curry powder. Bring to a boil, cover, and simmer 20 minutes or until carrots are tender.

Add salt and pepper to taste.

Put half the mixture into blender and blend until smooth.

Stir blended soup back into remaining soup, add chopped sprouts and heat until hot.

Makes 3 to 4 servings.

—adapted from **The Green Thumb Cookbook** *by Anne Moyer*

Potato Pea Soup

1 pound leeks
1 tablespoon butter
1 pound potatoes, thinly sliced
3 cups stock (made from Vegetable broth powder)
2 tablespoons lemon juice
1 cup peas (or 1/2 cup dried peas)
1 egg
1/2 cup milk
1 tablespoon dried parsley
1 tablespoon dill
1 tablespoon chives

Trim the green stems off the leeks and save for future bouquets garnis. Trim off the root ends. Cut each leek in half lengthwise. Wash under cold running water to remove the dirt between its layers. Slice thinly.

Place the leeks and butter in a large pot. Cover and cook over low heat for about 20 minutes or until the leeks are soft.

Add the potatoes, stock and lemon juice to the pot. Cook, covered, until potatoes are soft. Uncover, add the peas and simmer until they are just cooked.

Pureé in batches in a blender to the desired smoothness. Combine the egg and milk in a small cup, and, with the blender running, add the egg mixture to a single batch of soup. Then stir this into the remainder of pureéd soup.

Sprinkle with parsley, dill and chives.

Serves 4.

—adapted from **Cooking With the Healthful Herbs** *by Jean Rogers*

Cool Cucumber Soup
2 medium cucumbers
1 cup buttermilk
1/4 cup parsley
1 teaspoon chives
1/2 teaspoon dill
1/4 teaspoon mint
pinch of tarragon
2 teaspoons lemon juice
1 1/2 cups yogurt

If the cucumbers have been waxed, peel them. Cut in half lengthwise and scoop out the seeds. Cut the flesh into chunks.

Place the cucumbers, buttermilk, parsley, chives, dill, mint, tarragon and lemon juice in a blender.

Blend at high speed for 10 to 15 seconds or until finely chopped.

Transfer to a bowl. Whisk in yogurt and chill before serving.

Serves 4.

—adapted from ***Cooking With the Healthful Herbs*** *by Jean Rogers*

Chilled Peach Soup
4 large peaches
1 1/2 cups water
2 tablespoons honey
1 cinnamon stick
3 whole cloves
2 teaspoons cornstarch
1/4 cup water
1/2 cup yogurt or sour cream

Remove the peach stones. Add peaches and 1 1/2 cups of water to a blender. Purée until smooth.

Transfer the peach purée to a large saucepan. Add the honey, cinnamon stick and cloves. Bring to a boil and simmer for 10 minutes, stirring frequently. Remove the cinnamon stick and cloves.

Dissolve the cornstarch in a 1/4 cup of water, and stir into the pot. Cook for a minute or two longer.

Chill the soup. Whisk in yogurt or sour cream before serving.

Serves 4.

—adapted from ***Cooking With the Healthful Herbs*** *by Jean Rogers*

Bean and Corn Soup
1 cup dried white beans
4 cups water or milk
1 onion, chopped (or 1/4 cup onion flakes)
2 garlic cloves (or 1 1/2 teaspoons garlic flakes)
1 teaspoon turmeric
1 teaspoon cumin
2 cups corn
sea salt to taste

Cook beans with onion, garlic, and spices in simmering liquid. When tender, purée, then add corn and salt to taste. Reheat and serve.

Makes 4 servings.
*—adapted from **Stocking Up**, edited by Carol Hupping Stoner*

Black Bean Soup
1 cup dried black beans
4 cups water
3 bay leaves
2 garlic cloves (or 1 1/2 teaspoons garlic flakes)
1/4 teaspoon dry mustard
1 1/2 teaspoons chili powder
2 onions, chopped (or 1/2 cup onion flakes)
sea salt to taste
Add ingredients except salt to boiling water and simmer until tender. Pureé. Salt to taste and serve.
Makes 4 servings.
*—adapted from **Stocking Up**, edited by Carol Hupping Stoner*

Greek Lemon Soup (Avgalemono)
6 cups concentrated chicken stock (made from chicken-flavored broth powder)
1/2 cup raw, brown rice
sea salt to taste
1 egg
2 egg yolks
1/4 cup lemon juice
2 tablespoons parsley
1/8 teaspoon cayenne
fresh dill to garnish (dash of dried dill weed may be substituted)
Put chicken broth into heavy saucepan or soup kettle and bring to a boil. Add brown rice to soup, season with salt and cook until rice is tender - 15 to 20 minutes.
Put whole egg and two egg yolks into medium-sized bowl; beat with rotary beater or wire whisk until light and frothy. Slowly add the lemon juice, beating together thoroughly.
Just before serving: dilute the egg-lemon mixture with one cup hot broth, beating constantly with wire whisk until well blended. Gradually add the diluted mixture to the remaining hot soup, stirring constantly. Bring almost to the boiling point - do not boil or the soup will curdle. Stir in the parsley and cayenne; adjust seasoning.
Remove from heat and serve immediately, garnished with freshly chopped dill.
Makes about 6 cups.
*—adapted from **The Rodale Cookbook** by Nancy Albright*

Cream of Pumpkin Soup
1 1/2 tablespoons onion, finely-diced (or 2 teaspoons onion flakes)
3 tablespoons oil
2 tablespoons rye flour
4 1/2 cups chicken stock (made from chicken-flavored broth powder)
1 1/2 tablespoons cornstarch
1/2 cup water
2 1/4 cups pumpkin pureé
3/4 teaspoon ginger
1/4 teaspoon nutmeg

1 cup skim milk powder
1 cup water
sea salt to taste
white pepper to taste
3 egg yolks, lightly-beaten
parsley for garnish

Saute' onion in oil until tender. Stir in the rye flour and cook over low heat, stirring constantly. Gradually add the chicken stock, stirring with wire whisk until mixture is smooth and boils. Mix cornstarch with water and add to mixture, stirring until it begins to thicken and boils again. Add pumpkin purée and spices. Transfer to the top of a double boiler at this point.

Combine skim milk powder with water, using a wire whisk. Add to soup and heat thoroughly. Add salt and pepper, to taste. Shortly before serving time, add some of the hot soup slowly to the beaten egg yolks, stirring constantly. Then add this mixture to the hot soup gradually.

Keep soup warm but do not overcook or the soup will curdle. Garnish with chopped parsley. Makes about 8 cups.

—adapted from ***The Rodale Cookbook*** *by Nancy Albright*

Toppings

Toppings can be used to enhance and individualize even the simplest of dishes. Use herbs and spices to prepare delicious dressings, dips, and sauces, and you'll go a long way towards becoming a great cook. Below are some guidelines and suggested seasonings for making basic toppings. Be sure to look to your herb and spice rack for inspiration, as well, and experiment often!

Salad Dressings

Salad dressings are a perfect place to start. Anyone who enjoys an array of greens from the local market or her/his own garden can whip up a complementary dressing at a moment's notice. Keep a good quality oil on hand. Olive, safflower, sesame, or any vegetable oil is fine, if the taste is delicate and not overpowering. Also stock vinegar or lemons. Here again, there are several options— apple cider vinegar, wine vinegar, white vinegar, herb vinegar, and lemon juice.

To make an herb vinegar, simply place a handful of a favorite herb in a wine bottle filled with vinegar. (White vinegar works best here.) Cork and store in the sunlight for about three weeks. Strain and bottle. Some of the most suitable herbs for such vinegars are tarragon, basil, elderflower, chives, mint, savory, lemon balm, thyme, lemon thyme, and oregano.

The ratio for preparing a basic salad dressing is 1/2 cup of vinegar or lemon juice per cup of oil. To this standard recipe, you may add infinite variations of herbs and spices. Try alone, or in combination: paprika, mustard, garlic, basil, thyme, dill, celery seed, chives, tarragon, marjoram, parsley, and oregano. A small amount goes a long way. Blend well and taste. Perhaps it needs a touch of tamari, or a pinch of salt and pepper, another herb, or a dab of honey. If you prefer a creamy dressing, add yogurt, buttermilk, skim milk, mayonnaise, or sour cream. Homemade mayonnaise, made with herbs and spices in your own kitchen, is special enough to serve alone as a salad dressing.

For a very simple creamy salad dressing, mix equal parts yogurt and mayonnaise. Add a touch of vinegar or lemon juice, a dab of honey, and your favorite herb. Mix well.

Recipes for salad dressings are bountiful, ranging from simple oil and vinegar dressings (as described above) to luscious blends using fresh vegetables or condiments such as pickles and catsup. Try a new one with your salad each day!

Dry Toppings

Green salads and many other foods may be topped with other ingredients as well. Try roasted sesame or sunflower seeds, poppy seeds, nutritional yeast, or natural cheese flavoring powders. Gomasio, an excellent salad topper, is made by mixing ground roasted sesame seeds and a small amount of sea salt.

Sauces

Many salad dressing ingredients are also used to prepare tasty sauces to serve on grains, potatoes, pasta, fish, or vegetables. Use the sauce recipes from your favorite cookbooks, but learn to individualize them, too. Delete salt or sugar, if it suits your needs. Add your favorite herbs and spices, and nutritious ingredients such as sesame seeds, psyllium seed, carob powder (for dessert sauces), or nutritional yeast.

As a rough guideline for preparing sauces, use about 1/4 teaspoon dried herb for each cup of vegetable or grain, etc., to be served. Rub the dried herb in your hand before measuring. Add one ingredient at a time, tasting after each addition. To most sauces, add herbs and spices at the start of cooking, since they generally cook for only short periods of time and will not lose their aroma and flavor. When blending uncooked sauces, dressings and dips, add well ahead of serving time to allow the flavors to meld.

Sauces are extremely versatile, and the variety is enormous: white sauces, pestos, tomato sauces, cheese sauces, dessert sauces, sweet and sour sauces, yogurt sauces, barbeque sauces, salsas, lemon sauces...

A simple sauce to serve on vegetables is made by blending one stick of softened butter with one tablespoon of lemon juice. Add an herb or two, whip, and store in the refrigerator. Serve whenever you need a sauce for boiled potatoes, cooked spinach, or any hot vegetable. Good additions to this easy sauce, as well as many white, cheese, or yogurt sauces, are: parsley, oregano, basil, dill, fennel, tarragon, chives, thyme, and savory.

Tomato sauces favor garlic, oregano, and basil, of course, and hot sauces a variety of mild to hot peppers. Try some of the pre-blended herbal combinations available: Pizza seasoning, Italian seasoning, curry powders, salsas, Bar-b-quick, Herbal seasoning, Mexican seasoning. Consider pre-mixing your own blends, too. You might stock your herb and spice rack with your own blends for quick dressings, sauces, and dips. Be sure to keep notes in your recipe file so you can duplicate recipes when the jars are emptied.

Dips

Dips are similar to sauces and can also be used in a variety of ways. When used for fresh raw vegetables, chips, crackers, cheese cubes, or fruit slices, dips make lovely hors d'oeuvres out of otherwise plain snacks. Cottage cheese, sour cream, yogurt, mayonnaise, mashed beans or tofu, and avocados all make excellent bases for dips. Once your base is the right consistency, all you need do is flavor with herbs and spices and/or other condiments. Dips are very easy to make, and great fun for creative cooks. Unusual combinations such as chick peas and orange juice or avocados and tahini really add zest to a cracker or pepper slice! Salsa, mentioned as a sauce above, is a great dip when mixed to a thick consistency. When preparing any dip, blend your base with the herbs and spices several hours in advance. While chilling, the flavors will distribute evenly. For creamy dips, try savory, thyme, onion, chives, caraway seeds, lovage, rosemary, parsley, dill, sage, and basil (just for starters!). Basil and oregano work well in tomato dips, while bean dips are enhanced by garlic, cumin, ginger, coriander, hot peppers, mustard, and parsley.

Fondues

Remember fondues? Once popular as a dip for French bread slices, this hot cheesy dip is also excellent for topping fruit pieces, vegetable slices, cakes, crackers, and a variety of whole wheat breads. Let's reintroduce fondues with a healthy, interesting twist. To any basic fondue recipe, add roasted sesame or sunflower seeds, and of course, a delicate sprinkling of herbs and spices. Paprika, tarragon, parsley, lemon thyme, nutmeg, and white pepper come to mind.

Learn to spice up your dishes with herbal toppings. Experiment to determine your favorite herb and spice uses and combinations, and you will find yourself becoming a more interesting and successful artisan in the kitchen.

Recipes

Poppy Seed Dressing
1/3 cup honey
2/3 cup oil (safflower, olive, etc.)
1 1/2 teaspoon prepared brown mustard
1-2 tablespoons poppy seed
1/8 cup cider vinegar
1/8 cup lemon juice
1 teaspoon tamari
Combine all ingredients in jar or shaker. Cover tightly, shake vigorously.
Yield: 1 cup.
This is especially good on delicate leafy greens. Try adding strawberries as an added plus to this salad. A taste surprise!
—P. Kaplan

Curried Chervil Dip
1 teaspoon curry powder
1 teaspoon butter
1 teaspoon yogurt
1/2 cup sour cream
2 teaspoons lemon juice
1 tablespoon minced parsley
1 tablespoon snipped chives
1 tablespoon minced chervil or 1 teaspoon dried chervil
In a small pan cook the curry powder in butter for 2 minutes to release its flavor. In a bowl, whisk together the curry power, yogurt, sour cream, lemon juice, parsley, chives, and chervil. Chill.
Makes 1 cup.
—from ***Cooking With the Healthful Herbs*** *by Jean Rogers*

Tofu Dip
1 16 oz. block tofu
1/2 cup Vegetable Deluxe Soup Blend
1/2 teaspoon Bar-B-Quick
1/8 teaspoon garlic powder
1 cup water
1/4 teaspoon salt
1/2 teaspoon sesame oil
1 tablespoon dried chives
Mix vegetables, water, oil, and salt together and set aside. Place tofu in processor and process until very, very smooth. Pour into bowl. Add vegetable mixture, blending well. Add spices; then fold in chives. Refrigerate. Taste after dip has been chilling for 2 hours. Spices may need to be adjusted for your palate. Add water for desired consistency.
—P. Kaplan

Pickling

Pickling is thought to have been invented by the Chinese, who carried salted vegetables with them while working on the Great Wall of China. In America, the Pennsylvania Dutch are well known for their pickle recipes, and each meal served by this ethnic group is accompanied by complimentary pickles and relishes.

There are four kinds of pickled products, classified by the ingredients as well as method of preparation used:

BRINED PICKLES - Brined pickles, which go through a three week curing process, usually include sauerkraut and pickling cucumbers. The brine draws the moisture and natural sugars from the foods and forms lactic acid to preserve them. Brined (fermented) pickles are made in a low-salt brine (3-5% salt) and do not require desalting. Cucumbers may be cured in a high salt (10% salt) brine and are soaked in water before processing.

FRESH-PACK OR QUICK PROCESS PICKLES - These pickles are the easiest to prepare. They are usually soaked for several hours in a low-salt brine, drained, and processed with boiling hot vinegar, spices, herbs and seasonings. Cucumbers, green beans, mushrooms, and mixed vegetables may be prepared in this manner.

FRUIT PICKLES - Whole fruits— pears, peaches, watermelon rind— are simmered in spicy, sweet-sour syrup, then processed. They are delicious served by themselves, or with other foods.

RELISHES - Prepared from a combination of chopped, seasoned, and cooked fruits and vegetables, relishes are most attractive when uniform in size and brightly colored. They may be hot and spicy or sweet and spicy. Relish products include piccalilli (salted fruits or vegetables and spices and vinegars), chutneys (oriental mixture of chopped fruits, vegetables, nuts, and berries eaten as a condiment), corn relish (corn combined with small amounts of other vegetables and spices), catsup (tomatoes, chopped vegetables, and spices), and horseradish (a hot relish made from horseradish root).

Ingredients

FRUITS AND VEGETABLES - Use freshly picked, tender fruits and vegetables in perfect condition. Cut cucumbers from the vine to prevent rotting where the stem is broken from the skin. Clean carefully, being careful not to bruise.

VINEGAR - Use only a good grade of 40-60 grain strength vinegar. Distilled vinegar is clear and does not discolor white produce such as onion or cauliflower, as cider vinegar will. Many prefer cider vinegar, however, for its digestibility, flavor, and aroma.

HONEY - Light honey is generally preferred to dark for pickling because the strong flavor of dark honey can be overpowering. Add honey after the syrup has been boiled, to prevent a change in color and flavor in the honey.

WATER - Because the iron or sulphur in hard water will darken pickles, soft water is recommended.

SALT - Iodized salt may cause darkening of pickled products, while table salt can cause cloudiness. Sea salt, dairy salt, rock salt, or pickling salt are all acceptable.

SEASONINGS - The seasonings chosen are what give pickled products their characteristic flavors. Always use whole, fresh spices and herbs. Tie them in cheesecloth or a bag if they are to be removed before packing. Ground herbs and spices tend to darken pickles and whole spices may cause an off flavor if left in the jar after canning. Because spices vary in strength, test your liquid before canning and adjust the seasonings. A grape leaf added to each jar will insure crispness.

Here is a list of the most commonly used pickling seasonings:

allspice	cloves	cinnamon
mace	celery seed	turmeric
fennel	garlic	pickling spice
dill	onion	mustard seed
cayenne	ginger	peppercorns, black and white
bay leaves	horseradish	caraway seed
red pepper		

Recipes

If you are unfamiliar with canning, be sure to study the directions in a reliable cookbook. The following pickling recipes are taken from the excellent reference book, ***Stocking Up**, edited by Carol Hupping Stoner.*

Fresh-Pack Dill Pickles
(unsweetened)
17 to 18 pounds cucumbers, 3 to 5 inches in length (pack 7 to 10 per quart jar)
2 gallons 5 percent brine (3/4 cup salt per gallon water)
6 cups (1 1/2 quarts) vinegar
3/4 cup salt
9 cups water
2 tablespoons whole mixed pickling spice
2 teaspoons whole mustard seed per quart jar
1 or 2 garlic cloves per quart jar
1 tablespoon dill seed per quart jar.
Wash cucumbers thoroughly, scrub with vegetable brush, and drain. Cover with brine. Let set overnight. Drain.
Combine vinegar, salt, water, and mixed pickling spices tied in a clean, white cloth bag or spice ball. Heat to boiling. Pack cucumbers in hot, sterilized quart jars. Add mustard seed,

garlic, and dill to each jar. Cover with boiling liquid to within 1/4 inch of top of jar. Adjust seals and process in boiling-water bath for 15 minutes.
Makes 7 quarts.

Bread and Butter Pickles
30 medium-sized cucumbers
10 medium-sized onions
4 tablespoons salt
Slice cucumbers and onions and sprinkle with salt. Let stand 1 hour. Drain in cheese-cloth bag. Make a spiced vinegar using the following ingredients:

5 cups vinegar
2 teaspoons celery seed
2 teaspoons ground ginger
2 cups honey
1 teaspoon turmeric
2 teaspoons white mustard seed
Let spiced vinegar come to a boil, add cucumbers and onions, and bring to boiling point. Pack in jars, leaving 1/4 inch headspace. Adjust seals and process 10 minutes in a boiling-water bath.
Makes 8 pints.

Pickled Beets
1 gallon small beets
water to cover beets
1 tablespoon whole allspice
1 long stick cinnamon
1 quart vinegar
1 cup honey
Cook beets with roots and about 2 inches of stem left on in water to cover. Cook until tender; dip beets into cold water and slip off skins. Put beets in large preserving kettle. Combine the spices and vinegar, pour over beets and simmer 15 minutes. Then add the honey. Pack hot into sterilized jars. Cover beets with boiling syrup, leaving 1/4 inch headspace. Adjust seals and process pint and quart jars 10 minutes in a boiling-water bath.
Makes 3 to 4 quarts.

Sweet and Sour Cabbage
4 quart finely shredded red cabbage
4 tart apples, diced
1 1/2 quarts cider vinegar
1 or 2 cups water (sufficient amount for juice)
4 teaspoons sea salt
1/2 teaspoon peppercorns
2 teaspoons caraway seed
1/2 teaspoon mace (optional)
1/2 whole allspice
1/4 teaspoon cinnamon pieces
1 cup honey
Place spices in a spice bag and simmer with all the ingredients except honey in a large

pot for 20 to 25 minutes. Remove spice bag and add honey. Pack into hot pint jars to within 1/4 inch of the top. Process in a boiling-water bath for 15 minutes.

This cabbage will be much too stout for most people to eat from the jar, but it is delectable when the juice is drained off and it is simmered in a small amount of water.

Makes 4 quarts.

Spiced Sweet Apples

1 quart vinegar
2 cups water
1 ounce allspice
1 ounce cinnamon stick
4 cloves
4 cups honey
7 pounds sweet apples, quartered and cored

Put vinegar, water, and spices in pot. Bring to a boil. Add honey and apples, bring to a boil, and simmer gently until the fruit is tender.

Place the apple quarters in hot, sterilized jars, bring syrup to a boil, and pour over the apples, leaving 1/4 inch headspace. Adjust seals and process 10 minutes in a boiling-water bath.

Makes 4 pints.

Herbal Crafting

Herbal Crafts

There is a special satisfaction in making things with herbs and spices. Crafts items can individualize and warm your home, and while everyone appreciates hand-made gifts, the addition of scent so often found in herbal crafts makes them seem particularly "homemade." As with any crafts projects, herbal crafts range from extremely simple to fairly involved. Here I'll describe just a few projects to get you started. With a little imagination, you'll be designing many herbal craft items yourself.

Before starting any of these projects, gather all your materials and arrange them in an orderly fashion before you. Be sure to use quality items— to insure vivid colors, distinctive scents, and beautiful results.

Pomanders

In Medieval times, pomanders were small, round combinations of herbs and spices, worn on the person to ward off disease, and provide relief from the many foul smells. While they were most often worn around the neck, or attached to the belt, they were sometimes placed in ornate, open containers. This carefully-blended concoction of perfumes and fixatives resembled an apple, or "pomme."

Today pomanders are most often found hanging in closets, and are made in the following manner:

—In separate bowls, assemble whole cloves, a mixture of ground spices (cinnamon, cloves, nutmeg, and ginger work nicely), and a fixative such as orris root powder.

—Select a firm, unbruised orange, lemon, lime, or apple.

—Push the whole cloves into the fruit, covering the surface by setting the cloves head to head. It is best to accomplish this task in one sitting, as overnight drying of the fruit will make the task more difficult.

—Roll the clove-studded fruit in ground spices, covering thoroughly.

—Roll in the fixative.

—Set aside to dry for about one month.

To use the pomander, run a string or ribbon around it and hang in a closet or room. (You may instead pierce the top with a needle to run a string through for hanging.) Or wrap the pomander in a fancy net or fabric and place in drawers or chests. A bowl full of pomanders will add drama and a sweet fragrance to any room.

Sachets and Pillows

Sachets are another way to add scent to your closets, chests, and drawers. Basically, sachets are very small pillows, filled with lovely-scented herbs and spices. Ground mixtures work best for sachets, as compared to coarse or whole pieces often used in potpourris. You might want to buy a pre-blended sachet mixture, or specially concoct your own. You may follow directions for potpourri blending, although simple sachets may be made by using one of the following dried herbs alone: lavender flowers, lilac, rose, mints, rosemary, and thyme (See *Potpourri Blending*, page 171). Be sure to try the herbal blend "Herbal Mothless" in sachets for clothes in storage.

For a simple sachet, make a bag by measuring and cutting fabric to the desired size (small squares are common). Sew the fabric, right sides together, on three sides. Turn and press. Fill with your sachet blend, and hand sew the fourth edge closed. Remnants of decorative fabric such as satin, silk, lace, cotton, or muslin work well. To really individualize your creation, decorate with fringe, lace, ribbons, beads, or embroidery.

You can even make a sachet without sewing a stitch! Simply place your blend in a piece of fabric with pinked edges. Fold up the corners and tie with a ribbon. A pretty handkerchief may be used instead of the pinked fabric, and it looks especially nice when tied with satin or velvet. Tiny manilla envelopes, filled with sachet herbs, also do the trick, and may be decorated as well. Herb pillows were customarily used to help people sleep, and were thought to induce dreams. They still make lovely gifts, and children love them.

To make an herb pillow, measure and cut your fabric to desired size - eight inches square seems to be a good average. Sew the fabric, right sides together, on three sides. Turn and press. Fold blended herbs and fixative into an appropriately-sized piece of batting. The batting will make the pillow soft, while enclosing the herbs. Slip the herbs into the sewn fabric and hand sew the fourth side closed. To strengthen the scent, place the pillow in a plastic bag for about 24 hours before using.

Here's a good dream pillow recipe:

Combine equal parts mugwort, mint, chamomile, lemon verbena, and two teaspoons of orris root powder for each eight-inch pillow.

Wreaths

Depending on the desired effect, wreaths may be made using a variety of materials. Grapevine wreaths, decorated with dried flowers and ribbons, are very popular now. You can create a wreath suited for a special season or holiday, or for year-round use. Here are directions for a simple straw wreath. (Plain straw or grapevine wreaths are available in craft shops.)

Dissolve any pleasing combination of fragrance or essential oils in alcohol and spray a straw wreath until it is saturated, then allow to dry. Glue on spices, whole bay leaves, pine cones, whole dried flowers such as strawflowers, globe amaranth, and life everlasting, or other materials in patterns. String cinnamon sticks on florist's wire and zig-zag them around the form. Additional wire can be used to hold the sticks in place. Vanilla beans, long cinnamon sticks, and licorice root pieces can be combined with silk flowers and foliage to make an attractive display. You may even want to pin sachet or potpourri wrapped in bridal netting to the wreath for an additional touch of fragrance. Circle the wreath with ribbons and lace, and pin to the back with T-pins. Give a final touch to your creation by adding a colorful bow.

—from ***Potpourri, The Art of Fragrance Crafting*** *by Louise Gruenberg*

Incense

Incense is used to perfume a room and is easily made. Here is an easy recipe:

Stick incense
7 parts sandalwood powder
1 part ground cinnamon

1/2 part saltpeter
a few drops ylang ylang or nutmeg oil
gum arabic or tragacanth

Mix first four ingredients. Dilute gum in water to form a thin paste. Add to other incense ingredients. Use enough gum to form a consistency to adhere to splints. Dip splints in the mixture and stick them in a polystyrene block or limp of modeling clay to dry.

Here are two more recipes, both from ***The Rodale Herb Book*** *by William H. Hylton.*

Frankincense Incense

Combine: 2 tablespoons frankincense powder, 1 tablespoon orris root powder, and 1 tablespoon clove powder. Stir 1 tablespoon lemon oil thoroughly into the powdered mixture. Place in a cool dark area for 2-3 months. To use, sprinkle a little on some burning charcoal.

Light Floral Incense

Combine: 2 tablespoons ground rose petals, 2 tablespoons ground lavender flowers, and 1 tablespoon vetiver powder. In another small bowl mix 1/2 teaspoon lemon oil and 1/2 teaspoon lavender oil. Blend oils through the dry mixture. Store several months before using. Use by sprinkling on a piece of burning charcoal.

Holiday Decorations

Many of the crafts items mentioned above make perfect holiday gifts, and some may be crafted especially with the holidays in mind. Decorate wreaths with small pine cones or mistletoe, tie pomanders with red and green ribbons, make herbal pillows using holiday fabric. Other decorations may also be made by using herbs and spices. Small cinnamon sticks wrapped in ribbon look pretty on a tree, while long ones tied with Holiday ribbon make a nice centerpiece. Paint pinecones to use for tree decorations, or hang them in bunches from thin ribbons. Use your festive imagination!

There are many other herbal crafts to indulge in— herbal candles, rose beads, scented lining paper and writing paper, catnip mice, herbal toys for children. Leaf through craft books and think about how many of the projects can be adapted for use with crafts. Keep a folder of your ideas— you'll have so many you'll never remember them all!

Potpourri Blending

Potpourri is a scented blend of dried plant materials. These beautiful aromatic concoctions can be purchased ready-made or blended at home to suit your personal tastes and needs. You might develop a clean and minty blend to set in an old teapot in your kitchen, a flowery and sweet blend in a basket for your bedroom, or a blend containing lavender sewn into small pillows or "sachets" to scatter in dresser drawers. Potpourri blending is creative, fun, and easy to do.

No fancy equipment is required. A large stainless steel, ceramic, or glass bowl, measuring cups and spoons, a wooden stirring spoon, and glass jars with tight-fitting lids are all you will need. After you've become an avid potpourri blender, you may want to purchase a heavy mortar and pestle reserved for potpourri crafting.

Most dry potpourri blends contain a mixture of herbs and spices, a fixative, and essential oil. (Wet potpourri is a process in which moist plant materials are combined with fermenting agents such as salt, brandy, or orange peel and set in a ceramic pot for several weeks. Dry potpourri, as described here, is a more popular method today.) The herbs and spices used may include flower petals, or blossoms, leaves, seeds, barks, and roots. Citrus peels are often used as well.

Recipes will specify ingredients by volume. The following equivalents may prove helpful to you:

1/3 cup of powdered or ground items yields about one ounce.
3/4 cups of fine dried herbs, such as rosemary, yields about one ounce.
1 cup of dried petals or leafy herbs yields about one ounce.

You may choose to follow specific recipes in the beginning, and develop your own blends as you become more comfortable with the craft.

A *main scent* is usually chosen as a base for the blend. Choose a fragrance which pleases you and suits your purpose. Rose petals, jasmine flowers, lemon verbena, and lavender are often used singly or in combination for this purpose. *Secondary* or *additional scents* are combined to modify or enhance the main fragrance. While almost any plant material can be used, keep in mind the results you hope to obtain. *Color, texture* and *aroma* are all important considerations in judging the success of your final product.

In fact, your primary concern in developing a blend may be aesthetic. Many beautiful products are available to help you create with color and texture in mind. Crafting a potpourri in this manner may involve blending a product that which looks appealing and then adding spices and essential oils to imbibe it with a pleasing scent. Scents are volatile and quickly evaporate without the use of *fixatives*, mandatory ingredients for long-lasting potpourris.

Fixatives hold the scent, releasing it slowly over a long period of time while adding their own subtle aromas. Orris and veviter roots are common fixatives. Fixatives are generally used in the proportion of 1/4 to 1/2 cup (depending on the strength of the fixative) per quart of potpourri.

Essential oils are concentrated plant distillates, and are added to potpourris to intensify the scent. One to three oils may be added for a total of up to 15 drops per quart. Add these oils slowly, as a final ingredient. After allowing your potpourri to sit a while, you may determine that the scent needs to be strengthened; oil quantities may be increased at that time. The addition of several drops of essential oils may be also be used to revitalize old potpourris.

For those who like to experiment with scents, concocting potpourri blends is very rewarding. The method is simple and the possibilities are endless. Mix the ingredients carefully, using the wooden spoon and non-metal container. Start with a basic scent and add secondary substances as you develop the blend. Add the fixative and then the essential oils, one drop at a time. Gently mix. Remember that the overall scent will mellow with age. Place in a jar, cover, and store in a cool, dry, dark place, stirring occasionally. After several weeks your mixture will be ready to use. Place your new potpourri in an imaginative container (open bowls, baskets, pottery finds, antique jars, etc.) or sew into small pillows.

Simmering potpourris are becoming very popular because of their ability to quickly scent your entire home. As they need not be very attractive, these potpourris may be easily blended from herbs, spices, and oils whose scents appeal to you. Simply place your special blend in a pot of water and bring to a boil. Reduce heat and simmer, allowing the fragrance to envelop your home. Simmering potpourris are especially appreciated during the holiday season. Have fun experimenting!

Here is a recipe to get you started:

Floral Base

Allspice whole	*1/3 cup*
Balm of Gilead buds	*1/3 cup*
Lavender flowers	*1 cup*
Orange blossoms	*2/3 cup*
Pennyroyal	*1/3 cup*
Rosebuds-pink	*1 2/3 cups*
Rosebuds-red	*3 1/3 cups*
Woodruff c/s	*1 2/3 cups*
Malva flowers-blue	*1 cup*

Fixatives

Oak moss	*1 cup*
Orris root	*1/3 cup*
Sandalwood chips-yellow	*2/3 cup*

Oils

Carnation	*1/2 tsp.*
Jasmine	*1 tsp.*
Rose	*1 1/2 tsps.*
Total	***13 cups***

For more information on potpourris refer to the *Potpourris* section in this handbook. For more information on potpourri blending refer to ***Potpourri, The Art of Fragrance Crafting**, by Louise Gruenberg* and the *Crafts Botanical Chart* in this section.

Crafts Botanical Chart

BOTANICAL	COLOR	AROMA	TEXTURE	PRIMARY USE	OTHER USES
ALLSPICE	dark brown	spicy	small, round	texture	aroma
ANGELICA ROOT	white & brown	celery, herbal	small chunks	aroma	color, fixative
ANISE SEED	green-tan	sweet, licorice	small oblong seed	aroma	texture
ANNATTO	brick red	none	small flattened seed	color	texture
STAR ANISE	orange-brown	sweet, spicy	1" star-shaped	texture	aroma, color
ARNICA FLOWER	toast with gold flecks	delicate, carob	fuzzy	texture	color
BALM OF GILEAD	glossy orange-green-brown	beer, balsamic	1" cone shape	texture	aroma, color
BARBERRY BARK	turmeric yellow & tan	faint	small pieces	color	texture
BAY LEAF	green	spicy, menthol	2" oblong leaf	texture	aroma
BAYBERRY BARK	brown	bitter, woodsy	small chips	aroma	texture
BOUGANVILLIER	purple or white	none	1 1/4"-1 3/4" tissue thin	texture, color	
BROOM FLOWER	gold & brown	sweet grain	1/2" petals	color	aroma
BUCHU LEAF	green	pungent, earthy	1/2" lance	aroma	texture
CALAMUS ROOT	tan-brown	warm, woody	1/4" chunks	fixative	aroma, texture
CALCATRIPPAE	purple & green	light floral	strands of stem & petal	color	texture
CALENDULA	orange-yellow	light, corn	1" aster-like	color	texture
CARDAMON PODS	light green & tan	menthol	oblong 1/2" pod	texture	aroma
CEDAR CHIPS	red and white	woodsy	thin 1/2" shavings	aroma, color	texture
CELOSIA	purple/rose	none	1/2"-3/4" velvety, fan	texture, color	
CHAMOMILE FLOWER	white &yellow-green	softly fruity	small globes & petals	color	texture, aroma
CHAMOMILE, ROMAN	white	none	1/2" round, many rayed	color	texture
CINNAMON CHIPS	red-brown	spicy, warm	small to large pieces	aroma	texture, color
CINNAMON STICKS	chocolate brown	spicy, warm	1" long	aroma, texture	color
CLOVES	dark brown	spicy	1/2" torch-shaped	texture	aroma
CORIANDER SEED	brown & tan	faint	small ridged balls	texture	color
CORNFLOWER	blue-purple & green-brown	faint	1/2" tubular	color	texture
CUBEB BERRY	black & grey	spicy, peppery	small bead on a stem	texture	color
DAISY FLOWER	white, green & yellow	faint	small feathery	texture	color
DEER'S TONGUE	dark muted green	sweet, vanilla	3/4"-1 1/2" elongated lvs.	aroma	
ELDER BERRY	dark purple	sweet, fruity	small raisin-like	aroma, texture	color
ELDER FLOWER	yellow-tan	faint	tiny flowers	texture	color
EUCALYPTUS LEAF	green	menthol	1/4" pieces or 2" leaf	aroma	texture
FEVERFEW FLOWER	white	faint	3/4"	color, texture	
FRANKICENSE TEARS	translucent yellow	sharp, balsam*	1/4 - 1/2" clumps	aroma	texture
GINGER ROOT	tan-white	spicy, sharp	1/4" chunks or 2" roots	aroma	texture
GLOBE AMARANTH	pink-white or red-purple	none	1" spheres	color	texture
GUARANA SEED	dark brown	faintly sweet	1/4"-1/2" buckeyes	texture	color
HAWTHORNE BERRY	deep red	faint fruit	1/2" oval	texture	color
HEATHER FLOWER	lavender & green	none	tiny flowers	color	texture
HIBISCUS FLOWER	deep red to pink-red	faint citrus	1"sturdy flower	color	texture
HOP FLOWER	pale green	light, grassy	papery 1/2 x 3/4"	texture	color
JASMINE FLOWER	yellow-tan	light sweet	1/2" flowers & petals	texture	aroma
KESU FLOWER	brown & yellow & orange	faint	1" swirl	color	texture
LAVENDER	blue-purple	sweet, perfume	small lance-like	aroma	texture
LEMON GRASS	green	sharp lemon	1/4" grass pieces	aroma	texture
LEMON PEEL	brown-yellow	citrus	1/4" pieces	aroma	texture
LEMON THYME	bright green	soft lemon herbal	tiny leaf	aroma	color, texture
LEMON VERBENA	medium green	lemon	lancelike 3"	aroma	texture

Crafts Botanical Chart

BOTANICAL	COLOR	AROMA	TEXTURE	PRIMARY USE	OTHER USES
LIFE EVERLASTING	bright yellow	faint	1/2" flower clumps	color	texture
LIME PEEL	brown-tan	lime, citrus	1/4" irregular slices	aroma	simmering pot.
MACE (C&S)	orange brown	spicy, nutmeg	strips 1/2" or 1" fronds	aroma, color	texture
MACE (WHOLE)	pumpkin orange	spicy, nutmeg	1/2"x2"smth., hard fronds	aroma, color	texture
MALVA BLACK	black & pale green	sweet raspberry	1" flower	color	texture
MALVA BLUE	purple	faint, sweet	1" papery flower	color	texture
MINT LEAF	green	sweet menthol	small leaf or leaf pieces		
MOSS DYED GREEN	dark bright green	light pine, woody	soft, membrane-like	color	
MYRRH GUM	brown-red	sweet*	1/2" rough chunks	aroma	texture
NUTMEG PIECES	light brown	spicy, warm	1/2" chunks	aroma	texture
NUTMEG WHOLE	brown	spicy, warm	1" sphere	aroma	texture
OAK MOSS	silver-dark grey	soft sweet moss	1/2" feathery strips	color, texture	aroma, fixative
OLIVE LEAF	green-silver	faint	1 1/2" spears	texture	color
ORANGE PEEL	orange-brown	orange	1/4" or 1/2" pieces	aroma	texture, color
ORANGE PETALS	yellow-tan	very sweet, orange	1/2" lance petals	aroma	color
ORRIS ROOT	tan-white	sweet floral, violet	1/4" chunks	fixative	aroma
PATCHOULI	dark brown-black	earthy, pungent	1/4" herb pieces	aroma	
PENNYROYAL	green	menthol, mint	small	aroma	
PEPPERMINT WH.	muted green	minty, fresh	1/8"-1" leaves	aroma	texture, color
PEONY FLOWER	deep red with yellow	faint	2" clump	color	texture
PINE CONES	various	none	various	texture	color
POPPY FLOWER	deep red & burgundy	faint	large papery flower	color	texture
ROSEBUDS	red or pink	soft floral	1" flower	aroma, color	texture
ROSEHIPS	red	faint fruity	1/2" teardrop	color, texture	
ROSEMARY	medium green	herbal, menthol	3/4" needles	texture	aroma
SAFFLOWER PETALS	red-orange	faint, saffron	1/4" threadlike petals	color	texture
SAGE LEAF	grey-green	woodsy, sharp	1/2" leaf	aroma	color, texture
SANDALWOOD RED	bright red	faint	1/4" shreds	color	texture
SANDALWOOD YELLOW	tan & red-brown	woodsy	1/4" chips	aroma	texture
SASSAFRASS	red-brown	root beer	1/4" chunks	aroma	
SAW PALMETTO	black	sharp, cheesy	1/2" oval	texture	color
SENNA PODS	green/brown	none	1 1/2"-2" flattish pods	texture	
SOUTHERWOOD	green/yellow/brown	lemony	very small leaf pieces	aroma	moth mixtures
SPEARMINT WHOLE	muted green	minty, fresh	1/8"-1" leaves	aroma	texture
SPINA CRISTI	light green & tan	none	1" conical hats	texture	color
STATICE FLOWER	purple/pink w/ tan/green stems	none	1/2" fanlike	color	texture
STRAWFLOWER	bright fall shades	none	1" crisp	color	texture
SUMAC BERRY	rosy red	fruity	small flattened berry	texture	color
SUNFLOWER	golden-brown	faint	1" narrow petals	texture	color
TILIA STAR	red-brown	none	rigid 1/2" flower & stem	texture	color
TONKA BEAN	black	vanilla, sweet	1" bean	fixative	aroma, texture
UVA URSI LEAF	green	faint	1/2" teardrop	texture	color
VANILLA BEAN	dark brown	sweet, vanilla	6" narrow bean	aroma	
VETIVER ROOT	tan	woodsy	1" shreds	fixative	aroma
WOODRUFFF	dark green	sweet, hay	1" lance-like	aroma	texture
YARROW FLOWER	yellow-tan	faint	1" clumps	texture	

* These items give off their aroma only when heated.

Body Care

Hair & Skin Care

Since ancient times, herbs have been used as beauty aids. Perhaps Cleopatra's regimen included rosemary hair rinses, henna conditioners, rose petal baths, mint steams followed by clay masks. In fact, until the substitution of chemicals a century ago, herbs were the primary constitutents of cosmetics. A concern for what we put in our bodies has led to a return to natural, whole foods; a similar concern for what we put on our bodies has led to the re-introduction of natural methods of skin and hair care. Making your own herbal body care products is fun, effective, inexpensive, and usually very simple. Here are some guidelines to get you started.

Note: Although all of these products are natural, any of them could produce allergic reactions in some people. A skin patch test is recommended, particularly for people who tend to be sensitive, before applying unfamiliar products to the skin.

To conduct a skin patch test, apply the facial mask mixture, hair rinse, or whatever you plan to use, to a clean, one inch area on the inner part of your arm. Allow to dry. Leave undisturbed and uncovered for four hours. Rinse. Examine the area periodically during this period, looking for reddened, burning, or itching skin. Do not use the product if you seem sensitive to it.

Herbal Baths

Almost everyone enjoys luxuriating in a long bath now and then; the addition of herbs can enhance the experience! There are several methods of adding herbs to the bathwater, and depending on the herbs used, the result may be invigorating, soothing, relaxing, moisturizing...

Method 1 - Make a tea of one cup of herbs and one quart of water. Allow to steep about 15 minutes. Strain and pour the strong tea (or "infusion") into your bathwater.

Method 2 - Fill a mesh tea ball or infuser with herbs and put directly in your bath. If it has a chain with a hook on it, hang it from your tub faucet and allow the water to pour through the herbs. You can even hook it to your shower head for an herbal shower!

Method 3 - Use cheesecloth to wrap a handful of herbs. Steep in boiling water for 15 minutes, then add the tea and wrapped herbs to your bath.

Suggested herbs for baths (select combinations for desired effects):

Peppermint (cooling and astringent)
Chamomile (tranquilizing and moisturizing)
Rosemary (rejuvenating)
Lavender (stimulating)
Linden flowers (soothing and relaxing)
Roses (aromatic and moisturizing)

Orange blossoms (aromatic and moisturizing)

Facial Steams

To thoroughly cleanse and soften your face and neck, try an herbal facial steam. Place a handful of herbs in a large bowl. While boiling one quart of water, cover your hair and cleanse your face as usual. Pour boiling water over the herbs and hold your face over the bowl, making a tent with a heavy towel over your head and the bowl. Steam for up to ten minutes.

Rinse with warm water, then cool. Pat skin dry. Note that facial steams are not recommended for people with very dry skin, asthma, or breathing difficulties.

Below are some suggested herbs for facials steams:

Sage (refreshing)
Lemongrass (cleansing)
Chamomile (moisturizing)
Peppermint (cooling)
Fennel (softening)
Roses (softening and aromatic)
Lavender (stimulating)

Facial Masks

Combining herbs directly with oil, yogurt, or clay and applying this "mask" directly to your face is a simple way to nourish your skin herbally. These masks are especially effective if used after a facial steam.

Method 1 - Yogurt Mask - Add a strong infusion of fennel seeds and honey to yogurt. Massage onto face for an invigorating tonic. For oily skin, use yarrow instead of fennel.

Method 2 - Clay Mask - Mix clay with lemongrass and water (or oil if skin is dry). Apply directly to clean face and allow to dry if using water.

(If using oil, leave on approximately 15 minutes.) Rinse with warm, then cool water.

Method 3 - Oil Mask - Avocado and olive oils are beneficial for dry skin. Add to them small amounts of your favorite herbs. Warm gently. Cool and allow to stand several hours. Warm again and use cotton balls to apply to face. After ten minutes, rinse with warm, then cool water.

Suggested herbs for masks:

Sage (refreshing)
Horsetail (reduces large pores)
Lady's mantle (tonic, healing)
Linden flowers (softening)
Lovage (cleansing, deodorizing)
Nettle (tonic)
Elder flowers (soothing, slightly bleaching)
Dandelion (healing)

Hair Rinses and Conditioners

While concocting a successful herbal shampoo can be pretty tricky business, herbal rinses and conditioners are very simple and immediately effective.

Method 1 - To make a vinegar rinse, make an infusion by steeping one ounce of herbs in one cup of apple cider vinegar. Cover and set in a dark place for one week. Combine with an equal amount of water and pour onto hair as a next-to-final rinse.

Method 2 - Simply make an infusion of selected herbs and allow to steep until the correct temperature for rinsing. (One-half cup of herbs to one quart of water is a good guideline.) Strain and pour over hair as a next-to-final rinse.

Suggested herbs for hair rinses:

Sage (used to darken hair - leave on 1/2 hour, then rinse.)
Chamomile (healing, used to give blond highlights - leave on 15 minutes, then rinse.)
Nettle (hair tonic, said to strengthen)
Rosemary (excellent conditioner, adds luster)
Lemongrass (cleansing, good for oily hair)

Introduce herbs to your body care routines and read some of the books listed in the bibliography of this guide to learn more about the properties of various herbs and methods of developing your own products.

Henna Treatment

Pure henna contains hennatannic acid, a resinous substance which coats the hair shaft when applied as a hair treatment. This coating seals in the oils and reflects light, causing the hair to shine. It also creates a smoother, more protected surface.

Frontier's red henna is a completely natural plant product. It may be used to condition the hair while imparting it with red highlights.

Precautions:

—Do not use henna on hair that is grey or very light blond, hair that has been chemically dyed, or hair that has had a permanent using alkaline solutions.

—Twenty four hours before applying a henna treatment to your hair, do a skin patch test on your arm, and a dye test on a swatch of your hair. To conduct a patch test, mix a small amount of the henna powder with hot water. Apply over a one inch, clean area on the inner part of your arm. Allow to dry. Leave undisturbed and uncovered for four hours. Rinse. Examine area periodically during this period, looking for reddened, burning, or itching skin. Do not use the henna on your hair if you seem to be sensitive to it.

To dye a swatch of hair, snip and tie a small amount of your hair with a thread. Soak the swatch in the henna mixture you plan to use. Rinse after 30 minutes and dry. Check results in direct sunlight. Experiment with lengths of time until the desired shade is achieved.

Now you're ready:

—Measure henna (six ounces for short hair, eight ounces for shoulder length or longer).

—Select a modifying agent, if desired. An egg will add conditioning. A glass of red wine, ground coffee or cloves will vary the color slightly. Lemon juice or vinegar will aid the release of the dye, increasing the coloring effect.

—Mix the modifying agent and henna with water to form a thick, creamy, paste. Heat until hot. Cool slightly.

—While cooling, apply cream or vaseline to hairline, ears, and neck.

—Wear rubber gloves to prevent staining of hands.

—Apply comfortably warm henna paste to clean, dry hair, one section at a time. Cover entire strands, from roots to ends.

—Wrap the hair in plastic to seal in the henna and maintain a warm temperature.

—Wrap a towel around the plastic and sit in a warm place. The longer the henna remains on the hair, the greater the color change. For brown hair, begin with an absorption period of 30 minutes. (Light hair will absorb the color faster.)

—Rinse hair several times and shampoo.

A henna hair treatment may be repeated periodically (once a month, for example) to keep the hair beautifully conditioned.

FRONTIER
COOPERATIVE
HERBS

Frontier History

February of 1988 marks Frontier's 12th anniversary. It has been 12 years of tremendous growth and change— in facilities, personnel, product line, sales, and organizational structure.

In Frontier's first location, a small cabin on the Cedar River in Iowa, business began with the sale of a small line of herbs and spices to cooperatives and buying clubs in the Midwest. Initial orders arrived from Wisconsin, Missouri, Ohio, Michigan, and Colorado. The original staff of two grew to a handful.

The next location was in the basement of a food cooperative in Cedar Rapids— it was also quickly outgrown. The purchase of an old grocery store in Fairfax seemed expansive when the business first moved in during the summer of 1978. By 1980, however, Frontier products were filling not only the one building, but neighboring buildings and tacked-on trailers as well. In this location, we pulled orders from the basement, where the aisles between storage shelves were only 18 inches wide. By the time we left Fairfax, office workers were sitting on bags of mustard seed and using full boxes of parsley flakes for desks. The staff had grown to 35.

In the spring of 1982, Frontier purchased 10 acres of land near the small town of Norway. Here building began on what has now grown to roughly 30,000 square feet of warehouse. The warehouse itself is located off a gravel road, and is bordered on one side by a stand of pine trees. It is of passive solar construction, and is wood-sided. Also located on the property is a barn, a workshop, two well-used volleyball courts, and a farmhouse. Frontier renovated the house, which currently holds its childcare and lunch programs. At our licensed childcare facility, workers' children play with one another under the loving guidance of our childcare staff. The lunch program provides a meal to workers each day at noon.

In 1987, Frontier purchased an additional 50 acres of surrounding farmland for future expansion.

With growth in other areas, Frontier's organizational structure also underwent a number of changes in 10 years— from a worker collective in which all "collective members" met to make all business decisions, then to a management team, made up of several key managers, two elected worker representatives, and an elected personnel coordinator, to the present structure in which Frontier is managed by a General Manager (Rick Stewart, an original founder). Frontier's staff, which has grown to about 80, still meets regularly as a group to discuss business goals and performance.

Sales during the 12-year period grew from $18,003 at the end of fiscal year 1977 (for both 1976 and 1977 combined) to $5.4 million at the end of fiscal year 1987. Frontier's current growth rate is approximately 30% annually, and in 1983 it was number 78 in the Inc. 500 list of the fastest growing companies in the U.S. The product line has grown as well, from a small line of herbs and spices, to the present list of over 400 herbs and spices, 40 blends, 20 potpourris, baking products, dried broths and vegetables, 100 essential oils and fragrances, 30 teas, cosmetic and craft ingredients, and a wide variety of health and beauty aids. From its inception Frontier has functioned as a cooperative, with the basic mechanics of ownership and capitalization still in effect today.

Frontier as a Cooperative

Cooperatives are people and businesses working together for a common purpose. The Frontier Folks and the businesses we serve work together to bring consumers the best possible herbs, spices and related products in the most honest and professional manner.

Frontier Cooperative Herbs is unique as an herb company because of our cooperative structure. We are a member-owned cooperative with a governing board of directors elected by our members. Our members are comprised of retailers, distributors, manufacturers, and organizations. Put simply, Frontier is owned by the businesses who use our products.

Quality products, quality work, and the desire to provide optimal service to our customers are the driving forces at Frontier Cooperative Herbs. The cooperative system, combined with these driving forces, has proven very beneficial for Frontier, our members, and the consumers who enjoy our products.

Being part of a cooperative is a way of life and a great way to do business. We love it and we are honored to serve you.

Regulations & Quality Control

FDA Regulations

While the use of herbs and spices has a long and rich history, their use in the U.S. has only recently been legally regulated.

The increased use of chemical additives by food manufacturers in the 1950's prompted Congress to pass a Food Additives Amendment to the Food and Drug Cosmetic Act in 1958. The purpose of this amendment was to assure the safety of food by requiring pre-market approval of a food additive by the FDA before it could be used in foods.

In order to facilitate the enforcement of the amendment, the FDA drafted regulations (in both 1958 and 1960) which included a list of approved food additives. The list, which included some herbs, was based on the FDA's knowledge of safe, common uses of herbs for food flavoring at that time.

As herbs grew in popularity, so did the lists of regulations created by the FDA. In 1976 the Compliance Policy Guide (CPG) 7117.04 was drafted. This list served as a guideline for FDA officers on the use of herbs as teas. It listed herbs in three categories: unsafe, undefined safety, and safe. The safe section was no more than a relisting of the herbs in the regulations published in 1958 and 1960. The term undefined safety was used to label those herbs which were not yet researched by the FDA. The unsafe section listed 27 herbs determined to be poisonous due to various toxins produced by the plant.

In July of 1986, the CPG 7117.04 was revised. The new CPG 7117.04 states that any herb sold for food use must be shown (by appropriate means such as toxicity studies) to be safe for such use. If no such documented evidence exists, the burden of proof lies with the company selling the product. Herb companies now have the right to promote herbs for tea if they can prove they are safe for this use. Other sections of the regulations prohibit the sale of harmful, or potentially injurious, substances for food use.

The regulations and the list of unsafe herbs from the old CPG are neither complete nor consistent. They are, however, the best guidelines available at this time, and are the guidelines we have used to label the products in this handbook.

In order to best interpret the regulations, keep the following information in mind:

—For identification purposes, special attention should be given to the botanical name, the plant part (such as flowers, leaves, roots), and the form (such as extract or whole herb). For example, elder flowers are approved for flavoring but elder berries are not. A focus on botanical names is important in many cases. The common name "heal all" for example, has been used to name four different genus-species of plants. In the Herb and Spice section of this handbook, we have included specific botanical names, plant parts, and forms.

—The regulations are inconsistent. For example, yarrow flowers may only be sold if they contain less than 2% thujone. Sage, on the other hand, may contain up to 50% thujone and remain approved for food flavoring. Some herbs are approved for flavoring "alcoholic beverages only" because that was the common use for them in 1958. Other herbs are restricted for use only in a particular form (such as an extract), because only that form was commonly recognized as safe in 1958.

—Because an herb is listed as an approved food flavoring does not mean it is safe under any conditions and in any amounts, and those items labeled "undefined safety" may range from perfectly safe to potentially lethal. Our notations, based on the findings of the FDA to date, are meant to guide you, but it is up to you to make a well-informed decision. When using herbs and spices, consult reliable reference sources and carefully make your own decisions regarding their use.

Below is a list of the FDA regulations we have used in the *Herbs and Spices* section of this handbook.

FDA approved for flavoring foods. (This label most commonly applies to herbs which have been proven safe for use in foods.)

FDA approved as a spice and for flavoring foods. (This label applies to spices and essential oils. Substances approved for use as spices tend to be safe and more commonly used than substances approved as flavorings.)

FDA approved for flavoring foods when used as an extract or tea. (This regulation states that only the plant's extract, not the whole herb, is approved.)

FDA approved only for flavoring alcoholic beverages. (Some herbs and spices fall into this category because the only safe use known to the food industry at the time the regulation was enacted was for flavoring alcoholic beverages.)

FDA prohibited for use in food due to naturally occurring toxins. (This applies to plants which contain naturally occurring toxins. Frontier does not promote the use of these items for internal consumption.)

No FDA designation for safe use in food. (This is used to label herbs which are not listed in the FDA regulations. It does not imply that these herbs are safe, nor does it imply that they are unsafe.)

Quality Control

High standards of quality have been established at Frontier for all of our herbs and spices. Specifications are continually being updated for each of our products. If a product does not meet our specifications, it is returned to the supplier.

Our purchasers are herb and spice experts. We personally visit every supplier we work with, and we only buy from quality-conscious suppliers. Pre-order samples are required for all major purchases to allow our experts to inspect the products before actually purchasing them. In addition, Frontier's quality control staff continually monitors our product quality to ensure customer safety and satisfaction.

Samples of all incoming products are examined and retained for a minimum of two years. Each shipment is assigned a lot number to specifically identify and trace the product from the time of its shipment to its arrival at the customer's door. All herbs and spices go through an identification process to screen out adulterated and mislabled products. Products are further analyzed for foreign matter, correct processing, correct plant parts, and optimum harvest time. In-house testing for flavor, color, size, aroma, and moisture are also conducted. Analysis by independent labs may include tests for bacteria, yeast and mold, pesticide/herbicide levels, and radiation.

Our new 384-square-foot quality control laboratory has a growing complement of modern testing equipment. Laboratory clearance is mandatory for all herbs and spices prior to packaging and shipping. In addition, our temperature and humidity-controlled facility provides ideal storage conditions for our herbs and spices by preserving the volatile flavor components and color.

Packaging materials are carefully selected to suit the individual product and retain optimum freshness. Herbs and spices are packaged in foil laminate pouches, or plastic bags enclosed in paper bags.

Frontier also mantains a complete herbal library containing more than 300 reference works and periodicals to help us provide you with ample information. New titles are added as they become available. For customers with questions regarding the quality of herbs and spices we offer our Quality Control Hotline. Don't hesitate to call on us at (319) 227-7991.

Food Irradiation

Currently, no food destined for consumption in the U.S. may be irradiated unless specifically allowed by the Food and Drug Administration. As of September 1987, 48 spices are on the approved list (see below). Gamma radiation levels allowed for spices may not exceed 30,000 Gray (Gy). Approved levels for other products are generally limited to 1,000 Gy. One Gy is equal to 100 rads. One thousand Gy of radiation would kill a human many times over.

Spices are allowed a higher treatment level for several reasons. The FDA considers them a minor part of your diet, and their effects on your body are diluted by the other foods. Their low moisture content is also said to make them safer to irradiate. Finally, spices are irradiated for the purpose of controlling both insects and microorganisms, which require high doses of lethal radiation.

A consumer food product which has been irradiated must be labeled "Treated with ionizing radiation" or "Treated with gamma radiation." Any wholesale package or invoice or bill of lading must be labeled "Treated with ionizing (gamma) radiation — do not irradiate again." Recent changes in the law allow the words "Picowaved," "Picowaved to control spoilage," or "Picowaved to extend shelf life" to be used on retail packages. Additionally, the international logo— the Radura (pictured above)— must be on all retail labels.

There is a catch, of course. Non-irradiated foods that contain irradiated ingredients do not need to be labeled as above. Given the loophole, many foods in the marketplace contain irradiated spices as ingredients and are not labeled as such.

Spice manufacturers are interested in the irradiation because of their need for low bacteria counts in certain applications. For example, high bacteria counts in spices used to make "fresh, homestyle salad dressing" can turn the product into a jar full of bacteria before the consumer has the chance to eat it.

Frontier does not, and will not, sell irradiated products. We have questioned our major herb and spice suppliers and are confident that we have never handled an irradiated product.

The following is a list of 48 spices approved by the FDA for irradiation:

Allspice, anise, basil, bay leaves, caraway seed, caraway-black (black cumin), cardamon, celery seed, chamomile, chervil, chives, cinnamon, cloves, coriander, cumin seed, dill seed, dill weed, fennel seed, fenugreek, garlic powder, ginger, grains of paradise (seleguta pepper), horseradish, mace, marjoram, mustard seed, mustard flour, nutmeg, onion powder, orange petals, oregano, paprika, parsley, pepper-black; pepper-white, pepper-red, peppermint, poppy seed, rosemary, saffron, sage, savory, sesame seed, spearmint, star anise seed, tarragon, thyme, turmeric. Blends of these substances may contain sodium chloride as a minor component.

Industry Information

MARCH & APRIL 1987

FRONTIER HERB & SPICE FACTS

Spring Issue!

FRONTIER COOPERATIVE HERBS
P.O. Box 299, Norway, IA 52318

New Policy Viewed As Major Shift

On July 1, 1986 the FDA released a new Compliance Policy Guide for botanical food products which suggests, in part, that the agency is shifting its emphasis from enforcement of product safety-related issues to product labeling.

In short, the new guidelines state that the FDA will [illegible] on a [illegible] of the [illegible] manufacturer's claims [illegible] knowledge about a the product. [illegible]

The FDA [illegible] will no longer, [illegible] regulatory action unless [illegible] there is a valid toxicological concern resulting from a complaint, injury, or research.

On the other hand, the FDA appears to have bolstered its authority in the area of manufacturer compliance if the therapeutic claims of a manufacturer's product is challenged.

Now, even if the manufacturer agrees to remove such claims from the label, the action must be accompanied by a campaign to disassociate the relabeled product from its history as a therapeutic drug. By adopting the new policy, the FDA has essentially abandoned the infamous *List of 27 Unsafe Herbs*— the controversial memorandum dictating FDA policy since 1975— which has been openly criticized by the herb and spice industry as shortsighted and inaccurate.

The list was derived from an FDA report entitled *Safe and Unsafe Herbs for Use in Herbal Teas* and has resulted in product seizures, confiscation of imported herbs and spices, and industry warnings.

(Please turn to page 8)

Store PROFILE

Marketing & Quality

Bread & Circus and Yes! Gourmet Food: Two Perspectives On Establishing Profitable Herb & Spice Departments

by Chris D. Baker

The philosophy is quite simple— absolutely no sugar, no artificial coloring, no preservatives. In short, nothing artificial is allowed in the products sold by the Bread & Circus whole food store chain in Massachusetts.

"We have to screen everything," says Karen Lewis, nutrition manager at the chain's youngest, and largest, store located in Hadley, Mass. "We simply do not pick up on the latest fads. In fact, we do not even use the word 'natural' anymore because it has been applied to so many different things."

As a result of such stringent standards, Bread & Circus has emerged as one of the most reputable whole food supermarket chains in the country meeting the needs of the enlightened and demanding consumers.

(Please turn to page 13)

Yes! Gourmet Food store of Washington, D.C. is definitely a positive force in the natural food industry accounting for more than one million dollars in sales last year.

That is quite an accomplishment considering the store lacks some of the crucial elements of a successful business profile.

For example, the store's location in Georgetown is obscure, there is no storefront, parking space is virtually non-existent and the mortality rate is high— five other natural food stores have failed in the past 16 years.

However, Yes! more than compensates for the lack of prime real estate by implementing a superior marketing campaign and carrying only the finest quality natural foods.

(Please turn to page 13)

Industry Publications

Here are some magazines and newsletters currently being published which contain credible information about various aspects of herbs and spices. Of course, this list is not comprehensive and we cannot guarantee that the subscription rates are as listed.

The Business of Herbs
P.O. Box 559
Madison, VA 22727
A 16-page publication focusing on the commercial growing of herbs and various ways to harvest, market, and distribute herbs and herb products. Bi-monthly. $18/yr.

Frontier Facts
P.O. Box 299
Norway, IA 52318
Published by Frontier Cooperative Herbs, this 12-page, bi-monthly newsletter includes feature articles on the uses of herbs and spices, business tips, recipes and other helpful information. $9/yr.

GRI Newsletter
Ginseng Research Institute
Box 42, Main St.
Roxbury, NY 12474
To receive this newsletter you must be a member of the Ginseng Research Institute. Contains current information on ginseng and its research. $25/yr.

Herbalgram
P.O. Box 12602
Austin, TX 78711
A quarterly publication of the Herb Research Foundation and the American Herbal Products Association containing industry happenings, research news, and market reports. $15/yr.

Herban Greenhouse News
Rt. 1, Box 130
New Hartford, CT 06057
A bi-monthly newsletter containing information about herbal crafts, gardening, and cooking. $18/yr.

The Herb Basket
The Practical Press
P.O. Box 1773
Brattleboro, VT 05301
Concentrating on practical information about growing herbs, and their culinary uses, this newsletter is published bi-monthly. $15/yr.

Herbletter
4974 Riverdale Rd. S.
Salem, OR 97302
A four-page newsletter dealing with herbal crafts and gardens. $2.50/yr.

The Herb Magazine
P.O. Box 722
Boulder, CO 80306
A bi-monthly newsletter directed toward people who buy, sell, grow, gather, or otherwise serve the world with herbs. $15/yr.

The Herb Quarterly
P.O. Box 275
Newfane, VT 05345
An excellent magazine featuring herb history, lore, herb gardens, recipes, and much more. Quarterly. $20/yr.

The Herb Report
P.O. Box 95-3333
Stuart, FL 33495
Bringing you the latest scientific research regarding the nutritional aspects of plants, this report is published monthly. $18/yr.

The Herbal Review
by Gordon Taylor
The Herb Society Newsletter
34 Boscobel Place
London, England SW 1 W 9PE
A 24-page herb magazine with articles on a wide range of herb topics. $15/yr.

The Herbal Thymes
39 Reed St.
Marcellus, NY 13108
A charming, well-written quarterly with a potpourri of recipes, herbal crafts, and games. $5/yr.

Potpourri From Herbal Acres
by Phyllis Shaudy
P.O. Box 428
Washington Crossing, PA 18977
Loaded with potpourri ideas, "herbal blurbs," and recipes, this is a quarterly newsletter. $12/yr.

Sprout Letter
P.O. Box 62
Ashland, OR 97520
A newsletter of unusual and useful information on sprouts, raw foods, and nutrition. Quarterly. $14/yr.

Thinking Naturally Publications
6739 W. 44th Avenue
Wheatridge, CO 80033
Complete research information for professionals and practitioners, or retailers. Monthly. $24/yr.

Today's Herbs
Woodland Books
P.O. Box 1422
Provo, UT 84603
A monthly publication focusing on herbs. $15/yr.

Update On Herbs
215 John Street
Santa Cruz, CA 95060
A Quarterly newsletter from the Journal of the Institute for Traditional Medicine on Oriental herbology. $16/yr.

Industry Organizations

Listed here are several herb and spice organizations which are working for the betterment of the herb and spice industry. If you are interested in receiving their publications, becoming a member, or just expressing your concerns, their addresses are given. Frontier is a member of each of these organizations except The American Spice Trade Association.

American Herb Association

The AHA is an educational and research organization. It is dedicated to increasing the public's knowledge about herbs and to increasing the use of herbs and herbal products. The AHA is also dedicated to rekindling the nearly forgotten virtues of herbs, for both health and pleasure. They publish herbal source directories which help locate herbs, herb seeds and plants, and herbal products. They also publish a quarterly newsletter. AHA, P.O. 353, Rescue, CA. 95672.

The American Herbal Products Association

This association, which began in 1981, deals primarily with the non-culinary herb market. The primary purpose of AHPA is to protect the interests and promote the welfare of the herb industry and to assume as a group those functions which the individual member firms cannot perform as effectively on their own. Their aim is to support the common good of the herbal products industry and to secure the respect and dignity the herb industry deserves. AHPA is currently working with the FDA on the safety status of several herbs for the purpose of adding those herbs to the FDA GRAS (generally recognized as safe) list. AHPA, 215 Classic CT., Rohnert Park, CA. 94928.

American Spice Trade Association

ASTA is comprised of exporters, importers, growers, processors, manufacturers, brokers, and agents involved in the trading or usage of spices worldwide. This organization is 80 years old and continues to grow in stature and helpfulness to its membership. ASTA works with the FDA to set standard specifications for the importing of spices. They publish extensive information about spices and their uses. ASTA also provides data on testing procedures and the quality control of spices. ASTA, P.O. Box 1267, Englewood Cliff, NJ. 07632.

The Herb Research Foundation

The HRF is supported by a Board of Directors made up of some of the country's most distinguished pharmacognosists, enthnobotanists, botanists and other academics and physicians. They are well qualified to find resources for herbal research and answers to specific questions. The HRF conducts ongoing reviews of current plant research, toxicity research on herbal products in commerce, and nutritional analysis of herbs. They publish the *Herbalgram* in conjunction with The American Herbal Products Association. HRF, P.O. Box 2602, Longmont, CO. 80501.

International Herb Growers and Marketers Association

IHGMA was formed in 1986 to unite those engaged in the production and marketing of herbs and to educate the public about herbs and herb-related products. Their purpose is to support growers, gatherers, marketers, and researchers. They publish a quarterly newsletter. IHGMA, P.O. Box 693, Greenfield, IN. 46140.

Bibliography

Adrosko, Rita J., *Natural Dyes and Home Dyeing*, Dover Publications, 1971.

Albright, Nancy, *The Rodale Cookbook*, Rodale Press, 1973.

Bach, Phillipia and Loewenfeldt, Claire, *Herbs, Health, and Cookery*, Award Books, 1965.

Barlow, Max G., *The Shepherd's Purse*, Spice-West, 1979.

Bricklin, Mark, and Claessens, Sharon, *The Natural Healing Cookbook*, Rodale Press, 1981.

Buchman, D., *Herbal Medicine*, McKay, 1979.

Castelton, Virginia, *The Handbook of Natural Beauty*, Rodale Press, 1975.

Chesman, Andrea, *Salsas!*, The Crossing Press, NY 1985.

Christopher, John, Dr., *School of Natural Healing*, Brivold, 1976.

Claessens, Sharon, *The 20-Minute Natural Foods Cookbook*, Rodale Press, 1982.

Code of Federal Regulations, Food and Drug Administration, Title 21.

The Condensed Chemical Dictionary, Reinhold Publishing Corporation, 1961.

Coon, Nelson, *Using Plants for Healing*, Hearthside Press, Inc., 1963.

Cue, Ann, *Wonderful Weeds, A Backyard Herbal*, Cues for Health, 1980.

Culpepper, Nicholas, *Culpepper's Complete Herbal*, W. Foulsham and Company Ltd., 1981.

Culpepper, Nicholas, *Physician and Complete Herbal* by Leyel, Wilshire Book Co., 1972.

Densmore, Frances, *How Indians Use Wild Plants for Food, Medicine, and Crafts*, Dover Publishing, 1974.

Dextreit, Raymond, *Our Earth Our Cure*, Bolder Books, 1979.

Dorland, Wayne E. and Rogers, James A., *The Fragrance and Flavor Industry* , Wayne E, Dorland Co., 1977.

Duke, James A., *Handbook of Medicinal Herbs*, CRC Press, 1929.

Farrell, Kenneth, *Spices, Condiments, and Seasonings*, AVI Publishing Co., 1985.

Fernald, Merritt Lyndon, *Gray's Manual of Botany*, Van Nostrand Reinhold Company 1970.

Fisher, Bonnie, *Way With Herbs Cookbook*, Keats Living With Herbs Series, 1980.

Furia, Thomas E., and Bellanca, Nicolo (editors), *Fenaroli's Handbook of Flavor Ingredients*, CRC Press, 1971.

Gabriel, Ingrid, *Herb Identifier and Handbook*, Sterling Publishers, 1975.

Genders, Roy, *The Complete Book of Herbs and Herb Growing*, Sterling, 1980.

Gerard, John, *The Herbal or General History of Plants*, Dover Publishing, 1975.

Gerras, Charles, editor, *Rodale's Basic Natural Foods Cookbook*, Rodale Press, 1982.

Gibbons, Euell, *Stalking the Healthful Herbs*, David McKay Co., 1966.

A Glossary of Spices, American Spice Trade Association.

Grieve, Mrs. M., *A Modern Herbal*, Dover Publications Inc., 1971.

Gruenberg, Louise, *Potpourri, The Art of Fragrance Crafting*, Frontier Cooperative Herbs, 1984.

Gurudas, *Flower Essences*, Brotherhood of Life, Inc., 1983.

Guenther, Ernest, PhD, *The Essential Oils*, Robert E. Krieger Publishing Company, 1972.

Hanson, Larch, *Edible Sea Vegetables of the New England Coast.*

Heinerman, John, *The Complete Book of Spices*, Keats Publishing, 1983.

Huson, Paul, *Mastering Herbalism*, Stein and Day Publishers, 1974.

Hutchens, Alma R., *Indian Herbology of North America*, The Homeopathy Press (India), 1970.

Hylton, William A.R. (editor), *The Rodale Herb Book*, Rodale Press, 1974.

Jones, Lester, *A Treasury of Spices*, American Spice Trade Association Publication.

Kirschmann, John D., *Nutrition Almanac*, revised edition, McGraw-Hill Book Company, 1979.

Kloss, Jethro, *Back to Eden*, Back to Eden Books, 1939.

Krochmal, Arnold and Connie, *A Guide to the Medicinal Plants of the U.S.*, Quadrangle, 1973.

L'MAJ Cuisine for Creative Cooks, Pluim Publishing, Inc.

Levy, Juliette de Bairacli, *Common Herbs for Common Health*, Scholken, 1974.

London, Mel, *Bread Winners*, Rodale Press, 1979.

Lust, John, *The Herb Book*, Bantam Books, 1974.

Magic and Medicine of Plants, Reader's Digest Assn., 1986.

Marshall Marcin, Marietta, *The Complete Book of Herbal Teas*, Congdon and Weed, Inc., 1983.

McKenny, Margarete and Peterson, Roger Tory, *Field Guide to Wildflowers of North Eastern and North Central North America*, Houghton Mifflin, 1974.

Meyer, Clarence, *The Herbalist Almanac, 50 Year Anthology*, Meyerbooks, 1977.

Millspaugh, Charles F., *American Medicinal Plants*, Rodale Press, 1974.

Moulton, LeArta, *Herb Walk*, The Gluten Company, 1979.

Newcomb, Lawrence, *Newcomb's Wildflower Guide*, Little, 1977.

Nickell, J.M., *J.M. Nickell's Botanical Reference*, Trinity Center Press and CSA Press, 1976.

Niering, William and Olmstead, Nancy, *Audubon Society Field Guide to North American Wildflowers*, Knopf, 1979.

Organic Gardening Staff (editors), *Encyclopedia of Organic Gardening*, Rodale Press, 1978.

Parvati, Jeannine, *Hygieia, A Woman's Herbal*, Bookpeople, 1978.

Pond, Barbara, *A Sample of Wayside Herbs*, Chatam Press, 1974.

Pratt, James Norwood, *Tea Lover's Treasury*, 101 Productions, 1982.

Prudhomme, Paul, *Chef Paul Prudhomme's Louisiana Kitchen*, Morrow Press, 1984.

Rankin, Dorothy, *Pestos! Cooking With Herb Pastes*, Crossing Press, 1985.

Redgrove, *Spices and Condiments*, Pitman and Sons, 1933.

Revolutionary Health Council of Human Province, *The Barefoot Doctor's Manual*, Madrona Publishers, 1981.

Rodale's High Health Cookbook Series, *No Salt Needed Cookbook*, Rodale Press, 1982.

Bibliography

Rogers, Jean, *Cooking with the Healthful Herbs*, Rodale Press, Inc., 1983.

Rose, Jeanne, *Herbs and Things*, Grossett and Dunlap, 1972.

Rose, Jeanne, *Jeanne Rose's Herbal Body Book*, Grossett and Dunlap, 1976.

Rose, Jeanne, *Kitchen Cosmetics*, Panjandrum / Aris Books, 1978.

Rosengarten, Frederic, Jr., *The Book of Spices*, Jove Publishing, 1981.

Sailly, Virginia, *A Treasury of American Indian Herbs*, Crown Publishing, 1970.

Sanderson, Liz, *How to Make Your Own Herbal Cosmetics*, Keats Publishing, 1977.

Scagel, Robert F., *Guide to Common Seaweeds of British Columbia*, University of British Columbia, 1921.

Schafer, Charles and Violet, *Teacraft*, Yerba Buena Press, 1977.

Shaudys, Phyllis, *The Pleasure of Herbs*, Garden Way Publishing, 1986.

Shook, Dr. Edward E., *Elementary Treatise in Herbology*, Trinity Center Press, 1974.

Shook, Dr. Edward E., *Advanced Treatise in Herbology*, Trinity Center Press, 1978.

Singh, Manju Shivraj, *The Spice Box, Vegetarian Indian Cookbook*, The Crossing Press, 1981.

Stobart, *Herbs, Spices, and Flavorings*, Overlook Press, 1970.

Stoner, Carol H., *Stocking Up*, Rodale Press, 1977.

Stuart, Malcolm, *The Encylopedia of Herbs and Herbalism*, Grosset and Dunlap, 1979.

Theriot, Jude W., *La Cuisine Cajun*, Pelican Publishing Company, 1986.

Thomas, Everett, *The New York Botanical Garden III Encyclopedia of Horticulture*, Garland Publishing, 1982.

Thompson, William A.R. M.D. (editor), *Medicines from the Earth, A Guide to Healing Plants*, McGraw Hill Book Company, 1978.

Tierra, Michael, *The Way of Herbs*, Orenda-Unity, 1980.

Tisserand, Robert B., *The Art of Aromatherapy, The Healing and Beautifying Properties of The Essential Oils of Flowers and Herbs*, Beekman Publishers, 1977.

Tolley, Emelie, and Mead, Chris, *Herbs, Gardens, Decorations, And Recipes*, Crown Publishers, 1985.

Tucker Fettner, Ann, *Potpourri, Incense and Other Fragrant Concoctions*, Workman Publishing Company, 1977.

U.S. Department of Agriculture, *Common Weeds of the U.S.*, Dover Publications, Inc., 1971.

Veninga, Louise, *Goldenseal, Etc.*, Ruka, 1976.

Vogel, Virgil J., *American Indian Medicine*, University of Oklahoma Press, 1970.

Walker, Elizabeth, *Making Things With Herbs*, Keats Publishing Inc., 1977.

Weigle, Palmy, *Ancient Dyes for Modern Weavers*, Watson-Guptill, 1974.

Weiner, Michael, A., *Earth Medicine Earth Food*, Macmillan Publishing Co., 1972.

Winn Ford, Marjorier; Hillyard, Susan; Faulk Koock, Mary; *The Deaf Smith Country Cookbook*, Collier Books, 1973.

Winter, Ruth, *A Consumer's Dictionary of Cosmetic Ingredients*, Crown Publishers, Inc., 1974.

York, Alexandra, *Back to Basics Natural Beauty Handbook, How to Make and Use Your Own Natural Cosmetics*, Van Nostrand Reinhold, 1977.